About Island Press

Since 1984, the nonprofit organization Island Press has been stimulating, shaping, and communicating ideas that are essential for solving environmental problems worldwide. With more than 800 titles in print and some 40 new releases each year, we are the nation's leading publisher on environmental issues. We identify innovative thinkers and emerging trends in the environmental field. We work with world-renowned experts and authors to develop cross-disciplinary solutions to environmental challenges.

Island Press designs and executes educational campaigns in conjunction with our authors to communicate their critical messages in print, in person, and online using the latest technologies, innovative programs, and the media. Our goal is to reach targeted audiences—scientists, policymakers, environmental advocates, urban planners, the media, and concerned citizens—with information that can be used to create the framework for long-term ecological health and human well-being.

Island Press gratefully acknowledges major support of our work by The Agua Fund, The Andrew W. Mellon Foundation, Betsy & Jesse Fink Foundation, The Bobolink Foundation, The Curtis and Edith Munson Foundation, Forrest C. and Frances H. Lattner Foundation, G.O. Forward Fund of the Saint Paul Foundation, Gordon and Betty Moore Foundation, The Kresge Foundation, The Margaret A. Cargill Foundation, New Mexico Water Initiative, a project of Hanuman Foundation, The Overbrook Foundation, The S.D. Bechtel, Jr. Foundation, The Summit Charitable Foundation, Inc., V. Kann Rasmussen Foundation, The Wallace Alexander Gerbode Foundation, and other generous supporters.

The opinions expressed in this book are those of the author(s) and do not necessarily reflect the views of our supporters.

STRATEGIC GREEN INFRASTRUCTURE PLANNING

STRATEGIC GREEN INFRASTRUCTURE PLANNING:

A multi-scale approach

By Karen Firehock and R. Andrew Walker
The Green Infrastructure Center Inc.

◯ **ISLAND**PRESS Washington | Covelo | London

Green Infrastructure Center

Library of Congress Control Number: 2015946810

By: Karen E. Firehock, Chapter Seven by R. Andrew Walker

Manuscript Editor: Tim Lewis

Select Illustrations: Reed Muehlman

Book Design: Whitney Glick

Funding: The writing of this book was funded by grants from the Virginia Department of Forestry, the U.S. Forest Service and the Blue Moon Fund.

Published by Island Press

ISBN: 978-1-61091-692-9

First Edition published by GIC in December 2012 under the ISBN: 978-0-615-75870-1

CONTENTS

PREFACE

This book is a product of many years of work by the Green Infrastructure Center (GIC). The GIC is a nonprofit organization which helps federal, state and local government agencies, conservation groups, land trusts and communities to make better informed decisions about how to balance growth and development with conservation of their highest quality natural assets.

The GIC seeks to ensure that land-use decisions about what to conserve and how to do it are well informed by the best possible data and objective information. Its overarching goal is to focus development into those patterns that maximize resource conservation and economic efficiency.

This book is intended to help people make land management decisions which recognize the interdependence of healthy people, strong economies and a vibrant, intact and biologically diverse landscape. Green infrastructure consists of our environmental assets – which GIC also calls 'natural assets' – and they should be included in planning processes. Planning to conserve or restore green infrastructure ensures that communities can be vibrant, healthful and resilient. Having clean air and water, as well as nature-based recreation, attractive views and abundant local food, depends upon considering our environmental assets as part of everyday planning.

While there are other books and guides about the benefits of green infrastructure planning, this book provides practical steps for creating green infrastructure maps and plans for a community. It draws from twenty field tests GIC has conducted over the past eight years to learn how to evaluate and conserve natural resources. These field tests were conducted in a diversity of ecological and political conditions, at multiple scales, and in varied development patterns – from wildlands and rural areas to suburbs, cities and towns.

During these field tests, the GIC determined three things:

- How to create green infrastructure maps that highlight the most significant resources for conservation.
- Steps to integrate those maps into local and regional plans.
- How to communicate the importance of this work to local officials, planners, developers and others.

While we also draw upon outside case studies, the steps and advice offered here are the GIC's own interpretation of the most effective ways to evaluate and conserve natural assets. We hope our advice and practical tips can help you become even more effective in your work.

ABOUT THE AUTHOR

Karen E. Firehock is the primary author of this book. She is the executive director and co-founder of the GIC and is on the adjunct faculty in the Departments of Urban and Environmental Planning and Landscape Architecture at the University of Virginia. She has worked in the environmental field for 30 years. In 1999, she became certified as a mediator to help groups realize common visions for their environmental plans. She also served as the national Save Our Streams program director at the Izaak Walton League of America, where she directed stream and wetland conservation and education programs. She has been the recipient of numerous local, state and national awards for her work, such as a National Greenways Award, a Renew America Award, a United Nations Environment Programme Award and a Virginia River Conservationist of the Year Award, among others. She holds a Bachelor of Science Degree in Natural Resources Management from the University of Maryland and a Master of Planning Degree from the University of Virginia.

R. Andrew Walker is the GIS Analyst and Spatial Planner at the GIC. He wrote Chapter Seven which describes tools for green infrastructure mapping and modeling. He specializes in the intersection of geospatial technologies and planning applications, database development, remote sensing for environmental applications, the development of custom GIS models and tools. He manages the GIC's mapping and land planning and provides technical assistance to local governments, regional planning agencies, communities, land trusts and conservation groups. He holds a bachelor's degree in Geography from Arizona State University and a Master of Urban and Environmental Planning degree from the Univeristy of Virginia.

SPECIAL THANKS

The GIC wishes to extend special thanks to the many partners and colleagues without whom this book would not be possible. While we cannot thank everyone who has supported the GIC – there have been many – we want to specifically acknowledge the GIC's past and present Board of Directors and the states of Virginia, North Carolina, South Carolina, Arkansas and New York which provided funds and opportunities to build models and field test them. We also want to thank the U.S. Forest Service's Urban and Community Forestry Program as well as the Blue Moon Fund for their sponsorship of this book's development.

Other field tests were funded by the U.S. Environmental Protection Agency's Healthy Watersheds Initiative, the Chesapeake Bay Program, the Virginia Environmental Endowment, the Robins Foundation, the Oak Hill Fund, the Altria Group, Dominion Virginia Power, several planning district commissions, and others. These partners, as well as community members of the regions, counties and towns in which we worked, have made this planning book possible. Many agencies and technical staff -- too numerous to mention here -- provided peer review of our methods and ensured that we utilized the best science in all of our analysis and plans.

INTRODUCTION

Imagine a world where clean water is plentiful, air in our towns and cities is clean and fresh, native species of plants and animals are abundant, access to outdoor recreation is plentiful, natural beauty and verdant landscapes envelop our communities, historic landscapes are well preserved and protected and locally grown food is easily accessible. And imagine that these resources are available to everyone, regardless of income or social status.

While this vision may seem difficult to achieve, it is not impossible. However, it requires greater awareness and more thoughtful attention to how we plan our communities and care for our natural resources. We can have communities that are healthful and people that are healthy – but only if we plan for it. And the time to do that is now.

As far back as 1863, George Perkins Marsh, long considered the father of America's conservation movement, cautioned in his book *Man and Nature* that, "The earth is fast becoming an unfit home for its noblest inhabitant... [and]...to threaten the depravation, barbarism, and perhaps even extinction of the species."

Since Marsh wrote that statement, the United States has come a long way in recognizing the need to actively protect its natural resources. It now has an impressive array of national and local regulations to protect and clean its air, water and soil which compliment voluntary actions, such as reforestation or adopt-a-stream programs. Yet we have been developing landscapes in patterns that are not sustainable over the long term and do not account for the many ecological services provided by forests, wetlands, rivers, aquifers, soils and geology.

Consider the enormously aggregated ecological consequences of more than 39,000 local government entities – counties, municipalities and townships – that are regulating the use of 70 percent of the U.S. land base. At the site scale, add to that those private landowners and consumers who are making decisions about how they develop or manage their land, such as which forest to harvest, where to channel water flow, or how to draw water from a river or aquifer or how to fertilize their lawns. Without offering all these decision-makers a comprehensive understanding of the interconnectedness of our air, water and land systems, we risk taking steps that could inadvertently compromise or damage the present and future health of our environment. Until we see our natural resources as being part of a connected infrastructure that supports our everyday lives by providing clean air, water and soil, we may not recognize the need to actively conserve them.

While most people would prefer to make land-use decisions that restore rather than deplete our environment, land planners and decision makers may still overlook key natural resources. Just as we plan for our gray infrastructure – roads, bridges, power lines, pipelines, sewer systems, and so on – so should we plan to conserve landscapes and natural resources as our 'green infrastructure.'

Green infrastructure is

"a strategically planned
and managed network of
wilderness, parks, greenways,
conservation easements, and
working lands with conservation
value that supports native
species, maintains natural
ecological processes, sustains
air and water resources, and
contributes to the health and
quality of life for America's
communities and people."

— Benedict and McMahon

GREEN INFRASTRUCTURE

Green infrastructure can be thought of as the sum of all our natural resources. It includes all the interconnected natural systems in a landscape, such as intact forests, woodlands, wetlands, parks and rivers, as well as those agricultural soils that provide clean water, air quality, wildlife habitat and food. In their book *Green Infrastructure*, Benedict and McMahon defined it as "a strategically planned and managed network of wilderness, parks, greenways, conservation easements, and working lands with conservation value that supports native species, maintains natural ecological processes, sustains air and water resources, and contributes to the health and quality of life for America's communities and people" (2006).

Conserving green infrastructure is critical to building and sustaining wildlife and human communities that are healthy, both ecologically and economically. For example, American Forests has estimated that trees in the nation's metropolitan areas contribute $400 billion in storm water retention by eliminating the need for expensive storm water retention facilities (Benedict and McMahon 2006).

This is *not* a guide about how to stop development or to limit population growth. Rather, it describes the steps a community can take to determine what is important and to develop a rationale for what to protect. Development can then occur in a manner that recognizes and protects the area's most important landscape resources. This guide presents a way to think about and catalogue a community's natural assets as its 'green infrastructure.' It shows how to evaluate the different natural assets and to prioritize them for long-term stewardship. This guide provides the steps for determining how to *facilitate* development in ways that reduce its impact on the landscape, or to restore environmental functionality where it has been lost. Its application can benefit residents, businesses and government.

AUDIENCE

The intended audience for this book comprises local land-use decision-makers, such as appointed and elected officials (planning commissioners, planning boards, boards of commissioners, boards of supervisors, city and town councils, town or city managers, and staff of planning district commissions or regional government councils); college students and faculty in fields such as architecture, natural resources management, conservation biology, environmental science and landscape architecture; natural resource agencies and professionals (rural and urban foresters, extension agents, game and inland fisheries, wildlife managers and conservation groups); associations that manage significant land holdings (land conservancies and land trusts); homeowner associations charged with taking care of open-space lands; and realtors, developers and builders.

While the above list covers an extremely diverse audience, it includes those people who make decisions on how, when and where to develop and conserve land. It is a challenging audience to address because the level of its members' knowledge of natural resources and planning regulations varies greatly. In order to ensure a level playing field for all readers, the book includes several definitions of the field's more common technical terms. Text boxes and sidebars are utilized whenever possible to avoid slowing down the more advanced reader.

This book also includes examples that demonstrate several different approaches to creating green infrastructure plans, as well as examples of the GIC's field tests. It is hoped that this book will spur its users to evaluate, map and conserve their natural assets. Finally, citizens who read this book can use its ideas to educate local officials about the importance of planning to conserve their community's natural assets.

STRUCTURE OF THIS GUIDE

This guide is structured as follows:

In **Chapter One**, we provide an overview of green infrastructure planning, its definitions and a short history of the field.

In **Chapter Two**, we provide the reasons for undertaking a green infrastructure planning process.

In **Chapter Three**, we provide the steps to organize a planning initiative including stakeholder engagement and expert consultation.

In **Chapter Four** we cover steps to evaluate and prioritize natural assets

Chapter Five provides case examples for mapping natural assets.

Chapter Six includes ideas to build community support for a green infrastructure plan, key messages and options for expanded engagement.

Chapter Seven covers essential data and processes for creating maps.

The Natural Assets
That Sustain Us Including:
- Forests
- Water Resources: Rivers, Wetlands, Lakes, Estuaries. Aquifers
- Soils That Support Agriculture
- Unique Geologic Features and Landscape Forms

CHAPTER 1 - Green Infrastructure

Chapter One provides a rationale for why we need to think of environmental resources as 'green infrastructure.' It includes a definition, explanation and short history of the term 'green infrastructure,' along with basic ecological concepts and the reasons for undertaking an inventory of natural assets to create a green infrastructure network.

WHY ARE ENVIRONMENTAL RESOURCES PART OF OUR GREEN INFRASTRUCTURE?

Thinking about environmental resources as 'green infrastructure' is a way to recognize that they have value to people. Unfortunately, many of us take natural resources for granted, even though they sustain our very existence. Without clean air, water and agricultural soils, we could not survive. How we manage our landscape directly translates into whether we have the high-quality air, water and nutrients to keep us healthy.

In addition, these natural resources are valuable to us in social terms – terms that are difficult to quantify, but include the social and emotional benefits provided by natural beauty and the open, unspoiled vistas that many of us appreciate. In short, they should be considered our 'green infrastructure.'

Thinking of natural resources as 'green infrastructure' helps us recognize that they provide life-sustaining functions, along with tangible economic and social benefits. It also emphasizes that these natural resources need to be connected as a network because they are interdependent and because connected landscapes allow species to recover and repopulate areas that may have been damaged by such disturbances as drought, forest fires, diseases and hurricanes.

"**Green infrastructure** (GI) planning is a strategic landscape approach to open space conservation, whereby local communities, landowners and organizations work together to identify, design and conserve their local land network, in order to maintain healthy ecological functioning."

In the wake of Hurricane Katrina which devastated New Orleans and Hurricane Sandy which bludgeoned states in the mid-Atlantic, states are looking to restore and protect their 'green infrastructure.' New York and New Jersey, which suffered many billions of dollars of damage from Hurricane Sandy in 2012, are beginning to look towards green infrastructure as a way to mitigate risk and prevent damage.

In New York they are looking to replenish the marshes that once acted as natural storm surge protectors and restore the wetlands that once provided water filtration and flood control. Many scientific studies demonstrate that restoring 'natural infrastructure' can reduce significantly the damage from storm surges. "A 2007 study of New Jersey's wetlands, for example, estimated that freshwater wetlands saved the state $9.4 billion per year in filtrating and flood control costs, while its saltwater wetlands delivered $1.2 billion per year in protection. Hackensack, NJ – one of the hardest hit states in Hurricane Sandy – lost more than 75 percent of its wetlands between 1889 and 1995, according to the US Geological Survey" (Cassin 2012).

WHAT IS GREEN INFRASTRUCTURE PLANNING?

The recognition of the need to plan for conserving our natural assets has led to the field of green infrastructure (GI) planning, in which local communities, landowners and organizations work together to identify, design and conserve their local land network to maintain healthy ecological functioning. In short, it is an organizing construct that enables us to think about our natural resources as a critical part of our life support system. They are 'green' because they are part of the natural environment, and they are 'infrastructure' because they provide those basic services that we all need for healthful and restorative living.

Green infrastructure planning evaluates the types of natural and cultural resources available today and prioritizes those assets that are most important to us, or that best meet our current and future needs. In other words, a green infrastructure strategy includes the process of identifying, evaluating and prioritizing those areas we deem critical to preserving a healthy community for the future. Most importantly, we need to not only prioritize them; we need to implement actions to ensure their conservation over the long term.

THE SIX STEPS

To create a green infrastructure plan, you should follow these six steps:

Step 1. Set Goals:
What does your community or organization value? Determine which natural assets and functions are most important to you.

Step 2. Review Data:
What do you know or need to know, to map the values identified in Step 1?

Step 3. Make Asset Maps:
Map your community's highest-valued natural assets that contribute to a healthy ecology and also support cultural and economic values –Based on the goals established in Step 1 and data from Step 2.

Step 4. Assess Risks:
What assets are most at risk and what could be lost if no action is taken?

Step 5. Determine Opportunities:
Determine opportunities for protection or restoration. Based on those assets and risks you have identified; determine which ones could or should be restored or improved? And which need the attention soonest?

Step 6. Implement Opportunities:
Include your natural asset maps in both daily and long-range planning such as park planning, comprehensive planning and zoning, transportation planning, tourism development and economic planning.

SIX STEPS FOR COMMUNITY GREEN INFRASTRUCTURE PLANNING

During its field tests, the GIC identified six steps necessary to create a natural asset inventory and strategy. The following is a summary of those steps; they are explained in more detail in the following chapters.

STEP 1. Set Your Goals: What Does Your Community or Organization Value? Determine Which Natural Assets and Functions Are Most Important to You.

All GI planning efforts must start with the establishment of goals. What does your community or organization most value about your natural resources? Is it:

- Forests that provide clean air, water filtration, wildlife habitat or wood products?
- Recharge areas to replenish aquifers used for drinking water supplies?
- Water quality to support healthy fisheries?
- The landscape settings around historic landscapes and battlefields?
- Working farms?
- Nature based recreation, such as hiking trails and recreation areas?
- Landscape features, such as key views and vistas?
- Connections across the landscape for wildlife corridors?

STEP 2. Review Data: What Do You Know, or Need to Know, to Map the Values Identified In Step 1?

Once you have established your goals, it is time to assemble and review all the existing relevant data for your local area:

- Research existing studies and available data: What are their findings and are they relevant? Are the data accurate?

  Examples of data include watershed plans, wildlife plans, open space plans, ecological inventories, groundwater studies and air studies.

- Determine what data are still needed if you are to implement your goals: If you are using a Geographic Information System (GIS), you will require data to be arranged spatially in digital layers, which can be analyzed by overlaying them to show patterns and priorities.

  Examples of data that you might need to collect include stream buffers, watersheds, key agricultural soils, recreation routes, forested areas, historic structures and wetlands.

A *viewshed* is a landscape that can be seen from a particular vantage point. It is particularly important in the context of historical sites, such as battlefields and historic houses, where it forms part of those assets' history or supports scenic vistas for nature-based recreation.

Photo courtesy of Peter Stutts

STEP 3. Make Asset Maps: Map Your Community's Highest-valued Ecological and Cultural Assets – Based On the Goals Established In Step 1 and Data From Step 2

Once you have assembled all the existing data and collected additional data to match your goals, it is time to create a natural asset map. This is not a map of all your natural resources, only those you rank as most important because they fulfill a key goal or are the most unique example of a community value. Depending on your goals, and what your community has valued as of high importance, your maps may include elements such as:

- Large intact forests that provide interior habitat for wildlife.
- Watersheds that provide municipal water supplies.
- Key geological features, such as unique rock outcrops or bluffs.
- High-quality agricultural soils that support farms and farming districts.
- Streams, rivers, wetlands and groundwater recharge areas.
- Nature-based recreational areas (for fishing, boating, hiking, biking, birding, etc).
- Tourist sites that depend on the landscape.
- Historic and cultural features (such as battlefields and historic landscapes).
- In urban areas: street trees, the tree canopy, parks and streams.
- Locations and routes for agritourism (such as pick-your-own fruit orchards and farms, wineries, honey producers, local beef, pork and chicken farms, and permanent vegetable stands).
- Scenic views (viewsheds) or routes through historic or cultural assets that should be protected.

Agritourism is tourism based upon local agricultural products, such as pick-your-own fruit orchards and farms, wineries, cideries, honey producers, local organic beef, pork and chicken farms, or fruit and vegetable stands.

STEP 4. Assess Risks: What Assets Are Most at Risk and What Could Be Lost If No Action Is Taken?

Once you have created your natural assets map, it is time to assess those assets most at risk:

- Which areas are zoned for development and do they overlap key natural assets?
- Where are new roads or subdivisions planned – will they fragment key assets?
- Which steams are impaired and need restoration or, which streams are in good condition but may decline in the future?
- Which historic structures are in danger of destruction if no action is taken?
- Are there impaired areas where habitat can be restored?
- What viewsheds are threatened?
- Is any mining, drilling or quarrying planned for your region that might affect air or water quality?
- Which assets are most impacted by present zoning and currently planned developments?

STEP 5. Determine Opportunities: Determine Opportunities for Protection or Restoration. Based on Those Assets and Risks You Have Identified; Determine Which Ones Could or Should Be Restored or Improved? And Which Need the Attention Soonest?

- Which forests or woodlands that are most threatened, or that offer the most value for forestry, recreation and wildlife habitat, are at risk? Specify why.

- Which historical structures are most important and most under threat? Again, specify why.

- Which recreational areas are of most value and are most threatened? (Perhaps an important hunting area is threatened by a new housing development, or is zoned for industrial purposes, or a trout steam is at risk of pollution from expanded land development and runoff.)

- Explore the extent to which current zoning adequately addresses your county's or region's land assets.

- Where should towns or developments be located in the future, so as to allow retention of key resources or to take advantage of access to outdoor recreation?

- Where are new roads or transportation projects likely to impact your assets – should those projects be modified to minimize or prevent impacts?

STEP 6. Implement Opportunities. Include Your Natural Asset Maps in Both Daily and Long-Range Planning

Based on how you have ranked the key natural assets in your area, and which assets are at risk, you may need to implement projects or policies or make changes in local laws, zoning and comprehensive plans to ensure that the priorities you have outlined are achieved. Here are some examples of questions to consider:

- Given your rankings of your landscape's top natural assets, where should towns or developments be located in the future?

- Should zoning or the comprehensive plan be changed to better conserve high-priority assets?

- How can the key forests, farms and waterways you have identified be preserved?

- Should funding be sought to acquire development rights?

- Should there be a landowner education program to encourage voluntary conservation action?

- Could the area's natural assets be utilized in marketing campaigns to expand tourism or attract new businesses?

- Can highly-ranked natural assets be used to prioritize locations for future parks?

- What further data need to be collected, in order to monitor future changes and threats to the area?

- How can local communities, businesses and farmers be best involved in your green infrastructure plan?

- Determine areas important for growth and development, as well as for conservation.

Photo courtesy of Peter Stutts

NATURAL RESOURCES ARE GREEN INFRASTRUCTURE

The following are examples of how you can think of natural resources as assets within a green infrastructure planning effort.

Forests and Wildlife Habitats

Forests play a key role in the water cycle, helping to evapotranspire water into the atmosphere while slowing overland runoff and providing better infiltration of rain into underground aquifers. New York City relies on the vast forests of upstate New York to filter its drinking water and provide some of the cleanest water in the country to its five boroughs. This slowing and storage of runoff water also reduces flooding, since water is released much more slowly from forested landscapes to surface waters than from open fields or impervious areas, such as parking lots.

A forest is not only its trees but also includes the structures and assemblages of forest soils, accumulated leaf litter – also known as the 'duff' layer – soil microbes, fungi and the myriad habitat niches provided by overstory and understory trees, shrubs and plants (e.g. herbaceous plants and vines).

Forest cover is the most effective land cover type for reducing runoff pollutants. Tree canopy breaks the energy of rain drops, while the duff layer of the forest floor acts like a sponge, soaking up water, reducing the velocity of overland runoff and breaking down pollutants. In addition, forests absorb air pollutants such as volatile organic compounds, sequester carbon (which helps to abate climate change impacts) and produce oxygen.

Forests also provide habitat for wildlife. Larger forests can support a greater diversity of habitat types and thus more wildlife diversity. In general, the larger an intact forested area, the more likely it is to support a greater diversity of species. In order to support a diversity of wildlife, plant and insect species, a good rule-of-thumb for the size of a forest in the eastern U.S. is a minimum interior size of 100 acres made up of native tree species (e.g. not a pine plantation, but a natural forest with a diversity of tree species). In the semi-arid and mountainous regions of the western and southwestern U.S., a much larger area is needed to support many native forest species. Consult your state's Natural Heritage Program or wildlife department to determine a good minimum size of forest to support a high diversity of native species in your locality.

Alternatively, some regions may recognize the value of non-forested areas as functioning ecosystems and habitat for viable suites of plant and animal species. For example, throughout the midwest, only minute remnants of native prairie remain, relative to pre-European settlement. As a result, conservation priorities in these regions are focused on preserving those patches that remain and on finding opportunities to restore native vegetation assemblages. In parts of the country, marshland and open water are the preservation priorities, and not forests, which may actually be encroaching on those areas. Natural resource agencies in your region can provide guidance on the priorities for your locale and the minimum size requirements for such areas.

Trees Within the Built Environment

Natural resources are not just found in wild and rural areas. They also protect and enhance our urban life. Street trees and woodlots keep cities cooler, reduce air-conditioning costs, absorb stormwater and provide habitat for birds and other wildlife. They also provide habitat values for people by producing oxygen and absorbing pollutants. Within new subdivisions, yard trees increase property values and wooded lots are advertised as an amenity.

By raising the attractiveness of an urban area, natural assets improve both aesthetic and economic values. Even individual trees have value. A recent five-city study discovered that, on a per-tree basis, cities accrued benefits from their trees ranging between $1.50 and $3.00 for every dollar invested in their management (McPherson et al. 2005). For example, a large mature oak can transpire 40,000 gallons of water per year; this is water that is not entering storm drains and thereby causing runoff, excessive stream flows and downstream erosion (EPA: *Reducing Urban Heat Islands: Compendium of Strategies*).

The main street in Charlottesville, Virginia is now an urban park.

Trees are also part of the ambiance of many shopping districts. On a visit to Charlottesville, Virginia, Ian McHarg, the Scottish landscape architect who wrote the landmark book *Design With Nature*, praised the city for replacing what was once the city's main street with a pedestrian walkway shaded by large willow oaks.

Forested urban green spaces, such as the well-known Central Park in New York City or Rock Creek Park in Washington, DC, are large urban parks that provide respite and enjoyment for people from every social and economic background. Even small parks – often called pocket parks – make some cities very special, as, for example, the green tree-covered squares and gardens of Savannah, GA, which create both an identity as well as a degree of connectivity. Similarly, urban river walks, such as the 13-mile Tennessee River Walk through Chattanooga, TN, or the river walk park along the Connecticut River through Hartford, CT, have led to the revivals of those area's downtowns, spurring new businesses and greater opportunities for community fitness.

Rivers, Wetlands, Lakes, Estuaries, Aquifers

Most people realize that water is vital to our existence. The cleaner the water available, the healthier our human population will be.

All types of surface water, such as streams, wetlands, lakes and groundwater aquifers, springs and seeps, support life: birds and mammals, aquatic plants, fish, invertebrates, crustaceans and mollusks, reptiles and amphibians and people. Estuaries support vital nurseries for young fish, clams and crabs, as well as provide wonderful places to enjoy water sports and scenic views. Surface water also generates opportunities for recreation, such as fishing, boating and birding, and provides aesthetic qualities, such as scenic beauty. Local governments know that rivers, lakes and other water features translate into higher property values and directly support their tax base.

Keeping water supply sources clean can be supported through a thoughtful green infrastructure plan. For example, New York City spent 1.5 billion dollars to acquire 80,000 acres of the watershed that provides its drinking water, in order to restrict development and protect water quality. While this was a large sum of money, it was far less than the $8 billion required to build an adequate filtration plant and an additional $300 million annually for its operating costs (Tibbets, in Benedict and McMahon 2006).

Soils

While soil is defined as the unconsolidated mineral or organic material on the immediate surface of the earth that serves as a medium for the growth of vegetation, we can also think of it as part of our infrastructure. It serves as a medium for growing food, supports vegetation, absorbs water, breaks down wastes and absorbs carbon.

In terms of food production, certain soils are better for supporting agricultural uses, such as row crops or forage for livestock. If we have a map of where those soils are located, we can ensure that areas designated for agriculture can best support those uses. USDA-classified agricultural soils are available as GIS data layers and can be used to evaluate where those soils are located. (For more on this, see Chapter Five.)

In addition, soil data can promote smart planning by showing where soils are well drained and viable for septic systems, or where rural development is not appropriate because the soil is not suitable for septic treatment. Even good soils are becoming important in urban areas as farming takes off in many cities, including Richmond, VA, Asheville, NC and Little Rock, AR.

Geologic Features and Landscape Forms

Geologic features such as rock outcrops, cave and karst features, mountain ridges and unique rock formations are part of what we consider natural assets. These landscape resources contribute to its aesthetic value, whether it is El Capitan in Yosemite, Carlsbad Caverns in Texas, or the Grand Canyon. People place an aesthetic value on types of rocks and minerals, as well as on vistas of ridge tops and valleys.

Geology can also determine the location and extent of unique natural communities/vegetation. The minerals within the rocks as well as physical elements of slope and aspect can determine whether it supports certain species. A landscape's geology of mountains, hills and valleys also plays a significant role in agriculture, especially for crops such as fruit, that do well on slopes, or those crops that need the fertility of lowlands where soils are deposited. In addition, many developers seek to take advantage of outstanding geological features and emphasize them to their prospective buyers.

Karst and limestone features, such as springs, sinking springs and caves, are also critical natural assets. Not only do those areas provide habitat for many rare, threatened and endangered species (such as cave arthropods or the Indiana bat), they are directly linked to groundwater quality. So are many other types of rock. As a result, impacts above ground might not only affect beautiful natural features, but may have quick and potentially detrimental impacts on drinking water and wildlife habitat. The residents of several coal mining areas in Tennessee,

Kentucky and West Virginia are acutely aware of this, as mountain top removal for mining and filling of narrow stream valleys have impaired water quality. Thus, an understanding of rock types and geologic resources in an area may help prevent a future need to mitigate impacts to the quality and supply of drinking water or wildlife.

Floodplains are also key natural assets because they absorb the energy of floodwaters by allowing them to spread out and slow down during high-water events; accordingly, they reduce the downstream erosive force caused by flooding. Similarly, dune systems buffer coastal areas from floods and erosion associated with storms and protect both man-made structures and coastal land from damage.

Areas that possess a unique geology, such as rare mineral deposits, might be included on a map of natural assets, perhaps for future extraction, but perhaps also for aesthetic reasons. Examples of this are the staurolite 'Fairy Stones' of southern Virginia, which are cross-shaped and were formed under the great heat and pressure of the Appalachian Mountain orogeny; the zircon crystal mines in the Wichita Mountains; and the shale barrens of Canada. These are all unique geologies that serve as hosts to suites of uncommon and rare plants found almost exclusively in these habitats.

Unique geologic features can span many states, such as the quartz crystal deposits that are 30-40 miles wide and run from Little Rock Arkansas to eastern Oklahoma. There are cliff escarpments and mountain ranges that run for hundreds of miles, each of which forms a unique geology that supports rare plant and animal assemblages, such as the Catskill Escarpment (referred to as the Catskill Front by geologists), a range forming the northeastern corner of the Catskill Mountains in New York state, or the unique vegetation of the "Islands in the Sky" of Arizona and New Mexico.

GREEN INFRASTRUCTURE PLANNING TODAY

Across the U.S., communities are mapping and evaluating natural resources as they recognize that their integrity and the interconnections between them are key to long-term community well-being. Historically, these efforts have been known by different names – greenways, greenprints, conservation plans and asset maps. They are often initiated by state agencies, such as forestry and park departments, but other organizations also promote them: natural heritage programs and regional planning districts; university departments; conservation groups, such as the Nature Conservancy, Defenders of Wildlife, the Conservation Fund, the Trust for Public Land and the Green Infrastructure Center; and associations such as the National Arbor Day Foundation and the American Planning Association.

Federal agencies, such as the U.S. Forest Service, the U.S. Fish and Wildlife Service, the U.S. Environmental Protection Agency (EPA), the National Oceanic and Atmospheric Administration and even the U.S. Department of Defense (as a large landholder of significant environmental resources) are taking an active role in supporting green infrastructure conservation and planning efforts. In 2006, federal agencies collaborated on a national publication called *Eco-Logical: An Ecosystem Approach to Developing Infrastructure Projects*, which was developed primarily to promote conservation and avoid habitat fragmentation by road projects.

Photo courtesy of the Virginia Outdoors Foundation

In 2007, a consortium of federal agencies supported the Conservation Fund to develop a national self-reporting database of projects (www.greeninfrastructure.net). Also in 2007, the USFS published *Forest Service Open Space Conservation Strategy: Cooperating Across Boundaries to Sustain Working and Natural Landscapes*, in which Strategy #10 calls for the "development of tools to help communities strategically connect open spaces to build a functioning green infrastructure." In addition, the joint USFS and EPA's *Healthy Watersheds Initiative* have supported the use of green infrastructure as a way to achieve watershed protection.

GREEN INFRASTRUCTURE PLANNING CONCEPTS

Green infrastructure planning is not an entirely new concept and its underpinning principles arise from multiple disciplines.

The term 'green infrastructure' was first coined in Florida in 1994 in a report to the governor about land conservation strategies. Combining the words 'green' and 'infrastructure' was intended to reflect the notion that natural systems are equally, if not more, important components of our 'infrastructure' and should be included in the planning process. Since it is generally accepted that we have to plan for gray infrastructure, the idea of planning to conserve or restore our natural resources, as in taking care of our 'green infrastructure,' was intended to help people recognize its key role in civil society.

Low-Impact Development

In 2007, twelve years after the application of the term 'green infrastructure' to refer to natural resources, the EPA began to apply the same term to site-scale best-management practices, such as biofilters (rain gardens), planted (green) rooftops and other stormwater management structures. Previously, these practices were primarily referred to as *low-impact development* (LID). An LID approach offsets runoff pollution from the built environment by the use of integrated best management practices, such as a series of rain gardens to slow and filter stormwater within recessed planting beds whose plants and soil break down pollutants.

The application of the term 'green infrastructure' to site-scale, engineered stormwater management has led to confusion. This guide employs the term strictly as it was first coined by Florida – as a landscape-level evaluation of natural assets for a region, county, town or city. We also introduce the term *natural asset evaluation and mapping* to more directly reflect the GIC's focus on evaluating *natural* landscape resources and conserving them first, before seeking engineered solutions to mitigate impacts from the built environment.

However, while this guide focuses on the larger landscape scale, it does not ignore the importance of these site-scale solutions at all. Rather, it explores how to think at *multiple scales* – from the site to the neighborhood, to the town, city, county, watershed and region – and then back again. In fact, it is important to realize that natural assets need to be assessed and reconnected at multiple scales. So *first*, protect natural assets and minimize land disturbance while keeping the landscape connected. *Then second,* employ LID features to mitigate stormwater runoff at the site scale.

GREEN INFRASTRUCTURE'S KEY ELEMENTS

Several disciplines have addressed the idea of a connected landscape and the importance of selecting and connecting large habitat areas, including the fields of planning, landscape architecture, ecology and conservation biology, forestry, and more recently, transportation. The following is a brief summation of the key concepts they have developed.

Green Corridors

The notion of a connected landscape was popularized by the greenways movement. In the late nineties, Charles Little wrote *Greenways for America (Creating the North American Landscape)*, which popularized an existing movement to get Americans out of their cars and into the landscape through what he called "greenways" (Little 1995). These were loosely defined as "linear open spaces that preserve and restore nature in cities, suburbs and rural areas…to link parks and open spaces and provide corridors for wildlife migration." Later, the concept of *green corridors* was introduced, with much the same meaning.

"**Green infrastructure planning provides an opportunity** for communities to approach land-use planning in a new way by evaluating, prioritizing and managing the landscape as a connected and interdependent system."

However, green infrastructure is far more than greenways.

A *greenprint* is another name for a green infrastructure plan. For example, Miami-Dade calls its GI plan *GreenPrint: Our Design for a Sustainable Future* and describes it as "a fully collaborative process among the many diverse stakeholders of our community."

A *greenway* is a strip of natural land or riverside that passes through areas where the public can walk, ride bicycles and horses, picnic, or otherwise enjoy recreation. It also serves as a wildlife corridor that provides species with access to the inner cities.

Green Corridors are "linear open spaces that preserve and restore nature in cities, suburbs and rural areas... to link parks and open spaces and provide corridors for wildlife migration."

Core Habitats

In the early 21st century, authors such as Benedict and McMahon defined green infrastructure as "a strategically planned and managed network of wilderness, parks, greenways, conservation easements, and working lands..." They defined this network in terms of "hubs" that were joined by "links." They also brought in the notion of *multiple scales*, and stressed the importance of connecting specific local sites into a wider system of links and hubs. Other writers then developed the concept, though they often used different terms.

Around the same time, Hellmund, Smith and Somers updated the notion of greenways to incorporate the connection of large-scale habitats in their book *Designing Greenways: Sustainable Landscapes for Nature and People* (2006). Significantly, they developed a more useful and wider description of green infrastructure that built upon the greenways movement but also incorporated theories of landscape ecology from earlier work by noted landscape ecologist R.T.T. Forman. They discussed Forman's notions of edges, patches, and why the shape and size of habitat areas are extremely important as drivers for the dynamic flow of materials, insects, plants and animals into and out of these habitats.

A Connected Network

Green infrastructure encompasses much more than river greenways or green corridors. While GI planning appreciates corridor greenways as critical connectors between habitats, it sets them within a wider structural context. Rather than regarding the corridors as the focal point of a green strategy, it emphasizes the role of those corridors as links between larger blocks of intact habitat that provide sizable, wildlife-sustaining cores capable of supporting a diversity of species. It places a significant value on these core habitats, depending on their integrity, size and quality. The corridors are important, but without the cores, there is significantly less overall diversity in the landscape.

Whether you prefer to use the terminology of "hubs, links and sites," "patches, cores, corridors and sites," or "cores, corridors and sites," (which we use in this guide), the principle is still to conserve large blocks of intact habitat that are connected by corridors that allow for species movement. Species use the corridors to forage, nest, breed, and move and disperse between core areas.

Note also that each core consists of two parts: a *central area* of undisturbed wildlife habitat, which is surrounded by an *edge area* that absorbs impacts from outside the core (such as erosion, wind, human intrusion and invasive species). This *edge habitat* serves as a buffer; protecting the inner core habitat from encroachment.

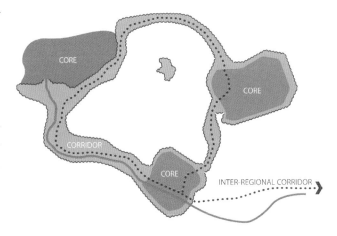

TERMS COMMONLY USED TO DESCRIBE THE COMPONENTS OF A GREEN INFRASTRUCTURE NETWORK

Patch: A relatively homogeneous, nonlinear area of natural cover (such as a forest, desert region, marshland, or grassland) that differs from its surroundings.

Core: A core is an area or patch of relatively intact habitat that is sufficiently large to support more than one individual of a species. Consider that the greater the number of interior species present and the greater the diversity of habitats, the more important it is to conserve the core intact.

Edge: The transitional boundary of a core, where the vegetation assemblage and structure differs markedly from the interior, such as forest edges. The structural diversity of the edge (with different heights and types of vegetation) affects its species diversity, as well as the prevalence or abundance of native or invasive species.

A hard edge, where the habitat changes abruptly is common along man-made fields. A softer edge can serve as a transitional zone or buffer and may support species specifically adapted to take advantage of edge areas.

Corridor: A more or less linear arrangement of a habitat type or natural cover that provides a connection between cores and differs from adjacent land. Corridors are used by species to move between cores, so they need to be wide enough to allow wildlife to progress across the landscape within conditions similar to their interior habitat. For this reason, it is recommended that these connections be at least 300 meters wide: a central 100-meter width of interior habitat, with a 100-meter edge on either side to protect safe passage and buffer against human intrusion and invasive species. Streams are natural corridors and the width of the vegetative corridor on either side should reflect the stream order (i.e. larger streams need wider forested buffers).

In addition to wildlife movement, corridors allow populations of plants and animals to respond to changes in land cover, surrounding land use and microclimate changes over the long term. For example, if a species in a core area is compromised because habitat conditions become unsuitable, it is more likely to survive if it can occupy corridors outside its core that provide some connection to surrounding areas. Thus, the larger a network of interconnected corridors and cores happens to be, the more likely it is that overall species diversity and functioning ecosystems can be maintained amidst a changing landscape.

Effects of sun, wind and human disturbance can cause impacts to the edge area. This disturbed area or edge is not counted as part of the interior of the habitat. The interior is mostly protected from these edge effects.

The edge width is determined by taking the average tree height, e.g. 100 feet, and multiplying that values times three. So in the eastern U.S. where average tree heights are 100 feet, the width of the edge is 300 feet. Whatever is leftover equals the interior habitat. Notice how the shape of the core affects the amount of interior. When there is more length of edge, there is less interior.

TERMS COMMONLY USED TO DESCRIBE THE COMPONENTS OF A GREEN INFRASTRUCTURE NETWORK

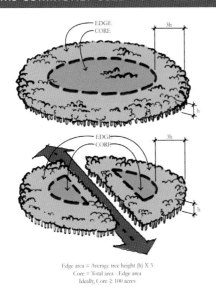

Edge area = Average tree height (h) X 3
Core = Total area - Edge area
Ideally, Core ≥ 100 acres

If you wish to ensure species diversity, particularly for native species, it is critical to identify, map and protect a series of intact core habitats and their connecting corridors, as well as identify those smaller areas of habitat that serve as stepping stones between larger cores.

In the image below left, a stepping stone has been lost. As a result, if something causes a decline of a species in an isolated core, such as a hurricane, forest fire, disease or over-harvesting of vegetation, the species may be unable to re-colonize it.

Although a similar scenario can occur when a corridor is breached, a cluster of closely-related stepping stones can provide substitute connections and alternate routes for plants and animals. The size and spacing of these areas will determine whether or not the species can cross between them and maintain viability.

Stepping Stone: Throughout this network of core areas and corridors, certain smaller areas can provide 'stepping stones' between cores. A stepping stone tends to be a smaller area of intact habitat that may not be large enough to sustain a species on its own, but is vital to a population's success over the network as a whole, as it provides a way to move across the landscape.

Fortunately, corridors can be restored through replanting. Also, some species have a remarkable ability to adapt and discover new paths between core habitats. There was a mountain lion that recently journeyed the hills and prairies of the Midwest from South Dakota to Connecticut, an incredible journey of 1,100 miles (Patch News, Greenwich Connecticut, July 26, 2011). In the summer of 2011, a similarly adventurous black bear migrated from the coastal plain up to Chapel Hill and Greensboro, NC, presumably using the riparian buffers along the Cape Fear River and its tributaries as corridors (Weakley 2012).

Together these cores and corridors form a network. A green infrastructure network seeks to connect habitats to allow species movement.

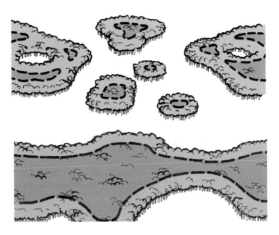

Stepping stones of habitat areas can facilitate animal movement. Roads or other impedances can block them sometimes.

Corridors can be restored by replanting bare areas between patches of core habitats.

GREEN INFRASTRUCTURE PLANNING IN THE UNITED STATES

Green Infrastructure Planning (GIP) is a rapidly growing field in the United States, yet there has been no consistent approach taken to it nationally. This is for several reasons. In part, it is because GIP tends to be practiced differently according to the landscape and the scale people wish to plan for. As ecology changes, so do the types of habitats people tend to consider. For example, an entire mountain range might be necessary to protect a species such as the California *condor* (*Gymnogyps californianus*), but a single cave system might suffice for the Texas Blind Salamander (*Eurycea rathbuni*). Other uses of the landscape may also influence the scale utilized for a GIP project. Forestry may be the main concern, or recreation, or a bird migration route – the scale of which might be international.

What Scale to Work At

In addition, the scale of landscape protected and the minimum size of habitat cores (patches) will depend on the goals set for a project. Part of assessing goals is determining the types of animals and plants for which protection is sought. This, in turn, will determine the approach people decide to take. For example, if a project in Michigan wished to protect the dunes bordering the Great Lakes, it would need to consider the scale required to sufficiently encompass that landscape.

While we have noted that, in the eastern United States, a good rule of thumb for minimum forested habitat cores is 100 acres of interior habitat (Weber 2006), this is not applicable at all scales and for all species. The actual size chosen should arise out of expert local knowledge and relevant studies of species assemblages, movement and habitat needs. If larger areas are present, they generally have even greater value as habitat, e.g. 1,000 acres of core habitat is far better when seeking to protect species.

However, not all landscapes are created equal. A single 100 acre landscape might contain unique wetlands or rare geology and soils that support endangered plants and animals not present on a far larger tract nearby, which might be an old ranch that has regrown into a forest and has severely depleted soils taken over by invasive species. This is why we recommend that both size and landscape characteristics be considered, along with data on species found, when considering the value of a core to realizing your green infrastructure goals. And, as already noted, landscape connectivity is a key factor in protecting biodiversity and ensuring species' resilience.

Thus, those habitats chosen for protection and the approaches adopted will depend on a project's conservation goals, which will differ greatly across the country and from project to project. Some species, such as the greater sage grouse (*Centrocercus urophasianus*), require open landscapes or vast expanses of desert and prairie to survive. Its range covers 186 million acres in 11 western states and two Canadian provinces. However, since three-quarters of the birds inhabit just 27 percent of that potential range, they are far more threatened by residential and commercial development, as well as roads

These dunes along Lake Michigan also provide recreation values.

and oil and gas exploration within that core habitat than overall figures would suggest. Indeed, greater sage-grouse habitat has been highly altered by development over the past century, which has resulted in declines in regional sage-grouse populations from 17–47 percent; in states such as Wyoming, it could decrease by a further 14–29 percent (Copeland et al. 2013) without conservation efforts. Accordingly, the approach taken by the U.S. Fish and Wildlife Service to conserve the species has been to approach every state within its range to coordinate efforts "under the Endangered Species Act and to inform the collective conservation efforts of the many partners working to conserve the species."

Planning at Large Landscape Scales

Today, satellite imagery and other new datasets allow us to look at the landscape at ever-larger scales. Agencies such as the U.S. Forest Service, the U.S. Fish and Wildlife Service, or large conservation groups such as The Nature Conservancy often consider multi-state landscapes when they look at how well the biodiversity for a certain species is being protected. For example, using remote sensing imagery, researchers at Colorado State University found that about a quarter of all the forested lands in the western U.S. could be considered "core patches" integral to a habitat network of forested landscapes. They also found that residential land use and the transportation infrastructure had effectively reduced the area of forested cores by 4.5 percent (20,000km²; 7,700mi²), and continued expansion of residential land by 2030 was likely to reduce forested cores by another 1.2 percent (Theobald 2011). Percentage

The greater sage grouse (Centrocercus urophansianusd)

wise, this is not a high number, but it encompasses thousands of square miles of forested land across 11 states.

There have been many efforts to create maps for large landscapes. At the Woods Hole Research Center in Massachusetts, researchers have identified every core habitat area in the north-eastern U.S., including impervious cover and forest cover. (See http://www.whrc.org/ecosystem/conservation/habitat_corridors.htm for further details.) Begun in 2004, Two Countries, One Forest is a Canadian-U.S. collaboration by conservation organizations, researchers, foundations and individuals focused on the protection, conservation and restoration of forests and natural heritage from New York to Nova Scotia, encompassing the entire Northern Appalachian/Acadian ecoregion. Meanwhile, in the southeast U.S., researchers are running region-wide models to determine the effects of climate change on vegetation dynamics and potential future habitat distribution for avian species (Constanza 2010).

Deserts are another unique environment in which huge ranges may be necessary to support an area's biodiversity. The *Sonoran Desert Conservation Plan* developed by Pima County, Arizona, identified two million acres of land as part of its Conservation Lands System. The plan established six conservation goals, all intended to protect the native species of Pima County. It utilized an extensive process of expert consultation that involved 150 subject-matter experts and engaged the public through 600 meetings. The concept for the plan was approved in 1998, after which it required a number of cooperative agreements to ensure all parties would continue to achieve mutual aims. By December of 2000, the Pima County Board of Supervisors, the Tohono O'odham Nation and various federal agencies agreed to create the Sonoran Desert Conservation Plan. The *Conservation Lands System Regional Plan Policy,* as well as conservation land categories, a policy and a map were adopted in 2005. Since then, they have been able to manage approximately 230,000 acres for conservation, with over 100,000 acres of it now owned by the county.

Land acquisition was funded through two bond referendums in 1997 and 2004, which provided funds to acquire key landscapes identified in the plan. The properties ranged in size from less than an acre to over 30,000 acres and represented the diversity of landscapes that continue to make Pima County unique. Rare species, such as the Cactus Ferruginous Pygmy-Owl (*Glaucidium brasilianum cactorum*) and the Mexican Grey Wolf

(*Canis lupus baileyi*) are just a few of the many species protected by this plan, which demonstrates the extent of expertise, engagement and scale necessary to plan for green infrastructure across a large landscape. (For more details, see www.pima.gov/sdcp.)

State Scale Habitat Models

Some states have created statewide models of their landscapes using the principles of habitat cores and corridors. As noted earlier in this chapter, Florida was one of the first to do so. The state's green infrastructure efforts date back to 1991, when several nonprofit organizations and citizens collaborated to develop the Florida Greenways program. In 1994, the program's successor, the Florida Greenways Commission, issued a report that called for a greenways system that comprised two networks: an Ecological Network, consisting of ecological hubs, linkages and sites along rivers, coastlines and across watersheds; and a Recreational/Cultural Network, with trail corridors connecting parks, urban areas, working landscapes and cultural/historic sites.

In 1995, the greenways initiative transitioned from an NGO-led program to a government-based program, funded by the state legislature, led by the Florida Greenways Coordinating Council (FGCC), and with the Florida Department of Environmental Protection (FDEP) as the state's lead agency. FDEP contracted with the University of Florida to develop the physical design of a statewide greenways system. Today, the role of the FDEP's Office of Greenways and Trails (OGT) is to establish a statewide system of greenways and trails for recreation, conservation and alternative transportation based on the findings of this work. Their greenways and trails system plan is on-going and in 2015 the state updated their Opportunity Maps.

The University of Florida continues its work though the Center for Landscape Conservation Planning, and in 2015 it began an expedition to study and map a 1,000 mile wildlife corridor from central Florida across the panhandle to Alabama. Florida demonstrates a key best practice: utilizing green infrastructure planning as an ongoing process.

Similar to Florida, Maryland's GreenPrint Program grew out of an emphasis on greenways. Maryland Greenways Commission was established in 1991; its purpose was to create a statewide network of greenways that would provide natural pathways for wildlife movement and trails for recreation and alternative transportation routes. The assessment was based on Florida's ecological network approach.

In 2001, Maryland created GreenPrint, a program designed to protect the state's most valuable ecological lands – largely by coordinating existing land conservation programs, easements and land acquisition. It showed the relative ecological importance of every parcel of land in the state. Prince George's County adopted the model and utilizes it to conserve green infrastructure at the county scale. Its first plan identified 92 strategies for conserving or expanding the county's green infrastructure, 80 of which are complete or in process, and it is now updating the plan to reflect new priorities and new data.

Virginia soon followed Maryland with the development of its statewide Virginia Natural Landscape Assessment in 2000, which was later updated in 2007. This model ranks habitat cores using a variety of factors, such as soil diversity, size, water acreage and elevations. It has been used by regions, cities and towns to prioritize natural assets.

In Virginia, the GIC stepped forward to ensure that the state's model could be used by regional and local governments. Beginning in 2006, it tested the state model's application at a variety of regional and local scales, incorporating local data to make the state model useful at the local level. It produced locally relevant green infrastructure network maps as well as themed overlay maps to highlight key issues for each locality, such as water resources, recreation, heritage, agriculture and other data. Since 2006, it has conducted 15 pilot projects in Virginia's regions, counties, cities and towns, and has provided consultation to five planning districts, in order to help them develop their regional plans. These encompassed Richmond, Crater, Rappahannock, Northern Virginia and New River planning districts. The GIC also worked with nonprofit groups to provide mapping and consultation services on strategic land acquisition for several land trusts, such as the New River Valley, the Valley Conservation Council, the Capital Region Land Conservancy and the Northern Virginia Conservation Trust.

Since then, the GIC has branched out into other states, where it has provided extensive consultation, teaching and training services and also built statewide habitat models. To date, it has created state habitat models for New York, Arkansas and South Carolina. In other states that do not have statewide models, the GIC has helped them develop some very useful online tools that can be used as a starting point. For example, in North Carolina, the GIC developed a training workshop in how to use the state's Conservation Planning Tool, which provides information on monitored habitats and their relative quality.

Check with your state's conservation division or natural heritage staff to learn what data and tools they may have created. The GIC can build a model for any state and also offers training workshops, technical guidance and modeling support to help you create your own maps.

In Chapter Seven we discuss the data and tools necessary to locate, map and rank habitats to determine which landscapes are most essential to support biodiversity. In Chapter Five and Seven we also discuss what to do in urban landscapes, where other environmental factors, such as stream corridors, tree canopy or urban woodlots become critical to achieving environmental benefits.

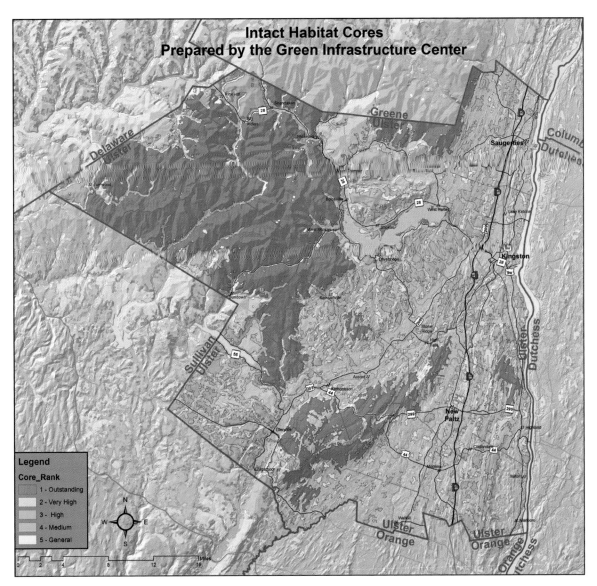

This map of Ulster County, New York, was created by the GIC which ranked habitats based on a variety of factors, such as size, degree of habitat intactness, significant natural communities, abundance and type of water resources, presence of rare species, and other factors. The map shows how cores were priority ranked.

KEY GREEN INFRASTRUCTURE PLANNING ADVANTAGES

There are several key advantages of a green infrastructure planning approach:

1. A green infrastructure strategy protects species. The key point to focus on when embarking on a GI planning process is to *think at multiple scales*. Begin with the wider landscape and consider how connections can be made across multiple areas. By thinking about connections in this way, your strategy will avoid isolating core areas and unintentionally aggravating species loss.

2. A green infrastructure approach can create a more resilient ecosystem. And a resilient ecosystem is better able to maintain its core functions. Here, 'resilience' refers to the amount of change a system can undergo and still retain the same controls on its function and structure. (Holling 1973). A resilient ecosystem has the ability to withstand more impacts, such as storm damage, human impact or diseases, and still maintain its core functions.

   In order to maintain resilience, it is critical to protect the natural state of an ecosystem as much as possible. Permit as little disturbance to it as you can: as little human intrusion, such as road building; as little fragmentation; as little noise; and as few introductions of alien species.

3. A green infrastructure strategy allows multiple objectives to be met at once. Often referred to as *multi-objective planning*, a green infrastructure plan should include multiple objectives for open space recreation, habitat conservation and biodiversity, tourism and economic development. Cores, corridors and other land areas that meet multiple goals can be targeted for conservation.

Pollinators also benefit from habitat protection.

Certain species, such as the scarlet tanager, prefer interior forests.

In this chapter we have covered definitions. In the next chapter, we will focus in more detail on the benefits of green infrastructure planning.

PLANNING WITH NATURAL ASSETS FIRST

- Avoiding Risk
- Ecosystem Services
- Cultural Assets
- Vibrant Communities

CHAPTER 2 - The Need to Evaluate and Map Natural Features

By considering environmental resources as 'natural assets,' based on the functions described in the previous chapter, we can begin to assign appropriate values to them and recognize their importance to our lives and livelihoods. Determining how to evaluate and manage these resources as key assets will help us meet important community values – for example, if you value wildlife or recreation, assessing your natural assets will help you protect them.

Other values you might wish to emphasize are stormwater treatment, energy savings, aesthetic values, improved community health or a sustainable local economy.

FIRST STAGE OF LAND PLANNING BEGINS WITH GREEN INFRASTRUCTURE

While the idea of natural resources as 'green infrastructure' (GI) has been around for several decades, most local governments are not familiar with it. As a result, it is important to articulate and promote GI's benefits to staff planners and both appointed and elected officials. We need to stress that these assets need to be evaluated and catalogued as the *first stage of land planning*, in order to ensure the long-term ecological, social and economic health of our communities, and to enable them to benefit from the considerable financial savings of a green infrastructure approach.

When Ian McHarg was putting forward his ideas in his book *Design With Nature* (1969), planners had to rely on trace paper, transparencies and long hours of coloring to show the relationships between the land's natural features, laying one transparent sheet over the other to see where critical drainage or key soils overlapped or intersected. Today, we have digital Geographic Information Systems (GIS), through which we can see these relationships almost instantly by turning on and off digital layers that are spatially related.

However, even with the advent of computer software, remote sensing technology and much faster computers that can analyze as much data on a laptop in seconds as it once took days to process on a mainframe, we do not always utilize the wealth of data available to us. But we need to. We need to do it consistently and *as a first step*.

Photo courtesy Peter Stutts

Right Order Thinking: Begin With a Map of Natural Features

A natural asset planning effort identifies and evaluates existing natural and cultural resources and prioritizes those assets that are most unique, or that best meet current and future needs. To achieve this, any strategy should include a *prioritization process* to select, rank and conserve those areas that are most critical to a resilient and healthy community.

Ideally, if enough natural assets are protected in the first place, there will be less need to build engineered structures to deal with such problems as stormwater runoff or sea encroachment over coastal areas. Once you have conserved your key natural resources and buildings have been sited to minimize impacts and landscape fragmentation, your focus can turn to mitigating the impacts from buildings and developed surface areas. For example, you can treat stormwater runoff through site-scale low-impact development approaches using rain gardens, green rooftops, permeable paving and a host of other best-management practices that contain, detain and filter runoff.

An illustration of the need to assess existing natural assets on a site as the first step was witnessed by the author. A developer of an affordable housing program proposed cutting down several mature oak trees and replacing them with rain gardens. The trees were already absorbing and filtering the rainwater, while also providing the proposed homes with shade and wind shelter. Fortunately, when the benefits of the existing trees were pointed out by the local planning commission, the developer changed his plans to cut them down. Whenever possible, natural infrastructure should be conserved before seeking an engineered solution to replicate its functions.

While saving a handful of trees on one site may seem to have a small impact, these site-scale conservation approaches can soon add up. A national study of the value of urban tree cover in reducing stormwater problems and improving air quality showed that the trees in our cities are worth more than $400 billion in terms of money saved by not having to build such structures as stormwater ponds or biofilters (Benedict and McMahon 2006).

While it is useful for future contingencies to map your natural assets, their links to key cultural resources and their desired future uses, it is also very useful for everyday planning. To quote a past president of the Virginia Homebuilders Association, when he was addressing county planners, "I just want to know what you want and where you want it. You can save us both time and money by telling me in advance what the community desires."

If you have your key assets mapped out in advance, it allows developers to propose projects that meet current and future community needs. It also saves time later by not having to make multiple reiterations of site plans when yet another key resource is discovered or a new community concern is brought up.

With a map already in place, your community can also choose to enhance its green infrastructure by proactively selecting areas to restore through new plantings, acquisition of land or the creation of new conservation easements that re-link disconnected landscapes.

A Map Avoids Future Risk

The key to maximizing a community's success is to ensure that it has as many choices and options available to it as possible. This is a similar approach to creating an investment portfolio – risk is minimized by having multiple kinds of investments.

In some respects, a healthy community needs to have a diversity of options to provide it with its necessary ecosystem services and ensure that today's decisions do not unduly foreclose on future options. Evaluating resources now and making sure there are enough of each type ensures that future populations can have abundant natural services and sufficient community character to build a successful community.

If you identify those assets that are at risk and that you wish to conserve, a map can mitigate against future economic challenges and threats to public safety. For example, if you identify those assets within floodplains and make them off-limits to future development, you can meet your needs to conserve wildlife corridors, while also preventing the loss of life and property damage.

Every community that has a zoning ordinance can decide whether or not to allow building in flood zones. However, those that choose to allow it must still follow federal regulations. The United States guaranteed flood insurance opportunities for communities through the Flood Disaster Protection Act of 1973 and amended

"**Whenever possible, natural infrastructure** should be conserved before seeking an engineered solution to replicate its functions."

Development has caused new backyard flooding and hazards.

regulations of 1994, but those laws only allow localities to develop their floodplains as long as they follow Federal Emergency Management Act (FEMA) guidance for floodwater ingress and egress.

You can also identify other areas of high risk, such as regions vulnerable to sea level rise, and you can include them on your map as areas to avoid. There are currently models and maps available from NOAA that identify these sections of coastline. For more, see Chapter Seven.

ECOSYSTEM SERVICES

In the past ten years, there has been a renewed interest both in landscape-scale planning and in linking ecological services and community needs. Increasingly, localities recognize that livable and healthy communities require the conservation and restoration of healthy forests, accessible open spaces and connected landscapes, in order to provide clean air, clean water, public fitness, wildlife diversity and aesthetic benefits. Often referred to as ecosystem services, these largely free environmental functions are key to creating livable communities. *Ecosystem services* have quantifiable economic benefits which reduce the cost of providing services within a community.

Ecosystem services are those positive benefits nature provides us, generally for free, that are essential for a thriving community. They include clean air and water, recreational opportunities, beautiful vistas, natural heritage sites, stormwater remediation, healthy foods and places to rest the soul and recuperate.

The notion of *ecosystem services* has now begun to gain credibility with economists and land planners. For example, as land managers and municipalities search for ways to abate the damage and costs of flood events, such as the repeatedly devastating floods of the Mississippi-Missouri river system, many are realizing that the most cost-effective way to alleviate future costs and minimize risk is to avoid building in hazardous areas in the first place, and to infiltrate a lot more water throughout our watersheds by planting far more forested land. Instead of continually trying to flood-proof buildings, some managers are realizing it is cheaper to let floodplains perform their natural function of absorbing floodwater. As a result, the economics of a green infrastructure approach have gained increased recognition, even though we may not always realize that we need to expend time and effort to ensure that these ecosystem services are well maintained. See the text box on page 23 for an example.

If land planning begins within the context of a local ecological system, it ensures that development is channeled into the most appropriate areas, while environmental functions are protected. This saves both money and energy. In already developed areas, green assets can be reconnected while new development takes place in more suitable areas. And you can even begin to restore lost areas vital to the ecosystem.

AVOIDING FLOOD RISKS

A very wet fall in 1992, followed by heavy snowmelt in 1993, caused dramatic runoff to swell the banks of the Mississippi River and its tributaries. Streams and rivers overran the levees in the Dakotas, Minnesota, Wisconsin, Illinois, Iowa, Nebraska, Kansas and Missouri. The result was the death of 48 people and $15–$20 billion in property and land damage.

Flood waters covered 2.6 million acres of land. A total of 74,000 people became homeless as navigation was closed on the system's major rivers for almost two months. The government declared 525 counties in nine states – including all of Iowa – disaster areas.

As a result, the towns of Pattonsburg, and Valmeyer in Illinois and Rhineland in Missouri agreed to relocate to higher ground, thereby letting the floodplain perform its natural function of absorbing flood energies without placing people and property in the watershed at risk. (*Los Angeles Times*, July 12, 1998).

Lack of forest cover can lead to more flooding and damage to grey infrastructure.

Even at environmentally impaired sites where some contamination has occurred, natural systems and habitats can be restored. And, more importantly, plans that seek to conserve natural assets can create or sustain linkages so that animals and people are able to move across the landscape.

We need to consider the values that these natural resources provide, in order to ensure that we can be intentional about conserving, protecting and restoring them. We need to understand where these natural assets are located, how abundant they are and what is their current condition. This will enable us to determine how best to manage them.

FISCAL CONSIDERATIONS

Perhaps the greatest long-term obstacle to local governments adopting new ways of planning that include evaluating and conserving natural assets are the fiscal challenges they face. An often-heard refrain is, "We can't afford to do more planning in these tough economic times. We need to get rid of rules, plans and regulations in order to attract more development."

However, that is a false economy. Local governments, chambers of commerce and others should be aware that green infrastructure planning is not an additional burden; it is a way to plan more efficiently and effectively. Having better information at one's fingertips can both *speed up* the planning process and make it easier to develop in a way that benefits *both* the environment and the economy and avoid pitfalls from poor decisions later on. They need not be seen as enemies. Rather, they are compatible elements that will improve our communities if they are *both* considered.

We can think of 'green infrastructure' as an environmental insurance policy that enables traditional economic growth and development in focused growth areas without compromising the health and well-being of the community. If we identify key watershed recharge areas, the best agricultural lands and the most unique and productive forests as a first step, we can ensure that growth does not deplete the resources upon which we all depend for healthy and strong communities. This is especially true when trying to ensure a long-term water supply or seeking to comply with mandates for clean water. If we avoid damaging our best areas and identify opportunities for restoration, we will save both our ecological and economic health over the long term.

> "We can think of 'green infrastructure' as an environmental insurance policy that enables traditional economic growth and development in focused growth areas without compromising the health and well-being of the community."

Economic Value of Green Assets

If a community wants to be more effective in luring businesses and growing during tough economic times, it should remember that green communities attract companies. Sound planning also helps to ensure predictability for those locating to a new area.

This is also true for real estate development; studies have shown that those who include green space or natural areas into development plans sell homes faster and for higher profits than those who take the more traditional approach of building over an entire area without providing for community green space (Benedict and McMahon 2006).

There is one other compelling fiscal reason for planning the conservation of natural assets as part of a green infrastructure strategy: avoiding costly natural disasters. By including the natural landscape as part of infrastructure planning, it is possible to reduce the threat of extensive flooding by identifying and protecting floodplains, allowing for natural drainage and avoiding building in hazard areas. The risks and costs associated with wildfires can also be reduced or eliminated by evaluating where forests are most sensitive to disturbance and avoiding overdevelopment in those areas. And, if you live in an earthquake zone, you can put strict building codes in place that are intended to mitigate future damage and seek to avoid building close to or on top of fault lines.

GI PLANNING *SAVES* MONEY

It is not a new idea to evaluate natural assets at the beginning of the land development process. Ian McHarg published his seminal book *Design With Nature* in 1969, in which he proposed that planning must begin with a consideration of the land's natural features: its soils, slopes, waters and drainage. He proposed the notions of *layering information* and considering landscape features as *resources that must be evaluated in tandem,* in order to create a development plan that worked *with* nature instead of against it.

His approach actually *saved* money, since it avoided problems of improper site development – such as poor drainage and flooding – and created developments that were more attractive and less destructive.

Land Values

A study by the National Association of Realtors found that 57 percent of voters surveyed were more likely to purchase a home near green space and 50 percent were willing to pay 10 percent more for a home located near a park or other protected area. A similar study found that homes adjacent to a greenbelt in Boulder, Colorado were valued 32 percent higher than those 3,200 feet away (Correll et al. 1978). Ensuring property values are maintained is important for localities that need stable tax revenues and for homeowners who need to maintain the investment value of their properties.

Jobs

Preserving open space helps attract companies that offer good jobs. Small companies, especially those that have a well-paid and skilled workforce, place strong importance on the 'green' of the local environment (Crompton Love and Moore 1997). The creative class – artists, media workers, lawyers, and analysts – makes up 30 percent of the U.S. workforce and its members place a premium on outdoor recreation and access to nature (Florida 2002).

In addition, many jobs are dependent on large intact landscapes. A high proportion of forest lands that are suitable for harvest are within a zone denoted as the *wildland-urban interface* – the zone where human encroachment occurs within a largely forested landscape – making it more difficult to harvest trees and manage forests there. For example, prescribed burns may be needed to restore forests or encourage native species. When people live

close to or within these areas, such management practices become unpopular or unsafe (*2003 Southern Wildland-Urban Interface Assessment*). For many states in the Southern U.S., forest industry revenues are in the billions of dollars, so continued urban encroachment into rural areas threatens their rural economies. In North Carolina, smoke impact zones are mapped to let residents know they live in an area where controlled burning will be done.

A *wildland-urban interface* (WUI) is a zone of transition between unoccupied land and urban development where development begins to encroach upon and within previously undeveloped areas.

SAVING COSTS OF MITIGATION AND WATER TREATMENT

A survey by the American Water Works Association found that a 10 percent increase in forest cover reduced the chemical and treatment costs of providing safe drinking water by 20 percent (Barten and Ernst 2004). Since half of the country depends on surface waters for its potable water supply, reducing treatment costs will benefit more than half the nation and have considerable cost savings.

There are multiple studies of the benefits of urban forest canopy in mitigating the cost of urban impacts. For example, USFS researcher David Nowak studied Washington, D.C.'s urban canopy and found that it stored about 526,000 tons of carbon, which he calculated provides benefits to the city of $9.7 million. The urban canopy also removed about 16,200 tons of carbon per year, at an estimated value of $299,000, along with 540 tons of air pollution, estimated to be worth an additional $2.5 million per year (Nowak 2006).

For those who depend on well water, forests recharge aquifers by holding water, filtering it and allowing it to slowly infiltrate down, instead of running off quickly (and causing other problems, such as downstream flooding). The longer a well can remain in service, the lower the cost, since it will not need to be relocated or re-drilled to reach a deeper water table.

URBAN TREES PROVIDE MULTIPLE BENEFITS

American Forests has estimated that "the value of urban tree cover for reducing stormwater problems and improving air quality in cities is worth more than $400 billion." (*Human Influences on Forest Ecosystems: The Southern Wildland-Urban Interface Assessment, 2003.*)

MEETING REGULATORY REQUIREMENTS

The federal Clean Water Act, the Safe Drinking Water Act and a host of other state and local regulations require us to protect the quality of our environment. We can reduce the costs of pollution prevention and cleanup by ensuring that our landscape is as forested as possible. We can also prevent pollution in the first place. Forested landscapes are the most effective land cover for infiltrating water and for filtering and cleaning polluted runoff. Sediment, nitrogen and phosphorus are the three primary types of pollution targeted for reduction as part of the mandatory plan to clean up the Chesapeake Bay, which affects the states of Maryland, Virginia, West Virginia, New York and Pennsylvania, as well as the District of Columbia. And trees and forested landscapes are the most effective way of reducing all three of those pollutants in our waterways.

Protecting watersheds with forested land cover and buffering streams from runoff also help prevent future water quality impairments that are expensive to mitigate under the Clean Water Act's Total Maximum Daily Loading (TMDL) provisions. These mandate modeling and clean-up plans for waters found to be impaired, something that affects every state. Planning, with water issues in mind is far less costly in the long run, than trying to rehabilitate an impaired stream.

IMPROVING HUMAN HEALTH

Forest cover reduces surface temperatures, which keeps cities cooler and more livable. Furthermore, trees absorb volatile organic compounds and particulate matter from the air, improving air quality.

Forests and other natural areas also benefit people who suffer from Attention Deficit Hyperactivity Disorder (ADHD). A study of children who moved closer to green areas found that those who relocated tended to have the highest levels of improved cognitive functioning following the move, regardless of level of affluence (Wells 2000). Green outdoor settings appear to reduce ADHD symptoms in children across a wide range of individual, residential, and case characteristics (Kou and Taylor 2003).

Kids who spend time outside have lower rates of ADHD.

NATURAL ASSETS SUPPORT CULTURAL ASSETS

As you evaluate your natural assets, it is important to consider how they link to or support *cultural assets*. A cultural asset is a place or feature that is important to the human experience. It forms part of the daily life of a community and is supported by, or includes, natural assets. For example, an historic plantation manor home and its associated outbuildings are set within a landscape. Both the structures and the setting of trees and vegetation are what we consider to be assets.

A *cultural asset* is a place or feature that is important to the human experience. It forms part of the daily life of a community and is supported by, or includes, natural assets.

A cultural landscape has been defined as "a geographic area, including both cultural and natural resources and the wildlife or domestic animals therein, associated with a historic event, activity, or person, or exhibiting other cultural or aesthetic values" (Birnbaum 1994). For more, see the text box on page 26.

While National Register nominations document the significance and integrity of historic properties, in general, they may not acknowledge the significance of the landscape's design or historic land uses, and may not contain an inventory of landscape features or characteristics. Additional research is often necessary to provide the detailed information about a landscape's evolution and significance that is useful in making decisions for the treatment and maintenance of a historic landscape. Existing National Register forms may be amended to recognize additional areas of significance and to include more complete descriptions of historic properties that have significant land areas and landscape features.

Cultural and Historic Features

When creating a map of natural assets, it is important to identify which natural features also support cultural assets.

A cultural asset is a place or landscape resource that is important to the human experience and is landscape dependent. For example, an historic plantation, a battlefield or an historic district are not simply the obvious and immediate features, but are dependent on the landscape that surrounds them. Imagine Vicksburg without the Mississippi River.

It is important to identify those natural assets that surround and support key cultural and historic features, in order to preserve their content and setting and to buffer them from intrusion. Taken together with other natural and culturally important structures and land uses across a larger scale, these features may comprise a particular cultural landscape.

A historic plantation home depends upon the landscape context.

Photo courtesy Sara Hollberg/Valley Conservation Council

This gas station destroys the historic context for this historic home's site.

Photo courtesy Sara Hollberg/Valley Conservation Council

An example of such a landscape surrounds the Jamestown Settlement in Virginia, where the neighboring James River, the surrounding tidal marshes and the small island itself need to be preserved to maintain the feel of those early settlement years.

CULTURAL LANDSCAPES AND CULTURAL ASSETS

A *cultural landscape* has been defined as "a geographic area, including both cultural and natural resources and the wildlife or domestic animals therein, associated with a historic event, activity, or person, or exhibiting other cultural or aesthetic values" (Birnbaum 1994).

There are four general types of cultural landscapes, but they are not mutually exclusive: historic sites, historic designed landscapes, historic vernacular landscapes, and ethnographic landscapes.

- Historic sites: These are particular structures or highly localized areas, such as battlefields, colonial houses, historic bridges, Indian mounds, lighthouses and tobacco barns.

- Historic designed landscapes: These are wider, more encompassing landscapes that offer an historic context to an important aspect of our past, such as that around the Cahokia Indian Mounds in Illinois.

- Historic vernacular landscapes: These evolved through use by the people whose activities or occupancy shaped them. Their alterations to the landscape determined its current physical, biological, and cultural character. The cultural region of the Ancient Pueblo in southern Arizona and New Mexico, encompassing such sites as Chaco Canyon and Canyon de Chelly, is one example. The Oregon Trail is another.

- Ethnographic landscapes: These contain a variety of natural and cultural resources that people have defined as heritage resources. Contemporary settlements, religious sacred sites and geologic structures can comprise these landscapes. Small plant communities, animals, subsistence and ceremonial grounds are often components. For example, Acoma Pueblo in New Mexico is such a landscape as it is a settlement carved into a massive rock formation that is occupied by indigenous peoples. Another example might be Bear Lodge (Mathó Thípila, or Devil's Tower) in Wyoming, which is sacred to the Native Americans of that region.

Community Character

Oftentimes, when people think about what makes their community special, they have difficulty in pinpointing exactly what makes up its character. When they say they like the rural character or the feel of their neighborhood, it can be challenging to define exactly what they mean. This is due, in part, to the fact that the landscape they see is made up of an assemblage of features that are so familiar, they take many of them for granted.

When asked to define rural character in GIC's workshops, participants often reply vaguely, in terms similar to, "It looks like home." In urban areas, community members may say imprecise things like, "The street where I live and my neighborhood are important," "I like the sunset from that bridge," or "That's the place where we like to ride our bikes." No matter how non-specific these comments are, they are part of the notions that build an individual's and a community's sense of place.

Indeed, the character of a place largely comprises familiar, non-specific stimuli that create these vague individual feelings – such as a pretty view where you went on your first date, a tree filled streetscape that you helped plant as a child, the park where you've walked your dog for the last ten years, or an historic area where your grandfather lived – along with the memories, stories and shared community experiences that together create something indefinably special. Many of these special or unique experiences are tied to our immediate surroundings – the built and natural resources of our landscape. Their vagueness does not mean they should be disregarded. Rather, we need to find ways to define them and incorporate them into our planning.

It is important to identify these culturally significant landscapes, natural features and settings as part of a green infrastructure planning effort. A Civil War battlefield, the spot where people were sold into slavery, or the view from a family-run orchard can be essential to a community's sense of identity. For example, a 2012 ceremony recognized the importance of the Rappahannock River in central Virginia, across which hundreds of slaves escaped to freedom during the Civil War. The river is a natural resource, but it is also a cultural artifact that is part of community history and identity. Recognizing that natural resources serve as a context for the built environment and often serve as the historic feature themselves, is key to evaluating the importance of natural assets.

Viewsheds

Often, those areas that can be seen from a particular vantage point are referred to as *viewsheds*. A viewshed is made up of key landscape features and includes those iconic components – cultural resources, ridgelines or geology – that form part of a landscape's context. An important viewshed can be identified by a community and included in a map of its natural and cultural assets. It may be an attractive view from a scenic road or include cultural resources such as an old barn, a 19th century church or an historic mill.

A few years ago, a large, privately owned observation tower was removed from the viewshed of Gettysburg in an attempt to restore the view looking across the battlefield. At Monticello, President Jefferson's former home in Virginia, the summit of a nearby hill was recently purchased to prevent any development taking place on it that would ruin the view Jefferson once appreciated. Similarly, at President George Washington's home, the Mount Vernon Ladies Association, which owns and runs his estate, worked with the State of Maryland and landowners across the Potomac to avoid building in ways that would mar the view from Mount Vernon across the river.

Usually, a community will have already identified those iconic views that are important to its character and provide the context for the statement that, "It feels like home." However, they may not have been recognized as such by the local government in its policy or planning documents, nor be protected by regulations. An historic house may be protected, but the land around it might

remain open to a variety of possible developments, such as a quarry or huge retail distribution warehouse.

A *viewshed* is made up of key landscape features and includes those iconic components – cultural resources, ridgelines or geology – that form part of a landscape's context and can be seen from a particular vantage point.

A common refrain often relayed in community meetings and public hearings is, "Why did someone put that eyesore (a billboard, cell tower, giant gas station canopy, etc.) in the middle of our favorite view?" Oftentimes, it is because the viewshed was not identified on any maps or planning documents. Yet, once the damage is done and the view is obstructed, it is often very difficult to restore it.

While those who own the resources in a viewshed have certain rights to develop their properties (based on existing regulations, such as zoning), there are many steps that can be taken to reduce visual impact to other users while still allowing development. Buildings can be shielded from view by putting them in places that take advantage of topography (low areas or areas screened by hills), or they can be screened with trees and vegetation to hide or disguise those built resources that would otherwise detract from the scenic view. For example, structures can be positioned below grade or towers can be disguised. Furthermore, the need for additional cell towers can be reduced by co-locating them with existing towers or attaching them to existing structures, such as grain silos and church steeples.

A view of The Priest and Three Ridges wilderness in Virginia.

Sky Meadows State Park in Virginia works with their neighbors to preserve this historic landscape view seen from the park.

Scenic Routes

From the standpoint of economic development, protecting the vistas that visitors can see from a scenic road is very important to ensure a positive experience for tourists. The first impression of an area often influences how long tourists stay and explore, which translates into direct financial benefits for the region in terms of the number of nights of lodging, meals purchased, visits to gift and craft shops, money spent on entrance fees and gas, and other travel-associated spending. Tourists are less likely to travel through blighted areas to reach an historic or natural area. However, if an area's scenic roadways are designed to enhance the locality's historic and architectural character and its beautiful landscape, they will be more inclined to stop and visit its towns and landmarks.

Photo courtesy capitalregionusa.org

Natural setting is very important to property values. They decline when areas begin to look rundown or overcrowded with signage and dilapidated buildings. It is important to have strong standards for signage size and design, as well as good building codes to address blight, in order to protect a landscape's natural beauty and its cultural and historical context.

In addition, many businesses depend on key views. Quite a few microbrewers have located to Nelson County, VA, to take advantage of its scenic vistas. People are willing to drive 40 or more miles to drink their beers, not just so they can enjoy a fine glass of malted hops, but to do so while gazing out at a beautiful forested mountain landscape. These microbreweries also depend on the mountainous forested landscape to absorb and filter the water they use in their brewing processes. Similarly, many hotels, inns and restaurants depend on their views to attract visitors. Wineries offer patios with vistas to entice visitors to spend a few hours imbibing both nature and their best chardonnays.

The challenge is to identify those supporting landscapes and natural features and ensure a mutual cooperation between landowners to protect them. The brewer or vintner depends on his view to lure customers, but he usually does not own it.

VIEWS ATTRACT TOURISTS

In Virginia, visitors spend $9.1 billion each year visiting historic and cultural sites (Hollberg and McMahon 1999). Most of them come to experience historic settings, such as Mount Vernon or Monticello, to visit Civil War sites such as Appomattox, The Wilderness and Chancellorsville, or to experience the wondrous vistas from the Blue Ridge Parkway. All of those sites are enhanced by preserving their viewsheds.

This viewshed attracts customers to the brewery.

In some Western states, landowners who want to preserve a viewshed will pay neighboring landowners to keep it that way. Some ranchers are reimbursed by adjacent homeowner associations to maintain their ranches because the viewshed is what attracted the homebuyers to the area in the first place, and is what continues to support their property values.

How to Determine Whether to Include a Cultural Asset on Your Map

When assessing cultural assets as part of your green infrastructure map, it is important to ask yourself two questions:

- Is this feature landscape-dependent?
- Does it need to be supported by neighboring green infrastructure resources, such as mature trees, a forest vista, protective sand dunes, an estuary, or any other unique geologic feature, if it is to retain its character?

If the answer to both is no, then the resource may not be critical to include on your green infrastructure map. If the answer to either is yes, you should consider preserving its viewshed in addition to preserving the feature itself.

If your community has already conducted an historic survey, then those maps can be overlaid with green asset maps (and possibly topography) to determine which areas are supported by the landscape and are dependent on landscape settings.

PROTECTING YOUR WATER SUPPLY

Water supply is another key application for natural asset plans. If a community is likely to need to draw from other surface or groundwater sources to supply future population growth, additional land use covenants may be needed now to protect any drainage area that will supply a future reservoir, groundwater aquifer or drinking water intake pipe. All too often, lax zoning regulations and overdevelopment around reservoirs mean that, when communities seek to tap those supplies, they learn that treatment costs have risen substantially or that reservoirs have silted in and lost capacity. Groundwater aquifers may also lose capacity when impervious paved surfaces prevent rainfall from filtering into the soil and recharging them.

An illustration of why you need to have a map of key watershed areas was witnessed by the author when a senior university environmental scientist asked the chair of a board of supervisors in 2007, "Why did you permit a large subdivision to be built on top of land that is the groundwater recharge area for our community's drinking water supply?" One can reasonably guess at the reply from the supervisor; "We didn't know it was a recharge area."

All too often, we plan first and ask questions later. This is not the result of a lack of caring; it is simply that local governments are not always in the habit of planning with natural assets in mind as a *first* step.

The consequences of considering environmental impacts too late in the game can be numerous and very expensive: impaired waters; expensive cleanup plans; higher costs to treat drinking water; flooded towns and neighborhoods; fires that inflict high property damage and loss of life; landslides that destroy neighborhoods; contaminated rivers; brownfield sites; dredging costs; new reservoirs and dams; deeper and more costly wells; lost opportunities for recreation, clean air, attractive landscapes and strong economies... The list goes on and on.

Conserving natural assets also avoids risk. One particular example of risk avoidance is to reduce exposure to wildfires in the high-risk areas of the wildland-urban interface (WUI), which include a large proportion of Southern forest lands. From a risk perspective, homeowners and firefighters face a higher threat when trying to save properties in these areas. Furthermore, the suppression of natural fires in WUI areas has other consequences. It reduces the diversity of the landscape while increasing the frequency of insect infestations. Avoid development in these areas to keep forests healthy and people safe.

This bridge forms part of a Nelson County, VA greenway trail which provides relaxation and fitness opportunities for nearby residents.

MANAGE YOUR NATURAL ASSETS AS PART OF A LOCAL LAND-USE PLANNING PROCESS

By better managing your natural assets as part of a local land-use planning process, you can:

• Preserve biodiversity and wildlife habitat.
• Combat climate change impacts (through carbon sequestration) and improve air quality.
• Protect and preserve local water quality and supply.
• Provide cost-effective stormwater management and hazard mitigation.
• Improve public health, quality of life and recreation networks.
• Ensure food security by conserving good agricultural soils and preserving local farms.
• Preserve cultural resources, such as historic landscapes and scenic vistas.
• Support rural economies dependent on forest products.

that could be future pocket parks, greenway or rail-to-trail pathways, not only will they serve a population that chooses to age in place, but they will provide extra habitat for wildlife, birds and pollinators.

Similarly, the younger generation, those under 30, who are sometimes called the "millennials" or "generation Y," are trending towards urban areas and yet they still want access to green spaces for hiking, biking, kayaking and other recreational activities. Growing populations demand new schools and walking routes that include natural trails, so that their children can walk to school and learn about nature and science locally.

CREATING A VIBRANT COMMUNITY FOR ALL AGES

If you want to create a vibrant and healthful community and incorporate demographic trends into your land conservation plans it is key to have a vision for how you want your community to look in the future. A well established trend being discussed today is that of 'aging in place.' Baby boomers (those born between 1946 and 1964) are tending to stay in their homes after retirement, rather than move into an elder care facility.

As people age, they are less able to drive to natural areas, parks and trails and they appreciate having them closer to their residences. If you can identify those areas

There are many abandoned rail lines, such as the one to the left, that could be re-purposed as trails. A *rail-to-trail pathway* or *bikeway* is an old railway line that has been converted into a hiking or biking trail. One notable recent example of this approach is the High Line Park in New York which took an abandoned elevated subway track in West Manhattan and turned it into a greenway that runs right through the heart of the borough. Another example is the American Tobacco Trail (ATT) which is a 20 mile long rail trail built from an abandoned railway that served the American Tobacco Company in the 1970s. Today it crosses through the city of Durham and the counties of Durham, Chatham and Wake in North Carolina. It then links into the larger East Coast Greenway spanning multiple states.

GREENING MID-MICHIGAN

The Greening Mid-Michigan project originated from the Tri-County Regional Growth Study released in 2005, which recommended that open space and resource protection be promoted through four region-wide principles that focused on farmland and other natural resources. These included pathways, sidewalks, trails and bicycle facilities that would provide transportation and health benefits, as well as park and recreation development to link facilities through greenways. The project also stressed the protection and enhancement of key buildings and the area's 'living heritage', which included historic and cultural sites.

The project established a clear vision to guide priorities: "Fundamentally, green infrastructure is key for creating and maintaining the sense of place we all desire for our neighborhoods, communities and the tri-county region. Ultimately, we envision the Tri-County region as a place where natural resource conservation is balanced with economic development and a healthy environment is broadly recognized as a critical component to our long-term prosperity. To realize this vision we will need to fully integrate these natural elements into our working lands (forest and farms), principal commercial districts,

neighborhoods, and social and cultural destinations." (Greening Mid-Michigan Map). At the site scale, the project promotes better stormwater management through low-impact development strategies such as installing rain gardens.

One example of parkland created through the project is Frances Motz Park. It was an abandoned sand and gravel quarry that has since been returned to a more natural site that includes a public swimming and boating lake. Hawk Island Park is another example. Formerly a dumping ground for yard and gravel waste, the park now boasts active-use areas and wild areas. In addition, Eaton County Lincoln Brick Park was created from an old brick factory. The ruins are now protected and the site feels like a wilderness, even though it's within a mile of the downtown Grand Ledge and the quarry is now a fishing and swimming area.

The project determined green infrastructure priorities by identifying potential conservation areas (PCAs). Its analysis was conducted for the Tri-County region using the Tri-County Regional Planning Commission *2000 Land Cover, Vegetation, BIOTICS (a biological database),* and the State of Michigan's Framework Streams and Roads data layers. The Land Cover data were derived from satellite imagery augmented by aerial photography and attributes were checked for accuracy and consistency. Older land cover data were updated by comparison with aerial photos.

The PCAs were determined by using GIS to analyze habitat intactness; wetlands and wetland complexes; riparian corridors; and forested tracts. Sites less than 20 acres were not included since they had less ecological value and a high probability of being misclassified when using satellite imagery.

The PCAs were then ranked by a combination of total size; size of core area; length of stream corridor; landscape connectivity; restorability of surrounding lands; vegetation quality; parcel fragmentation; and their bio-rarity score. Each criterion was divided into several different categories, or levels, which were translated into numerical scores. Finally, sites were assessed and their scores compared. Scores for the Tri-County Region sites ranged from 1 to 31 (out of a possible 45).

The inventory report noted that the Tri-County region had several high-quality natural areas that still appeared to function as they had done hundreds of years ago. Some of these, and other, high-quality sites were also likely to be harboring endangered, threatened, or special-concern animal and plant species. The green infrastructure strategy map and associated conservation project has helped conserve these areas and kept them connected (Paskus, 2008)

While the green infrastructure map is a work in progress, its first edition made significant progress since it included all of the area's priority hubs (cores), links (corridors) and sites. As a living map, localities and communities are continuously coming up with new ways to link key resources and to expand, protect and restore them. Furthermore, many localities have adopted the map as a planning tool. They make for an impressive list that includes Eaton County, Clinton County, Ingham County, Lansing, East Lansing, Meridian Charter Township, Williamstown Township, Delta Charter Township, Eaton Rapids, Delhi Charter Township, Watertown Township and Lansing Charter Township.

Implementation is well underway. Lansing riverfront has been refocused as the center of the city's revitalization and the Greening Mid-Michigan Project is leading the way to help the community reconnect to its riverfront. Shops and businesses are being concentrated near the trail and made accessible to trail users.

A great deal of focus has been on improving the quality of local streams and rivers. This has meant improving habitat for riparian species, such as reptiles, amphibians and waterfowl, and it has significantly improved water quality for local leisure activities. According to one local

paddler, "In the beginning I found [the river] to be kind of dirty, but now you can see the bottom and it's really beautiful. We see more birds on this river, we see blue herons…we see more birds on this river than we ever do on land." Another paddler noted that, "It's not the same river from 20 years ago…It's a cleaner river, it's a useable river, it's an enjoyable river…now we know the salmon are coming up in greater numbers, we know there's wildlife on the river, we know it's cleaner." A local woman who changed from being a self-described 'couch potato' to a tri-athlete credited her personal fitness achievements to the green resources now available: "If we're going to spend tax dollars, I can't think of a better way to spend them – okay! Infrastructure and our health! You are never too old, you are never too fat to get started!"

The project also includes working lands as part of green infrastructure. While much of mid-Michigan is urban or suburban, 60 percent is in agriculture, so its contribution to the overall green assets of the area is substantial. Furthermore, the local food movement is growing in mid-Michigan. Steve Gross, a local farmer noted that "It's important to support the farmers here in Michigan" and that is precisely what the Greening Mid-Michigan project is doing.

Like most successful projects, implementation is also on-going! Harmony Gmazel, a Senior Planner with the Tri-County Regional Planning Commission convenes the group's planning meetings every other month. According to Ms. Gmazel "They come up with fun and meaningful ideas and I try to make it happen. We've had a lot of luck putting the data into master plans and park and recreation plans." They are now in the process up updating the map with new data and setting up priorities. Over the coming year they will convene workshops to further engage people in the region – community leaders (neighborhood groups, local friends of the river groups, paddling groups and fishing groups), elected officials, and government staff. Ideas will also be posted on line for feedback. Focus areas will be agriculture, water conservation, habitat, and parks and trails. For updates see: http://www.greenmidmichigan.org/

Paskus, John. Clinton, *Eaton and Ingham Counties Potential Conservation Areas Report. Michigan Natural Features Inventory.* Lansing, MI September 2008

Thanks to the Eaton, Clinton and Ingham County Conservation Districts, Eaton, Clinton and Ingham Parks Departments, the Ingham County Farmland and Open Space Preservation Board and the Greater Lansing Regional Committee for Stormwater Management.

Now that we have laid out the reasons for undertaking a green infrastructure planning and mapping process, we can delve into the steps for organizing your initiative, which is the focus of Chapter Three.

CHAPTER 3 - Organize Your Initiative

In this chapter, we focus on two key steps to organize a green infrastructure planning initiative: first, how to create a process to engage stakeholders; and second, how to formulate relevant goals.

However, before we start, it is important to consider two other points: the scope of your effort – how extensive it will be; and the geographic scale of your effort: will it cover your community, county, city, region, or an even wider area?

DETERMINE THE SCOPE OF YOUR EFFORT

It is vital that you consider the amount of work you are prepared to do, the amount of time and effort you are willing to put in, the resources you have available, and the finances you have to see it to completion. You need to assess these factors before you delve into data collection and analysis. You should develop a clear rationale for what you want to achieve and why you feel there is a need to evaluate and map certain critical natural assets. Otherwise, you may become lost and collect too much, or not the right type of data.

Plan for Green Infrastructure Conservation at Multiple Scales

As part of discussing the scope of your project, you need to consider the geographic scale of your effort. There are various scales you can consider, bearing in mind that it is often best to take a multi-scale approach. This means seeing your local effort in terms of a wider regional, or multi-state connective scale. So, even though you may be simply considering your local community park and a river greenway, be aware that it fits into a larger network of green spaces. By taking a wider approach to your green infrastructure plan, you may be able to achieve far more than otherwise.

When considering how best to develop a particular site, a developer should consider how it links to neighboring sites and into the

Site visits are important to help evaluate landscape health.

larger landscape. Similarly, when planning at a regional, county or city scale, a planner should consider how areas of regional or county-wide importance can link to and influence individual sites. No matter which scale you start from – large to small or small to large – you need to think about impacts and influences at multiple scales.

Regional, Landscape and Cityscape Scales

Even when working at the level of a specific landscape or defined area, it is helpful to consider the overall distribution of natural assets in the region and determine how your area fits into such ecological systems as wildlife migration routes, watersheds, bird flyways or other cross landscape features. How does a city or town park fit within a wider scheme that allows wildlife to move into and out of the city, or that allows for a variety of recreation opportunities and wildlife interactions for your population (both people and wildlife) as a whole? For example, could individual parks be linked to regional trails? Frederick Law Olmsted's 'Emerald Necklace' was an early attempt to think of Boston's city parks as a connected network. Today, we can think about linkages across a city to the region beyond. The Appalachian Trail is a multi-state trail to which there are many spur trails and links to other parks.

In practice, mapping your natural assets as part of a green infrastructure scheme should focus at a landscape scale, looking across multiple parcels and ownerships.

Ideally, this occurs before land development begins. This allows land managers, landowners and planners to consider which areas should be selected for protection or restoration, in order to provide such ecological services as wildlife habitat, recreation areas, stormwater treatment, energy savings, aesthetic values, improved community health and a sustainable economy. This ensures that areas are not cut off, or that ecosystem functions, such as groundwater recharge, are not unintentionally disrupted.

Even inner suburbs, towns and cities can contain unique habitats within them, as well as substantial open spaces. In such urban areas, green infrastructure planning focuses on different scales and types of data. For example, it assesses the citywide tree canopy and the condition of public trees, riparian habitats and stream corridors, as well as the trees and streams in a local district, neighborhood or watershed. It looks at where there are connected blocks of habitat, such as large city parks, trail systems, good locations for community gardens and opportunities for small-space habitat restoration, water features or water infiltration.

Site Scale

Once your plan has identified the types of resources that are important at your chosen scale, you will need to prioritize which resources to conserve and to determine how these resources can best be connected or restored.

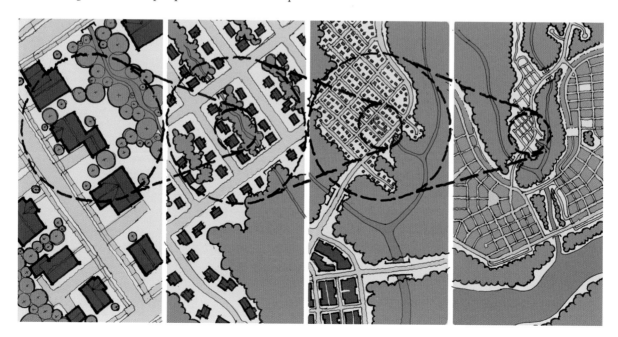

Then, once you have prioritized those assets, you should evaluate what opportunities you have to implement your goals at the site scale. If specific sites are proposed for development, you should determine how to best connect their natural resources to your area's larger, landscape-scale assets.

The illustrations to the right show why it is important to think regionally and act locally. In the first picture, each developer has independently established his own little parcel of green space, conserving green assets locally but fracturing the habitat at a larger scale.

In the second picture, land is developed more densely on the far-right parcel and at medium density in the middle parcel, while the far-left parcel has been entirely preserved as green space through the use of one or more planning tools.

Examples of tools that could be used to avoid development on the left-hand parcel include *purchasing development rights* (PDRs), *transferring development rights* (TDRs) and establishing *conservation easements* to restrict further development, while allowing some existing uses, such as farming or forestry, in exchange for a tax break.

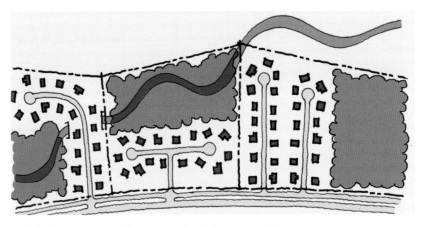

Each development conserved green spaces but did not connect them.

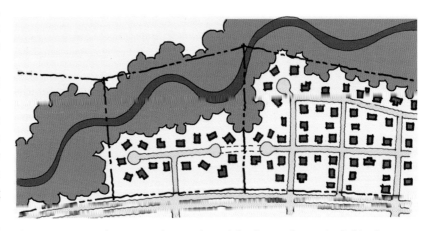

These sites maintained connections between them while achieving the same level of development.

HOW TO ORGANIZE A GREEN INFRASTRUCTURE PLANNING INITIATIVE

You are now ready to begin your community engagement process by engaging stakeholders and formulating relevant goals.

If you have already organized a group to evaluate and map your natural assets, or if your group consists of an appointed or elected body, such as a planning commission or city council, you may not need to read the following chapter sections. Similarly, your group may be a local land trust and you may be consulting primarily with your board of directors and not seeking broader community engagement. Or you may be conducting an internal evaluation of assets to decide on where to put a conservation easement. Whichever is your scope, you may still need to engage outside stakeholders to review your plan at some point, so you may want to at least skim this chapter for pertinent ideas.

Why Engage Community Members?

Community members should be engaged in a green infrastructure planning process as early as possible. They should not learn about the plan for the first time after it is completed. Local citizens should have a role in setting or reviewing a project's goals so that they have buy in. And they should be re-engaged before the plan is completed, while there is still time to provide meaningful input.

Deciding which natural assets are the most important to identify and conserve is a value-driven process. Determining what is valuable, requires some form of community engagement in order to determine which are the most important natural assets to include. For example, while the best available science can tell us the types of habitats that are important for wildlife, we must first decide that wildlife conservation is important. Furthermore, community support is usually needed for implementation, so establishing goals that meet community needs can be key to ensuring that any strategy to protect those assets is implemented. However, public engagement adds a layer of complexity to any mapping effort because of the multiple and often conflicting perspectives that will be offered.

Notwithstanding the difficulty of public engagement concerning issues that can be highly technical and may lead to conflict, there are many good reasons for engaging the broader community. Daniel Fiorino notes that there are substantive, normative and instrumental reasons why the public should be involved in environmental decision-making (1990). Substantive reasons are that citizens are often able to see problems, issues and solutions that experts miss. Community knowledge can inform and enrich environmental understanding of both problems and potential solutions. Normative reasons are that community engagement can legitimize the committee and its conclusions, while also legitimizing the citizens themselves; giving them a sense of ownership and control based on their participation. Lastly, instrumental reasons include citizens' ability to aid in implementing the chosen solutions. Simply put, communities are more likely to 'buy into' ideas that meet goals which they helped to create.

A good beginning is usually essential to a good ending, so how you begin and with whom you engage are worth careful consideration as a first step in your process. It is important to ensure that the results of your planning efforts will actually be utilized by the community by engaging stakeholders early in the process. If key stakeholders are not engaged at the beginning, they may not accept or adopt the final outcomes. For example, a state park agency developed a detailed green infrastructure map, but did not first gain agreement from end users that it was needed. The result was a plan that was nice to look at, but was not actually utilized (Duerksen and Snyder 2005). Citizens may even try to thwart the process because they were not part of its inception.

Lastly, change is often initiated from outside of local government. It may be that a community land trust, watershed coalition or other local stakeholder group is the one to begin a process and seek to engage their local government, so their involvement will naturally be from the beginning. The outside group may be able to foster new innovation and may become the key catalyst for green infrastructure planning.

Challenges of Community Engagement

While we have stressed the importance of community engagement; it is not without challenges. Often, when the public is engaged, it is difficult, if not impossible, to incorporate or address the multiple perspectives that are offered. Some ideas can be detrimental or run counter to a project's goals, while others may challenge you to achieve more with your plan than you first thought possible. However, even if you disagree with the public's comments or cannot fit their requests into changes or expansion of the project, it is important to allow time for *genuine* input. This is an important distinction. Genuine input means that each public comment will be considered thoughtfully and may potentially result in a change to the project.

When requesting public comments, it is important to understand that the public is not a monolithic body. Consider that there are actually many publics. Sometimes, they have been characterized as "communities of place," based on where they live, or as "communities of interest," based on a particular concern, such as hunters, hikers or heritage tourists.

The diversity inherent in the term "public" can result in conflicts over perspectives. Since communities are made up of individuals and organized sub-groups, they may offer suggestions that are polar opposites, such as, "Open this area to recreation," or "Close this area to protect rare species."

It is often possible to reach some common ground between differing opinions. In the above example, it may be possible to provide some public access while also protecting other, more fragile habitat areas.

Some opinions, however, might be impossible to reconcile, and a decision will have to be made about which route to take. For example, GIC staff heard these two non-resolvable comments arise in the same meeting: "Bring back the beaver!" and "Kill all the beaver!"

"Simply put, communities are more likely to 'buy into' ideas that meet goals which they helped to create."

While it is important to consider all comments, you should communicate to stakeholders that your project will not be able to solve or address all community needs and desires, nor should it. If possible, document all comments received, whether or how they were addressed and the reasons for the decisions made.

A Pre-assessment

Before you engage anyone, you may want to conduct a pre-assessment of the key issues and stakeholders for your effort. This can be useful in formulating or refining your project's vision. You may want to conduct interviews with those stakeholders to get a sense of community priorities and gain insights on which issues are accepted or controversial.

Some counties and states like the term 'green infrastructure,' while others prefer to use the term 'natural assets.' Some communities do not want to use the term 'green' for anything, out of concern that some members of the public will be afraid of a 'green agenda.' These types of hot button issues, which include climate change, green ideas and other terms you might want to avoid, can be learned about during the pre-assessment effort and can help you sidestep unnecessary conflicts later on.

To conduct a pre-assessment, utilize experienced interviewers who can maintain confidentiality. Encourage stakeholders to be as frank and open as possible by assuring them that their identities and responses are kept confidential. You may also decide to conduct several confidential interviews on your own as part of scoping your project. Who to interview is up to you, but one way to frame your assessment is to limit it to those who will have a say in implementing the project, such as the board of supervisors, city council, leaders of conservation groups and agency representatives.

Engage Potential Skeptics

It is advisable to engage potential skeptics early on. People often fear new initiatives because they are not sure what they are about. They may wonder, "Is this a plot to take away my property rights?" or "Is it going to raise my taxes or waste time?" Find out early on what are likely to be people's concerns. If it is property, development or hunting rights, make sure you have framed your project in a way that alleviates, rather than adds to, those fears. For example, a green infrastructure plan can help to connect habitats that facilitate wildlife movement. This benefits other users such as hunters who need populations of animals to be healthy and abundant to enjoy their sport.

INTERVIEW QUESTIONS

Devise questions based on what it is you need to learn and utilize interview responses to determine how to frame your project in a way that is non-controversial. You can also use them to ensure that you are consulting the key people and data sources, that you have thought through all the possible end uses for the mapping effort, and as a way to build support for your initiative. Prepare a short summary introduction about the project and share that with participants before seeking their input.

Examples of questions that could be used in a stakeholder pre-assessment to scope your project and mapping needs include:

- What is it you want to be able to do (that you can't do now) e.g protect sensitive watersheds or identify the best lands for agricultural uses?
- At what scale do you want to plan to restore or conserve your assets (town, city, region, watershed)?
- What is most important to you (clean water, forestry, scenic vistas, etc)?
- How would you like to be engaged (as advisors during the process, end-users, or both)?
- What themes (topics) are most important to evaluate and map (wildlife habitats, water, working lands, nature-based recreation)?
- What are some of the key sources of information that we should consult as we try to map our natural resources?
- What areas are at greatest risk from changes to their current land use and which areas might need greater effort to ensure they are maintained?
- Who should be engaged in a mapping effort and why?

Keep in mind that there are many ways and multiple venues you can utilize to gather community input, such as open houses, presentations, workshops and online questionnaires. These can be collated and used as part of on-going review and engagement.

Consider creating a "Frequently Asked Questions" document and add it to your website, if you have one, to answer questions or concerns that you have anticipated, or learn about during your pre-assessment. You can also conduct assessments periodically throughout your project by using a focus group or other surveys to gauge community support and address concerns before the project is concluded.

Misinformation can lead to a great deal of headaches for project organizers and conveners. Many times, GIC staff have observed people who come to meetings with the intent to protest a project, but who then change their minds and offer to support it once they understand what it is about. So, the best way to gain community support is to fully understand and address community concerns as early and as often as possible.

If you are inexperienced in running meetings where multiple and conflicting viewpoints may arise, consider whether you need to hire a professional facilitator. There are many excellent guides for how to facilitate groups, set clear agendas and goals, and resolve conflicts about what is important to include on a map.

All too often, GIC staff have been contacted by localities or planning districts who have created an overly long and impossible list of everything that is important (a.k.a. the kitchen sink approach) and have asked the GIC to help them map everything they have listed. Usually the GIC staff begin by first asking, what is important and from there help the community to determine what could or should be mapped.

In practice, the assets that can be mapped and the actions that can be taken are limited. One helpful approach can be to mine existing documents (such as the comprehensive plan, open space plans, vision statements from the board of supervisors or city council) to see what are their existing goals. Then ask, are these goals things that can be mapped and evaluated?

Chapter Four has more details about how to create goals that can be represented with mapping.

THE THREE STAGES OF THE ADVISORY PROCESS

Most advisory processes can be separated into three distinct stages – and you need to be aware of the different tasks allotted to each stage.

These three stages are visioning, asset evaluation, and implementation:

Visioning

At the start of any advisory process, agencies, community leaders, elected and appointed officials, and the general public should consider what kind of community process they want to create and what they would like it to achieve. These discussions will inform the process's values and goals and will highlight the type of natural assets participants feel it is important to map. Be sure to consider whether your community has an existing vision that can be utilized or modified to suit your project's needs.

Asset Evaluation

Following on from the visioning stage, scientists, land managers and designers need to evaluate and rank the area's natural and cultural resources according to the goals and values already set in place. Examples of such experts include landscape ecologists and architects; environmental and open space planners; wildlife biologists; floodplain managers; foresters; and agricultural experts. Those who will be most active in developing the asset map should also be engaged at this stage, so bring in your GIS analysts as well. If you are creating a local plan, you may want to engage laypeople who have local knowledge about where unique resources can be found. You will probably find that many such assets have not been monitored or evaluated and may be missed entirely if you only rely on existing data. And note that expert review will be required of any new data you collect.

Implementation

This final part of the advisory process involves federal and state land managers, local and regional conservation groups, land trusts, developers, sports groups and others who have a role in managing or conserving the land affected by your goals. At this stage, it is important to re-engage participants from the visioning stage, such as planning commissioners, landowners and local stakeholders, in order to help with implementation. Lastly, consider if the effort will require additional funds to carry it out – whether it is for staffing, land acquisition or public education and outreach.

STAKEHOLDERS YOU MIGHT WANT TO ENGAGE		
WHO TO ENGAGE	WHY	HOW TO ENGAGE*
Planning commission, planning board, environmental review board, appearance commission, agriculture advisory board or other relevant local planning group.	Responsible for comprehensive plans, zoning recommendations, land use and area plans.	Presentation to seek their input on goals and learn of key needs that could be met by a study.
Local resource agencies Extension Service Soil and Water Districts County/Regional Forester Game and Inland Fisheries Farm Bureau	Determine their priorities for resource conservation (specific types and locations) and programs to help with implementation.	Personal meetings or in one meeting.
Land trusts Agencies holding easements	Determine current land that is conserved. Determine if new maps can help them prioritize.	Personal meetings, or in one resource meeting. If working at a regional scale, consider one meeting with all land trusts.
Conservation and environmental groups or associations	Learn about conservation priorities and current programs to help with implementation. Some groups may have science experts and own or manage key land reserves.	Personal meetings, as part of a committee, or through meetings with individual groups.
Scientists and resource experts	You may need to consult with experts to rank the value of natural resources, such as which forests have more biodiversity or which rivers are most ecologically unique or at risk.	Personal visits or a committee meeting. May consider having committees by theme, such as water, agriculture, forests, recreation, history and culture.
Large land holders	May have a significant role in land management or may be able to add land to conservation (programs or easement).	Personal visits or a landowners' meeting.
Homeowners or homeowner associations	If working at smaller scales where joint or coordinated management of open space would make a difference.	Neighborhood meetings or a community workshop.
Developers and homebuilder associations	Those who are making plans to develop large tracts of land can help to ensure the right pieces are conserved and open space connections are made/maintained.	Participate on stakeholder committees and through personal contacts.
Representatives of local or regional financial institutions and potential funding organizations.	Engaging those who will or could fund the effort is important to do early on.	As advisors or on a committee.
Regional governance agencies Regional planning district commissions Watershed basin commissions Regional transportation agencies	If working at a regional scale or including resources that cross jurisdictional boundaries. If crossing state boundaries, consider agencies from other state(s).	Individual meetings or presentations to the board or regularly scheduled board meetings.

*Any of these groups may also be part of an advisory committee.

OPTIONS FOR STRUCTURING AN ADVISORY PROCESS

There are several ways to structure an advisory process. A key consideration is that people may not agree on priorities and may need some assistance to reach consensus and manage their competing perspectives. Given that possibility, consider what may be the best structure to enable consensus to happen.

The following are a variety of options to consider. For additional ideas – both traditional and unusual – about how to build support for the effort, see Chapter Six. Enlisting the help of a professional facilitator also can be a useful way to manage the process.

Stakeholders

Stakeholders include anyone with a key stake in the outcome of the process. This may include owners of large and significant land parcels, conservation groups or land trusts who are targeting lands for conservation and protection, managers of natural area reserves, farmers, foresters, hunt clubs, businesses engaged in forestry, tourism or outdoor recreation, or any category of people who will be affected by or have important knowledge to assist your mapping and prioritization process.

It is key to engage the owners of large land holdings early on. For example, if your plan depends on cooperation and collaboration with a national park or large timber tracts owned by a corporation, you may want to have them serve on your committee from the start. If they do not want to serve on a group, you may want to meet with them individually to share the project's aims and learn about their concerns and priorities. For example, a land developer may not want to serve on a committee, but may be amenable to adopting a land development plan that maintains a wildlife corridor, as long as they are consulted early on.

Implementation Stakeholders

If your group wants its green infrastructure maps formally adopted by an appointed or elected body (such as the planning commission, planning board, supervisors or town or city council) you may want to ask a representative of that body to serve on your stakeholder committee. In this way, they can ensure some level of buy in/support for the effort early on, as well as to help guide your committee and share key insights with your group. For example, if your group labels an area for conservation that the county has already identified as a future growth area, this conflict can be highlighted, discussed and evaluated.

Alternatively, the elected or appointed body may actually *be* your committee. During a project run by the GIC in Madison County, VA, the planning commission was the review body and it reviewed information, data and applications for the data over several meetings.

Also consider that not all stakeholders will be local, especially key funders such as foundations or state and federal grant-makers. It can be critical to your success to engage those funders early on.

One of the best examples of this was the Healing Waters Retreat initiated by Nancy Ailes, Director of the Cacapon and Lost River Land Trust in West Virginia. In 2002, before the trust began its work, she engaged both stakeholders and funders to create maps and formulate a unified vision. According to the trust, this approach was the foundation for its success, and it is now the largest land trust in West Virginia, and the seventh largest in the Chesapeake Bay Watershed.

Experts

It is unlikely that you will have all the expertise you need within your organization. Based on the types of things you may wish to map and the issues you may want to address, you should invite experts to serve as reviewers. For example, if you want to map key cultural assets, such as historic buildings, you may want to invite local historians to provide advice. Similarly, if you want to map key habitats, you may want to engage scientists from your state's natural heritage program. For an example see text box on the Northern Virginia Regional Commission on page 45.

NATURAL HERITAGE PROGRAMS

If you want to map key habitats, you may want to engage scientists from your state's natural heritage program. Some of these programs are run by a state agency while others are maintained by universities or libraries. To find your state's listing, see http://www.natureserve.org/visitLocal/

One key caution is that experts may want you to map everything or conduct extensive new surveys. You'll need to provide them with the limits to the project's scope. For example, when the GIC asked local historians to tell it what historic resources to include on a five county regional map, they got so excited they suggested we categorize resources into multiple separate data sets: as colonial, antebellum, post-industrial, and so on. This was too much detail for a map at a five-county scale. Later, when we asked a biologist which key landscapes to include his response was that, first, we needed to establish field plots in all the forests across all five counties, then create a map of forest diversity types, then... This was not necessary for the scale of the project or for the goals the group had established.

So, engage experts, but provide clear guidance for what you need to know, why you need to know it, and how the information will be applied. This will help them to give you the appropriate information at the right scale. Natural heritage programs (NHP) will advise on using the best available data instead of unnecessarily creating new data. Additionally, if new data are needed, NHPs may be able to assist in creating that data in a timely manner for that region.

Assigning Roles

A simple way to structure engagement in your project is to determine the role each person or group will play. You need to assign roles for everyone (advisor, reviewer, modeler, end-user) and determine who will make the final decisions. But note that, depending on the stage of your project, you may need to involve different persons with different types of input at different times. If you analyze your stakeholders by their role in each stage of the process, you can utilize each person effectively and efficiently. Essentially, you will be creating a vision for what you hope to achieve, evaluating your natural assets and developing an implementation plan.

While some organizations recommend that you form a multi-stakeholder committee at the beginning of your process that comprises all possible interests, it can be difficult for all these groups to agree on what to evaluate, how to prioritize and how to map landscape features. As a result, you may want to restrict your consultation with a multi-stakeholder group to just asking it: "How would you use a GI map?" Or, a thoughtful survey can be used to help gauge the interest and priorities from diverse groups.

Since you will almost certainly need some level of expert scientific help, it is important at the beginning of your advisory process to think about what types of expertise and what levels of technical knowledge are needed to inform your mapping effort – taking into consideration the awareness levels of your lay participating members, as well as the final product you want to see. If you are building a model that will rank natural resources, you will probably want a technical (science) committee that is familiar with the extent and importance of the area's natural resources. They will also likely be aware of available data that can be utilized. If you want to ensure that the information you map is in a form that can be readily applied, you will want to consult those who will be using the information regularly – the end users – such as planners, state natural resource agencies and land trusts.

In summary, you may want to form a technical committee and consult with stakeholders periodically. The technical committee made up of modelers, scientists and other experts can collaborate to actually create your map or model. You can re-engage your end users once you have a draft in hand, to learn if the way the information is presented is useful, applicable and accurate.

COMMITTEE OPTIONS

You may decide you want to set up a standing committee or you may choose not to utilize a committee at all. On the other hand, you might decide that you need *several* committees, or sub-committees, to handle different aspects of your process: for example, one committee can gather GIS data and create your asset map; another can provide a forum for stakeholders.

The following are examples of the types of committee you could utilize during your process, along with their pros and cons. They include the option to forgo a committee process altogether.

The process recommended by GIC is found in the text box on page 42.

A Technical Committee

A technical committee is a core group of experts who create a mapping protocol and map and evaluate the results. This committee can identify and evaluate the best available data, and identify any data gaps; this group can also document the methods used to evaluate and rank data for use in mapping.

It may include those scientists who can determine which landscape types are most significant for wildlife, water resources, agricultural uses, habitat corridors, and so on. It may also include those staff who will be responsible for the mapping, since data will need to be evaluated for consistency and whether it can be represented spatially on a map – for example, are the data consistently available, accurate and represented across the entire study area?

THE GIC'S RECOMMENDED PUBLIC ENGAGEMENT PROCESS

The GIC has found this four-part engagement process to be very effective in soliciting community input.

This process does not include all technical review. It gives you several options, depending on specific circumstances:

PART 1 - PRE-ASSESSMENT: Conduct preliminary interviews or surveys to determine which key issues to investigate, how to frame the project, and who to engage.

PART 2 - STAKEHOLDER REVIEW: Implement a stakeholder review committee, made up of key groups to help frame the project's goals. If the goals have already been established, move onto discussing what needs to be mapped to help achieve them

> Option 1: Form a small technical sub-committee to work on data and maps.

> Option 2: Have the review committee be the planning commission or other decision body.

This process involves three two-hour committee meetings with the following formats:

> Meeting 1: Introduction to Natural Asset Mapping and Discussion of Community Goals and Values
> • This meeting requires some prior research on what data are available and what could be mapped.
> • Which of the community's goals and values can be translated into a map?

> Meeting 2: Proposed Mapping Strategy
> • The strategy should be based on Meeting 1 outcomes.
> • During the meeting, review options for what to map and why, and gain agreement about how to create your maps.

> Meeting 3: Review Maps
> • The format of this meeting should include several aspects: a review of accuracy; a prioritization of assets; and whether the maps present their messages clearly.
> • During this meeting, make edits to your maps based on feedback; then create final versions for further review and final adoption.

> Option: Instead of the three-meeting process, have a focus group review the maps prior to public release of the information; then revise them based on the focus group's input.

Following the three meetings, you have several options before you:

> Option 1: Host a fourth meeting to review and adopt the final version. Celebrate!

> Option 2: Have a community open-house to show the draft maps, in addition to or instead of a committee meeting.

> Option 3: Make individual presentations to key stakeholder groups who cannot attend public meetings, such as sportsmen's groups and civic groups, in addition to or instead of a committee process.

PART 3 - FINALIZE YOUR MAPS: Make final changes to your maps based on feedback, and present them to the decision makers. Make revisions as needed.

PART 4 - STRATEGIZE AND BREAK INTO TASKS: Create a strategy for implementation of your goals and break it into specific tasks.

> Option: Form an implementation committee to ensure your strategy and its allocated tasks are completed. Establish a timeframe to achieve your strategy, as well as each specific task.

For ideas on strategies, see Chapter Five.

Keep in mind that your 'experts' may comprise citizens who are very familiar with the landscape, such as retired ornithologists or experienced birders who have kept accurate records of key nesting sites. The main challenge in consulting any person about the ecology or habitat of an area is to ensure that whatever knowledge is tapped, it represents an accurate and reliable picture of the entire region under investigation. It is important that one area not be labeled as particularly unique or important, simply because there were more data collected in that location. The area in question may be actually less unique; it may simply have been studied more.

A Stakeholder or Implementation Committee

This is a larger group of key-interest representatives who can inform the technical committee about what is important and why. For example, they may place a high value on nature based recreation -- sports that require a large and connected landscape, such as hunting, hiking or cross country horseback riding, or they may want to map key scenic vistas that are important to tourism, or areas that are important to future drinking water supplies (reservoirs or river intakes) or drinking water recharge zones.

A group such as this can be consulted both at the beginning of a process, to determine the community's key values, and again at the end, to evaluate if the mapping effort has met its needs.

It is important to note that not all values can be met and anyone running the stakeholder process should clearly articulate what can and can't be mapped or what is outside the scope of the project. For example, it is not uncommon for a group to identify something that is important to them, but for which no data exist. To put something on a map for a region two things must be true:

1. The data must exist (or be readily obtainable in the near term).

2. The data must be spatially represented and consistent.

A Focus Group

Rather than have a standing committee, you may instead (or in addition) enlist a focus group to test out ideas before proposing them to the broader public or to appointed or elected bodies. Focus groups are often used by marketing firms to test consumer preferences for products, such as cereal, or by political or advertising campaigns to test key messages. A focus group comprised of key interests can determine if current green infrastructure maps best represent key assets or to test the popularity of implementation ideas, such as conservation easements, land swaps or purchases of development rights.

Key messages or strategies can be tested within the group by having them react to ideas, either through discussion or by ranking them on charts or in ballots. This approach was one of several used by the GIC in Nelson County, VA. The focus group was appointed by the board of supervisors and was very helpful in pointing out how to best represent key messages on the maps. It also let GIC staff know which policy ideas would be more or less likely to be viewed favorably by citizens, businesses and elected officials. This information was then used to modify the data representation (graphics) of the maps and to inform a policy implementation document prepared for the county's planning commission.

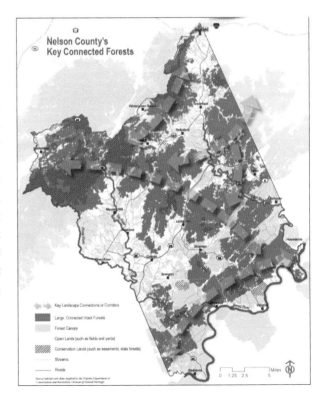

Another approach to diversify input, without having to form multiple committees and sub-committees or host focus groups, is to visit experts individually and then share their perspectives with the larger group. This allows you to focus the review on their particular area of expertise, such as providing wildlife corridors or choosing the highest quality agricultural areas.

No Committee At All

Lastly, you may not need to have any committee at all. Your effort may be for a government agency or other singular entity. For example, if you are conducting your study for a land trust or conservation group, your board of directors or your membership may already serve as your review group.

Alternatively, you may prefer to solicit input through a series of one-on-one meetings with key stakeholders and presentations (see the earlier chart on who to engage). In this form of engagement, you will need to consider the various functions of your stakeholders. A downside to this approach, however, is that experts will not be able to readily inform one another's views because they are not listening to each other and engaging in live dialogue. However, an upside to holding individual expert consultations is that interviewees may offer you more candid viewpoints when they are not being observed by others.

Instead of trying to have all needs met through one committee or focus group, you may want to base your engagement with them upon the needs and timing of your work. For example, if you need the planning commission and board of supervisors to adopt your plan or maps when they are completed, it is a good idea to engage them early on to review the goals and work plan. This will ensure that they agree with the project's direction and are prepared to play an active role in its implementation. If you need to prioritize your natural resources, you may require a science or technical committee to rank or rate the quality of various assets and assign weights or scores to them. For example, a waterway could be valued more highly by the community if it also provided drinking water.

A Last Word On the Benefits of a Committee

One advantage of a committee is that stakeholders can hear and learn from one another. A common refrain experienced in GIC's field tests was that developers will not support an idea, or that the board of supervisors would never vote for it. If you have a member of the body present to say, "Actually, we *can* support that," or "Oh, we never thought of things that way, let's see how we can make it work," then it can smooth the way for agreement within the stakeholder group, and for its adoption and implementation later on.

Another advantage is that most natural asset maps and strategies include lands that fall under multiple ownership, as well as numerous zoning or land use regulations that require cooperation amongst diverse interests to manage them effectively, in order to maximize conservation and community values. The committee brings these varied interests together under one aegis, which allows them to discuss differences and resolve them.

In conclusion, all projects will need to have some level of community consultation and coordination. However, each community is unique and coordinators of natural asset planning efforts will need to consider the best way to advance their goals for strategic landscape conservation.

Experts can be any age. In this picture from a workshop for the GIC's Walkable Watershed's Project in Richmond, VA, 5th graders identify their preferred new routes to walk to school. This helps to guide where re-greening projects will be implemented and tells project organizers where children are most likely to walk.

NORTHERN VA REGIONAL COMMISSION PROCESS

In the Northern Virginia Regional Commission (NVRC) project there were multiple levels of expertise needed to create regional themed maps. Rather than having every possible expert sit on one very large committee, they decided to have one core committee and create additional subcommittees to explore particular issues or themes in greater depth.

A standing committee was formed of representatives from the localities in the region, along with regional conservation groups and land trusts. They worked collaboratively to advise the NVRC about what to include or exclude from the regional asset map.

They convened subgroups of experts from the committee, as well as additional experts on the subject area – such as watershed health and heritage and culture experts to create overlay maps on particular themes. This allowed professionals to advise the project by providing their expertise in key areas.

The NVRC Natural Assets Committee meets to review their maps.

We have covered how to get organized and create a structure for your mapping process. In the next chapter, Chapter Four, we provide guidance about what can be mapped and how data can be evaluated in terms of meeting a community's goals.

SIX STEPS FOR GREEN INFRASTRUCTURE PLANNING

- Step 1: Set Goals
- Step 2: Review Data
- Step 3: Make Maps
- Step 4: Assess Risks
- Step 5: Opportunities
- Step 6: Implement

CHAPTER 4 - How to Identify, Evaluate and Prioritize Natural Assets as Part of a Green Infrastructure Plan

In this chapter, we present the steps you should take to identify, evaluate and prioritize your natural assets as part of a green infrastructure plan. These six steps were initially presented in Chapter One, but are expanded upon here.

This is a key chapter to read before Chapter Seven, where we present specific suggestions regarding the data and models to use when creating your maps.

There are Six Steps you should consider to identify, evaluate and prioritize your assets as part of a green infrastructure plan:

Step 1. Set Goals: What does your community or organization value? Determine which natural assets and functions are most important to you.

Step 2. Review Data: What do you know or need to know, to map the values identified in Step 1?

Step 3. Make Asset Maps: Map your community's highest-valued natural assets that contribute to a healthy ecology and also support cultural and economic values –Based on the goals established in Step 1 and data from Step 2.

Step 4. Assess Risks: What assets are most at risk and what could be lost if no action is taken?

Step 5. Determine Opportunities: Determine opportunities for protection or restoration. Based on those assets and risks you have identified; which ones should be restored or improved? And which need the attention soonest?

Step 6. Implement Opportunities: Include your natural asset maps in both daily and long-range planning such as park planning, comprehensive planning and zoning, transportation planning, tourism development and economic planning.

We will now outline these steps in detail.

STEP 1. SET GOALS: WHAT DOES YOUR COMMUNITY OR ORGANIZATION VALUE? DETERMINE WHICH NATURAL ASSETS AND FUNCTIONS ARE MOST IMPORTANT TO YOU

All GI planning efforts that involve the public must start with the establishment of goals. However, before asking people what their goals are for evaluating an area's natural assets, they may need an introduction on what natural assets are and why cataloging them is important.

Introduce Key Terms

It is likely that lay members of your community will be new to the concepts of green infrastructure (GI), natural assets and ecological services and not understand why it is important to evaluate and map them. In fact, some may not realize the need for mapping assets at all; they may assume that this information is already taken into account as part of everyday planning activities. It is worth spending some time at your initial meeting, or in your preliminary engagement process, to ensure that they fully grasp these – and other – basic ideas and understand their central role in the GI planning process. You may also need to explain the overall process to them, so that they can see how their interests and values are incorporated into your plans and will be realized on the ground.

Create a Vision

Before you discuss goals, you may need to spend some time helping your community develop a vision of what it would prefer its landscape to look like.

On the other hand, if you are a local authority or organization that already has a clear vision statement or comprehensive plan that includes a proposal for the future, you may not need to do anything more than reaffirm that vision and apply it to the particular process you now have in mind. However, you might still need to ensure that the community as a whole understands the inspiration and participates in translating it into specific planning goals.

Be Strategic

Since it is likely that you are being strategic in your approach, your mapping effort will not simply entail taking everything that is 'natural' and might be construed as an 'asset' and putting it on a map. Rather, the purpose of mapping is to identify key priorities based on the values and goals they fulfill. So, establishing your goals has to be your first step. And those goals should arise from the vision you have established, either as part of your established purpose, or from engaging stakeholders in a visioning exercise.

You may recall from Chapter One that a map of natural assets is a "strategically planned network," and is not simply an inventory of assets. Yet it is common for groups engaged in green infrastructure mapping to start by making lists, with statements such as, "Clean the water!" or, "Provide recreation." However, you need to give careful thought to how those values can be translated and represented on a map, as well as managed for long-term conservation or restoration. A list answers the question, "What do we have?", while a strategy answers, "Of those things we have, which are the most important to conserve and how can we do that?"

Green infrastructure planning involves the prioritization of catalogued assets to create a strategy for conserving what is most important. To prioritize, you must have some way of setting aside ideas that are not critical or relevant. The only way to achieve that is to strictly adhere to your goals. The more specific your goals are, the easier that will be.

Set Clear and Consensual Goals

When you initiated your mapping project, you clearly had a reason for doing so. In a rural area, your initial goals might have been as broad or vague as, "To identify large, intact habitats that will conserve our region's biodiversity." Or they may have been as specific as, "To identify critical natural resources, habitat areas and key viewsheds that can support and sustain a strong, natural resource-based economy."

Once people understand why you are undertaking a natural asset mapping initiative, they can consider what goals need to be addressed. However, before you begin

"**Green infrastructure planning involves prioritization** of catalogued assets to create a strategy for conserving what is most important. To prioritize, you must have some way of setting aside ideas that are not critical or relevant. The only way to achieve that is to strictly adhere to your goals. The more specific your goals are, the easier that will be."

asking your group or community to establish goals, be sure to avoid the pitfalls of generating a long, cumbersome laundry list. The challenge is to create some consensus around a limited, defined set of goals that everyone can agree on – in other words, which four or five goals can people agree are the most important?

You may want to utilize goals that already exist for the community by consulting existing documents, such as the comprehensive plan or zoning ordinance. Since these have been adopted already, it may make it easier for them to gain acceptance. Another simple way to begin is by asking stakeholders what is important to them.

A goal for an urban area might simply state, "To identify and protect the city's natural resources and restore habitat and natural area connections wherever possible, in order to create a livable, resilient, attractive and healthful city." Or it might specify particular natural aspects to focus on, such as stream buffers or the tree canopy.

A goal might focus less on wildlife and more on human-based ecosystem services, such as clean air, clean water or recreation, and might be framed in such a way: "To conserve the city's natural areas, urban tree canopy and forested stream buffers, in order to protect native species, keep the city cool, maintain clean streams, and provide abundant opportunities for nature-based recreation."

An example of linking goals to natural assets is to promote outdoor recreation by protecting landscape corridors for those activities, such as hunting, that rely on intact habitats – the better connected a landscape is, the easier it is for animals to move and repopulate areas and for hunters to enjoy their sport without conflict. Other non-consumptive outdoor sports, such as cross-country skiing or long-distance hiking also require a connected landscape.

Set Goals for Various Timeframes

As we have discussed, your community may have undergone a visioning process to determine what it wants to achieve. Now, you can set your goals for that vision over several time periods: say, 10, 20 or 50 years. For example, after 10 years, your goal might be to preserve the following natural assets and ecological services: abundant clean water; clean air, a strong natural, resource-based economy; an intact landscape that supports outdoor recreational activities; abundant and biologically diverse native species; attractive vistas; and so on. Then, after 20 years, it might be to have a truly connected landscape that further enhances all those assets.

Or your community might have a more singular goal in mind, which it wants to achieve relatively quickly, say over just five years. An example would be an immediate economic goal to protect an agriculturally-based economy by identifying and conserving areas with high-quality agricultural soils though zoning protections and support for farmers markets. Another example might be to map your city's tree canopy and target gap areas where canopy can be restored through city and citizen-based planting programs to meet a target canopy level.

EXAMPLES OF GOALS THAT CAN JUSTIFY CONSERVING KEY NATURAL ASSETS

- To preserve regional forests for wildlife.

- To ensure biodiversity and a healthy ecosystem.

- To protect a rural economy (that comprises, say, timber stands, farms and grazing lands).

- To maintain forested land cover in order to facilitate recharging groundwater aquifers for drinking water supplies.

- To conserve community character and heritage by protecting an historic landscape.

- To preserve and promote natural-resource-based recreation, such as hiking, birdwatching and hunting.

- To save money by directing development into areas where services (roads, schools, power lines) already exist.

- To protect public safety and prevent future hazards by identifying hazards such as unstable slopes, floodways and areas prone to sinkholes.

Do Your Goals Address Your Major Issues?

You will need to consider if your adopted goals address all the issues your community or organization thinks are important and whether they are specific enough to provide direction for your evaluation of assets. If not, you may need to modify your goals to add specific qualifying statements. For example, if you already have a community goal, "To keep the county's water clean," you may need to add specifics such as, "To keep the county's water clean by protecting forested buffers along streams." You may also need to add specific objectives, such as details of how wide the buffers should be and whether there are areas of higher priority, such as headwater streams or streams that feed into the drinking water supply. One way to flesh out specific parameters for your objectives is to have a panel or committee of topical experts discuss them and suggest refinements.

Also, you may not be exactly sure what your goals should be, without looking at existing data and assessing it. So use those maps and GIS layers you already have, or gather new data if you feel you need additional information to make an informed decision on what your goals should be. For example, your initial goal might be to protect core forest habitats and corridors, but you have little idea where they are, or which ones to prioritize. So you decide to consult existing GIS layers and county forest maps to make an initial determination of those that are the most important. You then enter a full data-gathering and mapping process, and as you do so, discover another key core piece of forest, or decide to remove one from your list.

Thus, you will probably need to take an *iterative approach* when establishing and refining your goals. An iterative approach involves setting goals, creating a map and then determining the condition of the resource and what should be prioritized. For example, you may find that forested land cover is more fragmented that you realized and that there are less cores than originally supposed. This may lead you to put greater priority on conservation actions for certain areas of the landscape. Or, you may determine new corridor possibilities to connect intact core areas.

Decision Metrics

One challenge that all projects face at some point is how to address conflicting perspectives. Some stakeholders will want to target an area for growth, while others will want to preserve it. One way to minimize this is to develop clear *decision metrics* early on.

A *decision metric* is a standard that helps you prioritize what to conserve first and why. Creating decision standards early on can help resolve potential conflicts in the future.

These metrics define priorities into a ranking of what is considered most important by the community, and might include such things as:

- Protect the area that shelters rare or endangered species first.
- Protect the habitat cores with the highest rankings first.

Decision metrics can provide a way to sort through data and decide more quickly which aspects of your landscape are most suited for conservation. Evaluating natural assets within a green infrastructure context means conserving those resources that offer the greatest conservation and community values first, and not simply trying to protect everything that is natural or green. You'll need to keep asking yourself, "Does this meet our highest priorities?" and "Will it ensure achievement of the multiple community values or goals we identified earlier?"

As described previously, an area may be deemed more valuable because it provides multiple community benefits, such as a forested area that helps with groundwater recharge and buffers runoff into an existing drinking water reservoir. However, you are likely to find more conflicts around such areas, because there will be more demands on them. For example, a high-value habitat area for recreation may also be indicated by the locality as the best location for a new school or shopping center, precisely because of its proximity to an existing population center.

Similarly, if you are evaluating your soils for food production as part of your green infrastructure network, you may find that the best soils for growing food are also the best soils for septic systems. This was the case in Accomack County, VA, where soils with lower clay content that were well drained were less common and were thus in high demand by both farmers and developers since both groups needed well-drained soil; one needed this for crops and the other for septic.

Achieving Your Goals

Next, consider how a green infrastructure map can help you achieve your goals. For example, if you map forest cover, that will help you protect your forests, which will help you facilitate groundwater recharge. If you map forest corridors, you can protect them and identify where there are gaps, which can help you promote biodiversity. Those corridors can also help you draw up plans to facilitate animal movement and support hunting, hiking and cross country horseback riding, since they all depend upon a connected landscape. Similarly, if you map your soils, you can protect your agricultural economy by identifying and conserving those landscapes that have the best soils for growing crops. The key is to match community needs and interests to the functions you want to achieve by identifying natural assets on a green infrastructure map.

Can Your Goals Be Mapped and Turned Into Actions?

You will need to determine if your goals can be evaluated spatially (on a map) and whether they can be used to create real on-the-ground actions. As part of this, you need to consider those resources you will have available to you to collect data and implement your goals. For example, if your community relies on local water from wells or from a stream-fed reservoir, both surface water protection and groundwater recharge may be important. However, you will need an existing study of groundwater recharge areas in order to map them.

If you do not have data on exactly which areas are best for recharge, you can still undertake actions to help your drinking water. It is well known that forests help with retaining and infiltrating water, so if you protect the forest cover across the headwaters of local streams, around your reservoirs and across watershed areas that are upstream of your reservoirs, you can link your goals for clean and abundant drinking water to land management actions, such as protecting your forests through easements, stewardship plans or replanting.

The aim here is to have realizable goals that are practicable, can be mapped and are actionable in order to help you realize the vision defined for your local landscape.

STEP 2. REVIEW DATA: WHAT DO YOU KNOW, OR NEED TO KNOW, TO MAP THE VALUES IDENTIFIED IN STEP 1?

Once your community, locality, land trust, or other organization has established the purpose of its project (what it is seeking to conserve or restore, and why), the next step is to determine how to implement that purpose. To do that, you need to assess what information you already have and what you still need to gather. Keep in mind that the goal is not to put everything on your map, but rather to prioritize. A green infrastructure map – a map of natural assets that support community functions – is most effective as a strategic tool if your natural resources are ranked in terms of importance for *achieving* your goals. It is not uncommon for communities to make long lists of what should go on their maps without having first investigated if the data are available. That is frustrating, time-wasting and ultimately pointless. Natural resources should be ranked in large part based on how well the data represent the conservation value of those resources.

> "A green infrastructure map – a map of natural assets that support community functions – is most effective as a strategic tool if your natural resources are ranked in terms of importance for achieving your goals."

Prioritization, Prioritization, Prioritization

If *everything* currently known is put on your map (such as all forested land and all agricultural soils), it is likely to result in a map that does not show priorities and is lacking in definable strategies. To avoid this, decide how the available data relate to each of your goals, and how they data can be catalogued, evaluated, prioritized and mapped.

For example, if your community decides that it values clean water, then rather than mapping all watersheds, it could identify and conserve just those with high levels of forest cover and intact stream buffers. This can be mapped in GIS by creating a watershed boundary layer, adding in forest cover and determining the highest value forest cover you desire for a watershed, e.g., at least 70 percent cover overall, with extra buffering for headwater streams.

Every community is different and you will need to evaluate whether or not such a simple mapping metric makes sense for your area. For example, in mountainous areas, it is not uncommon to have highly forested slopes that are not developed, since they are difficult to clear for farming or housing, and to have open lands with grazing or crops located alongside valley streams. This could mean that, even though you have a high-forest-cover watershed, it lacks adequate forest buffers in the right places – alongside streams where they can help protect water quality. So you could add an equation into your GIS mapping to select ('clip') areas of 100 feet alongside each stream and determine if they are also adequately forested for filtering land runoff.

Since forested streams often make good wildlife corridors, this is another reason to select them as a high conservation priority in your green infrastructure prioritization process. If you are also seeking to protect or create a wildlife corridor, then 300 feet on either side of the stream will be needed. In this case, both wildlife and water quality are supported.

If your community decides that locally-sourced food is important, you might want to map the locations of good agricultural soils. Thinking strategically, you should map only the highest quality agricultural soils instead of selecting every soil classification. Then compare these class IV and V soils (from the USDA) with land cover to ensure that they are actually available for farming (and not underneath a factory or urban area).

There are many other site-specific criteria for all types of crops. For example, vineyards may perform well on poorer soils and most fruit production does best on slopes between 1.5 and 15 percent and at higher elevations than valley floors, to avoid spring and fall frosts. Vineyards also do best in open areas with good airflow that avoid interaction between cultivated grapes and wild grapes (which carry a fungus that can harm cultivars). So, if you are interested in areas that are best for fruit growing, these can be included on your agricultural asset map as well.

With guidance from your local extension agent, you can identify areas suitable for each crop and include them on a map of key agricultural zones. In Madison

County, VA, the extension service mapped areas with soils and conditions most suitable for grape growing, to make it easier for prospective vineyards to locate within the county.

Find the Right Data

In order for something to be mapped, data must already be available. Stating this seems obvious, yet it is common for groups to identify things that they want to include in a map for which no data currently exist. A data table of available state data is found in the last chapter of this guide. You may also have additional local data such as a groundwater study conducted by your county.

Simple rules of thumb for what can be mapped are:

- The data must exist (or be readily obtainable in the near term).
- The data must be represented spatially.
- The data must be consistently available over the entire area.

If your group identifies something it wishes to map, but for which there are no data, consider how this data might be collected. Given that field studies could take years and require grant funds to support, think carefully about how to create a map with the data now available and how you might update and reprioritize the map in the future, when new or more accurate data become available. For example, can you map known high-value habitats now, and then update the map later when a more comprehensive inventory can be conducted?

If groundwater recharge is important to your community, a detailed study can take time and resources to complete. In the meantime, you could create a map that only includes watersheds that currently supply a large number of existing wells; that have community wells (usually those wells serving 20 or more users); or that feed into public reservoirs.

Proxies

When the desired data are not available, *proxies* may be used. A proxy is a way to simulate (create a surrogate for) what you want to map. For example, most localities have not completed extensive surveys of all of their wildlife. While it is likely that some rare species have been catalogued and recorded at your state's Natural Heritage Program, you are only allowed to show these data with large buffers around the sites, in order to blur the actual locations of the rare species. This is to prevent anyone from locating, stealing or destroying them.

Your state's wildlife action plan may have also identified locations that are *likely* to contain key species, but these areas may not have been monitored to confirm the actual existence of those species. Thus, even the wildlife mapping data that *are* available may not be very useful.

If you want to take a proxy approach and map likely locations that can support native species, pick areas of your landscape that are still intact (as undisturbed and unfragmented as possible) and large enough to support a diversity of habitat types or *niches*. For example, in Virginia, the state uses a proxy of 100 acres of intact interior forest as a minimum size and land cover type to support a diversity of native, interior forest species. The larger the area, the more likely there will be suitable habitat for area-sensitive species, such as forest-breeding migratory songbirds, black bears and mountain lions. Consult with your state to determine a minimum acreage. If you also know that a specific area supports rare species or rare habitat types, you may rank those areas higher.

A ***proxy*** is a way to simulate data that represent what you want to map.

Tying Data to Location

Since the mapping rule requires that all data be represented spatially, it must all be tied to location.

Some studies randomly select species in order to characterize abundance for an area, such as an entire county, and do not record actual locations. You will not be able to use that data for your map. Other data may cover too large an area, lacking in the precision necessary for mapping. An example of this is bird flyways, which are often represented as large swathes many miles wide. To make matters worse, these flyways can change year-by-year depending on weather, temperature, food sources and other factors. To learn more see http://www.birdnature.com/flyways.html

Another point to be aware of is that, when you look at the habitat demanded by a particular species, it may require the entire area of your project, making it difficult to prioritize one part of it over another. For example, when the GIC reviewed the bear habitat needs for one Virginia county, the entire county was highlighted.

If you face a similar problem in your locality, a better way might be to select those core areas and corridors that offer the very best of all possibilities. It is important to contact scientists/experts for guidance on what can be mapped, including natural heritage programs and wildlife resource agencies.

You also need to consider data consistency. This means that all your data must have been evaluated in a consistent manner, as opposed to collected sporadically. It is often a common desire for members of the public or local stakeholders to want to add something on a map that they happen to know about – such as their favorite duck pond or beaver dam. If you allow these personal *ad hoc* details to be included, as opposed to using data that were gathered consistently across a landscape or in all potential habitats, you will probably create an inconsistent mishmash on an inaccurate map that is not useful for identifying anything, let alone the highest priority areas.

Consider the following two examples (both are real examples):

In the first, a stretch of river had been included on a map as significant for bald eagles because canoeists had seen an eagle nest there and a single breeding pair; in the second, an area had been mapped as significant for trilliums because one particular researcher had established a study plot on a slope and noted that it had abundant numbers of the locally rare woodland plant.

The question is, why trilliums, why eagles? And why there? Putting data on a map just because it is available, absent of a defined rationale and protocol for doing so, can result in a map that is full of data points but lacks any clear way to prioritize those areas that need better stewardship or management.

While certain areas may, indeed, contain bald eagles and trilliums, there is no way to determine whether or not they represent the *best* areas for eagles and trilliums in the locality. In fact, eagles and trilliums may be far more abundant in other, less disturbed areas, or in areas with more suitable soils or more abundant food sources.

If these communities had wanted to create maps of the best bald eagle and trillium habitats, so they could prioritize them, it would have been better to conduct a county-wide eagle survey or an examination of soils and slopes where trilliums are most likely to be found. In addition, these data should be provided to natural resources professionals and heritage programs so that they can be included in broader inventories and incorporated into your state's existing assessments.

STEP 3. MAKE ASSET MAPS: MAP YOUR COMMUNITY'S HIGHEST-VALUED NATURAL ASSETS THAT CONTRIBUTE TO A HEALTHY ECOLOGY AND ALSO SUPPORT CULTURAL AND ECONOMIC VALUES – BASED ON THE GOALS ESTABLISHED IN STEP 1 AND DATA FROM STEP 2.

Once you have at least an initial sense of what data are available, consider which data could help you meet the goals you established in Step One. Then assemble them.

Once you have brought together all the existing data you want and collected any additional data that matches your goals, it is time to create your natural asset map. Depending on what those goals are, this map might include:

- Large intact forests, native meadows, marshlands.
- Key geological features.
- Farms and farming communities.
- Streams, rivers, wetlands and reservoirs and ground-water recharge areas.
- Recreational areas.
- Historic and cultural features.
- Viewsheds.
- In urban areas: street trees, the tree canopy, parks, community gardens and streams.

GIS Models

Although several states have models covering the entire state, each intra-state regional or community natural asset mapping project still needs to develop its own locally relevant model or base map. Some states that lack comprehensive models have statewide datasets, which are very useful for creating a local natural asset map. However, for any local project, whether or not there is a state model available, creating a local base map of natural assets will require the addition of new data from both state and federal sources and locally sourced data.

HOW GIS WORKS

In GIS, data are collated in layers. Each layer represents a specific type of data, such as forest cover, roads, or streams. These layers can be put together and symbolized (e.g. represent streams using blue lines) to form a map. Thus a map (or 'Map Document' in ArcGIS) is a series of data layers overlain to create a composite picture of a geographic area.

How Data Are Organized in GIS

In order to show as many pictures and patterns as possible, it is recommended that you keep your data sets in discrete *layers*, often called *themes* because each one focuses on a specific type of data.

In GIS, data layers are saved as *Map Documents*. A Map Document is a series of data layers which contain all the data you have input.

It is recommended that you keep each type of information as a separate layer of information so you can grab it and add it to any map to show new patterns and relationships. This will allow you to create new projects easily as you compare different data sets. For example, you may want to overlay your Protected Lands data layer onto your Highest-Quality Agricultural Soils layer to answer such questions as, "How many areas with high-quality agricultural soils are already protected from development under conservation easements?"

Another example applies to historic resources. You might add your Conservation Easement layer to your Key Cultural Resources layer to determine how many of historic sites are within landscapes protected from development or encroachment by incompatible uses.

Keeping your data as discrete layers allows you to use your data for multiple applications and to build maps as and when you want to, with the specific information you wish to have represented. You can combine these layers to see new relationships such as areas that are important for both water quality and habitat (water theme map + wildlife habitat map).

Data Tables

The data for each GIS layer are kept in a linked data table. Each table can then be used to sort and compare data, perform data analysis and create new maps. The data can also be used to run calculations and categorize and rank information.

A GIS user can run calculations or sort the data tables in those ways that are most helpful to your local needs. For example, you may be able to calculate the acreage of all habitat cores that have been given the highest ranking or sort the data for all habitat cores that contain rare, threatened or endangered species. Similarly, you may be able to select all habitat cores that intersect or are within 50 feet of a waterway that has a high priority for conservation.

Scalability

Green infrastructure maps have been created at many different scales. The mapping and modeling that have occurred in the past few decades have been made possible by advances in GIS software, as well as improvements and increased access to high-resolution satellite imagery, new data management tools and the increased processing power of the desktop computer. These all allow you to create data layers that are scalable and that enable you to view your data at various different 'heights' – much like zooming in and out of Google Maps.

This allows you to see connections at multiple levels, such as between core areas or development areas, over a regional as well as local scale, and to understand how your local efforts fit into a much wider network.

Using GIS Software

The approach recommended by the GIC requires that you use GIS software to overlay data, in order to see the emergence of patterns and priorities. You can use this GIS software and its associated data tables to establish your priorities. For example, if you want to protect water quality, you can overlay watershed boundaries with forest canopy to determine whether the canopy is sufficient to protect your water quality. Does the canopy cover most of the watershed (e.g. 80 percent) or just 10 percent? Will you need to reforest part of the watershed, or nearly all of it? Where is forest cover most needed? Are forests located along streams to buffer runoff and stabilize banks?

If you want to determine whether or not streamside buffers are adequate, you may want to draw a boundary polygon 100 feet either side of the center line of the stream to determine if adjacent forest coverage is adequate and if there are sections of the stream that would benefit from a reforestation effort.

IMPAIRED WATERS

Your state's Impaired Waters List will indicate if there are known impairments for your surface waters. Contact your state's department of environmental quality or department of conservation (or equivalent).

Which GIS Software Should You Use?

It is worth a reminder that, while there are several more simplistic mapping programs available to you, many of them do not include analytical properties available in GIS programs, such as the Environmental Systems Research Institute's ArcGIS software products.

Simpler programs, such as Green Maps, and graphic tools such as Google Maps, do not allow you to run more complex calculations such as, "Select all cores that include 200 acres of habitat and slopes greater than 20 percent."

ArcGIS is the easiest GIS software to use and is more translatable if you want to share your data with local, state or regional government agencies. It can also perform calculations that analyze information. Once you draw boundaries (polygons) around key areas, you can calculate the total acreage of those polygons, the distances between them, and so on. This is very helpful when you want to discover such information as, "What percentage of the region contains land protected by conservation easement?" or, "How many miles of rivers and streams have a linear forested buffer of 100 feet wide to filter nutrients?"

Metadata

Every data layer should have an associated set of *metadata* attached to it that describes where the data came from, as well as a data table that includes source data for the layer and other associated attributes, such as accuracy information (resolution) and details on how data were collected. Your GIS expert should help you with this, but make sure that he or she is including it in all your data layers.

Metadata is information about data that gives details such as where, how and when the data was collected. A data table is an Excel spreadsheet that lists every data unit in columns that you can select, compare and analyze, just like any other digital spreadsheet. An *attribute table* contains information about a set of geographic features, usually arranged so that each row represents a feature (such as soil type) and each column represents a feature attribute (such as loam, clay, sand, etc.).

You may find this web page useful. It is a dictionary of GIS terms:

http://support.esri.com/en/knowledgebase/ GISDictionary/term/attribute%20table

If you use existing data from another source, then modify or update it, you should make a note of this in the metadata and *attribute table*. For example, if your data layer maps water features, your metadata should always record the source of the data (for example, that it came from the National Hydrography Data Set), the year of the data collection (for example, land cover from 2014), and other key data regarding such attributes as resolution scale (e.g. 30-meter resolution).

Your attribute table will contain all the data in a map layer in tabular format. Since this is usually in the form of an Excel spreadsheet, you can open that spreadsheet and perform a number of different calculations from the table, such as adding up the total acreage of your parks or the linear length of your streams.

If you do not have GIS capabilities, consider hiring a consultant or a local university student proficient in GIS to work with you. There are new, low-cost software licenses available for just $100 for nonprofits from ESRI, so it is more affordable to own and use GIS than ever before. Universities and colleges usually have their own GIS licenses, so students can use their school's software to help create maps.

Your Base Map

The first step is to create a *base map*.

A base map is a master map of your prioritized natural assets. It is used to compare other key land use concerns or management needs. If you want to add more nature-based recreational trails, your base map can be used to determine if your trails take advantage of key natural assets, such as exceptionally unique forests or connecting wildlife corridors. Similarly, you can use your base map to overlay key cultural assets, such as tourist destinations, and ask, "Does this priority landscape also support key views from these sites?" In general, we recommend you begin with your state's model of intact interior habitats and connecting corridors – if it has one – and then create themed maps to show how this base map supports other cultural and community values. States such as New York, Maryland, Virginia, North Carolina, South Carolina, Florida and Arkansas have models and more are being created. Chapter Seven describes data sources to build a habitat model or you may want to hire a geospatial analysis firm such as the Green Infrastructure Center to build one.

Here, we give a list of the steps we recommend you follow to create your base map. Chapter Five provides case examples for mapping natural assets. We recommend you follow this procedure to create your base map for large landscapes. For urban areas you will want to also add other types of data such as tree canopy (see the section on urban restoration in this chapter):

1. Begin with your state's basic land-cover model of cores and corridors, if one is available, and determine the date of the version you are using to ensure you have the most up-to-date data available.

2. Consider core habitat distribution.

3. Consider what corridors and stepping stones you will need between cores to create a viable habitat network.

4. Identify those habitat cores and corridors that have the highest priority for conservation.

5. Identify gaps in the network of cores and corridors.

6. Identify and rank any additional local priorities.

7. Assess the risks to those areas.

8. Review the levels of protection you have assigned.

9. Reality test your model and finalize its data.

Determining Priorities

Once collected, your data can be utilized to demonstrate the relationship between your priorities. For example, if you overlay your digital layer of protected lands (such as lands under easement or within national parks), it may show you that the natural assets you have identified as key resources are not, in fact, as protected as you thought; in fact, they may be at serious risk of disappearance without concerted conservation action. You may also notice that a large tract of habitat ranked as average connects two highly ranked areas. As a result, you may decide to raise the ranking of that 'average area' and add it to your map as a priority area because it is a key corridor that helps connect your local landscape and facilitates a more resilient natural network that can better withstand change.

The more connections you have across a landscape, the greater its potential to ensure that species diversity is maintained. Likewise, expanses of connected areas of natural cover can also allow for recreational uses such as cross country sports (skiing, riding or hunting) which depend upon a connected landscape.

Using Data to Establish New Goals

Each natural asset map needs to include a map of the natural and cultural assets that are most significant and of highest priority to your local community. Determining 'significance' requires that you set goals for what is most important. This was covered earlier in this chapter.

The process of creating maps allows new priorities to emerge. You may discover that an asset you thought was abundant is actually in short supply, thus driving a new goal for restoration. Or you may find that overlaying additional data layers highlights previously unrecognized landscape features worthy of protection. For example, a forest may gain greater local significance because an historic event occurred there, such as a Civil War encampment, a Native American burial mound, or a battle at a frontier fort.

In one county, considering this historic data overlaid with the forest layer, turned an otherwise insignificant piece of woodland into one worthy of protection. It led the local county to prioritize that woodland for its historic significance. From an ecological standpoint, that piece of forest was not the most remarkable in the county, but its historic resources elevated its preservation importance. It also turned out that the site provided a wonderful setting for a newly constructed 'green' elementary

school adjacent to the woodland, because it afforded the children an accessible place to study nature while also learning about Civil War history. Without its historical significance and educational opportunities, it is likely that the woodland would have been developed long ago.

Similarly, an area could be ranked more highly based on local knowledge of its ecological function. For example, a local river or wetland could contain a unique feature such as a heron rookery (a place where many herons breed and nest) to be more highly valued at the local level and thus increase the ranking for that feature. In this way, overlays of data sets help bring out new priorities. Combining data sets in new ways can bring out hidden values and can lead to new conservation or restoration goals.

These examples show why it is important to use your data layers to look at land development patterns and compare that with known problems. In urbanized areas, even streams with wide forested stream buffers can be polluted by stormwater runoff, if there are pipes carrying untreated stormwater from urban areas directly into waterways.

For each problem known or suspected, use the data to help answer the question, "Can a green infrastructure strategy help address the problem?"

Mapping Ecological Assets

A community may hold in high regard certain intrinsic values, such as wildlife, or promoting a landscape that is biologically diverse. But how do you map such values? Well, you can map the desire to protect wildlife by including those habitats that support the greatest species diversity. But how do you do determine that?

Your community will need to establish a series of *metrics* and *protocols* for what types of habitats to conserve and where. A metric is a measurable quantity, such as buffer width, acreage, the number of tree species, the age of a forest, or water quality. A protocol is a scientific method that turns those measurable quantities into discrete spatial data that suit your needs.

When you try to capture community values on a map of natural assets, be sure to use appropriate and defensible scientific protocols. For example, to map corridors for wildlife, consult the academic and scientific literature. A local expert can also help – such as a qualified employee from your natural resources or wildlife agency. Use this information to determine how wide the corridors need to be, where might be the best locations, and so on. For example, as part of the 1996 federal Farm Bill, the Natural Resources Conservation Service (NRCS) encourages landowners to install buffer strips ranging from a minimum of 30 feet for some herbaceous filter strips to a maximum of 150 feet for forested riparian buffers (Fischer and Fischenich 2000). Most states have their own requirements as well. Similarly, if you wanted to protect drinking water intakes, your state likely has guidance on how far upstream the river needs to be protected, so use your legal standards when establishing protection zones on a map. The specific models, data sources and suggested methods for doing this are covered in Chapter Seven.

Your community will need to establish a series of *metrics* and *protocols* for what types of habitats to conserve and where. A metric is a measurable quantity, such as buffer width, acreage, the number of tree species, the age of a forest, or water quality. A protocol is a scientific method that turns those measurable quantities into discrete spatial data that suit your needs.

Mapping Cultural Assets

So far, we have discussed natural assets and the protocols for mapping them. But your project may also want to include assets that are valued for cultural reasons. Green infrastructure is a construct that helps us think about the importance of natural resources for people. Yet because people place an intrinsic value on nature and biodiversity – in other words, they value something because it exists, even if they have never experienced it personally – human use of a natural feature is not a prerequisite for including it in a natural asset map. That said, there are cultural resources and values that depend upon the support or context provided by neighboring natural areas.

It can be a complex undertaking to help communities make the link between culture and nature. However, when community members are asked to think about a cultural place that they really

enjoy, such as a plantation, a battlefield or an historic farmhouse, it is often the setting that makes it particularly special.

The setting can be made up of forested hills or mountains, large trees around a building, an adjacent river or marsh, or an uninterrupted vista of green. A view looking out from the structure is part of the experience of enjoying it. Similarly, many recreational pursuits depend upon nature and intact landscapes to make them possible – such as hunting, cross country horseback riding, skiing, landscape and nature photography, birding, canoeing and kayaking.

In Nelson County, VA, views of the intact forested landscape pay dividends to businesses that bring in clients largely to enjoy those vistas while eating or drinking their products. Several local breweries have sprung up in the past five years that depend upon on the county's clean, clear spring-fed streams, as well as on the breathtaking scenery that lures urbanites from nearby densely populated counties and cities. These views keep tourists, hikers, bikers and birders in the county longer, offering refreshment after a fun day in the field or touring local amenities.

According to one Nelson County brewer, "The water in this region is an integral part of the success of our brewery process." One forester called the all-important views of the mountains from the breweries, cideries and wineries "the brewshed" – those views afforded to each brewery that lure and retain customers throughout the seasons. In fact, Nelson County has combined marketing

for nature-based recreation on the Appalachian Trail and Blue Ridge mountains with enjoyment of beer in natural settings by creating a "Brew Ridge Trail," which links hikers, birders and boaters to the many breweries and wineries in the area.

Built Structures

Built structures, which include features such as plantation houses, historic log cabins, old, one-room schoolhouses and 18th century mills, are likely to have a country setting and their backdrop landscapes of hills, forests, marshes, or streams contributes to their historic character.

A simple way to identify these cultural assets is to contact your state's office of historic resources to learn the location of its historic features. It is then relatively easy to map them at a large scale (county or region), where you plot each point and create a buffer around it. Draw the buffer as large as it needs to be. One suggestion is to include contributing natural resources within 500 feet, with a 1300 feet (¼ mile) boundary around areas dependent on a larger setting.

A more accurate (and more time consuming) approach is to use digital mapping tools. There are several add-ons to GIS that can map elevations, and thus sightlines, such as using the GIS-based digital elevation model and Crystal Reports. These can map elevations, which determine where vistas are more or less visible and thus more or less important for a visitor's or resident's experience from a site. It only takes a few minutes to run a digital elevation model and output an elevation map. The time-consuming aspect is to analyze the results, which will likely require site visits to confirm what is actually visible. ESRI's web site provides guidance on mapping viewsheds as well.

PREVENT VANDALISM

Some cultural resources may need to have their locations masked, such as Native American burial mounds or other sacred sites where artifacts could be plundered or compromised by disturbance. Adding a buffer – say 1000 feet -- around those sites can hide their exact locations.

Another method of collecting data about culturally significant features is to ask community members and stakeholders about them. Just be careful to verify the data, as anecdotal information is not always reliable.

Linking Cultural and Natural Assets

The advantage of linking cultural and natural resources is that it helps a community recognize the importance of natural resources to its well-being, identity and sense of place. These natural resources may be taken for granted until they are destroyed. County boards are often asked, why did the cell phone company propose to put their tower (or other obstruction) in our most iconic view? Besides the obvious answer that the location was probably in a good reception area for cell signals, it may also be because most localities have not taken the time to create cell-tower location guidance that asks companies to try to avoid mapped viewsheds or to use designs that help conceal towers.

An important caveat when adding cultural resources to a mapping effort is to carefully bound the discussion; otherwise, people begin to add in 'everything.' At some GIC workshops, participants have even requested we map the locations where things *used to be* – as in the place where an old store burned down in 1942, or the location of the old school they attended before it closed.

It is important that people understand they are not making a map of *everything* they value, but rather those key cultural items that depend on a natural setting for their enjoyment and function. So nature-based recreation means a walking trail through the woods or along a river greenway trail, but does not mean a pedestrian walk through the mall; it means a field set aside for birding, but not one for drag racing.

'Favorite Places Maps'

If people in your community really want to put their favorite nature- and culture-based resources on a map, let them. The GIC calls these maps 'Favorite Places Maps' or 'Peoples' Maps.'

As long as a resource relates to green infrastructure in some way it can be recorded on its own GIS layer. Allow people to write on a map at a community meeting (or have them add their 'data' digitally through programs such as Green Maps). Create a common nomenclature or symbology (such as different colored dots) for the different classes of features on the maps, such as "fishing spots," "best hiking," "best sunset view," and use the

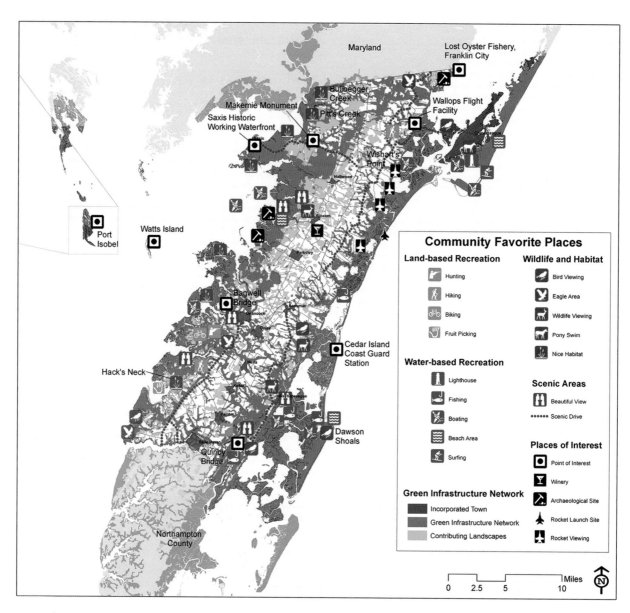

Accomack County Favorite Places Map.

symbols to create a coherent and readable map (see the illustration for Accomack County, Virginia above).

Such a 'favorite places map' can prove useful when it comes to evaluating your green infrastructure priorities. For example, you may find that it closely overlaps areas that had already been prioritized by your local county administration as natural assets and thereby provides community validation for what local government and conservation groups had already identified as priorities to conserve.

The following chart provides examples of goals and potential data sources to indicate spatially how values and goals can be translated into a map of natural and cultural assets. The degree to which they are achieved – for example, how much natural area is protected or how much acreage of intact forests are preserved within the locality – will be determined by the specific objectives you set to achieve each goal. The purpose of the chart is to help you match your goals with resources that can be represented and evaluated spatially.

EXAMPLE GOALS AND DATA			
GOAL	DATA TYPE TO MEET GOAL	DEFINITION/APPLICATION	SOURCE
Protect habitat for native species.	Intact Forests or other habitat types (i.e. large dune systems, wetlands, marshes, natural heritage areas)	Habitats that have adequate interior area which is unfragmented by intrusions such as roads or power lines that create edges which facilitate problems from invasive species or predators. In the eastern U.S., 100 acres of interior conditions (that do not include the necessary 300 foot buffer from surrounding land use) is a minimum size to accommodate a diversity of native forest-dwelling animals, bird and plants.	States such as VA and MD have mapped intact forested, wetland and dune areas (cores) already. The National Land Cover Dataset can be used to create a core layer. A fragmentation layer can then be used to determine which areas remain intact. Those areas that have at least 100 intact acres that are not bisected may form a new core.
Prevent urban heat islands. Protect aesthetics. Reduce stormwater (developed areas). Sequester carbon to mitigate climate change. Clean the air.	Forest Canopy	Canopy is the coverage by forests (bird's eye view) and is more commonly applied to urban areas where other values (besides forest interior) also become important, such as tree cover to keep cities cooler, aesthetic values of trees to downtown areas, and habitat for urban birds and other animals. Trees also mitigate urban stormwater and sequester carbon and clean the air.	Forest canopy may be available from the Department or Division of Forestry. In urban areas, along with the canopy (or if no canopy data, you can use street tree inventories, if available, or create your own). I-Tree is a software tool to help evaluate canopy.
Protect habitat. Protect water quality. Protect aesthetics. Support fish nurseries (if tied to waterways or ocean).	Wetlands	Wetlands include forests, meadows, bogs, shrub swamps, ponds, lakes, streams or bays, and depending on location, may be tidal or non-tidal. Many species can only thrive in wetlands and they provide nurseries for many birds, fish, crustaceans, insects and animals.	National Wetlands Inventory Data (NWI). The NWI may not be very precise. If local or county wetland data are available, add that to this layer.
Promote agriculture row crops.	Agricultural Soils	Prime (best) agricultural soils occur in certain locations. If crops are important to the area, then agricultural soils can be mapped.	USDA Soils Data Mart, select classes IV and V (top ranked). Use land cover to select and remove areas already covered by urban uses (cities, towns, industrial parks) since not suited to large scale farming.
Promote fruit orchards or vineyards.	Slopes Soil Type	Fruit trees and vineyards do best on south or west facing slopes in well drained soils. A local extension agent can help suggest the best areas for orchards or vineyards.	Use a digital elevation model to select slopes. Use the USDA Soils Data Mart, select appropriate soil classes.
Protect watersheds and clean water.	Watershed Boundary Forest Cover Stream Buffers Municipal Water Supply Watershed Boundaries Water Quality Data	Streams should be included in most GI maps as they provide habitat and are often good corridors for wildlife, as well as sources of drinking water. To determine how well forested the watershed is, the forest cover can be clipped in GIS to match up to the watershed boundary and used to determine the percentage of area covered by forests. For water quality, map stream buffers by using GIS to find center lines of streams and map 100 feet widths on either side to see extent of forested stream buffers for buffering runoff. For large rivers use stream edge if known. If using streams for wildlife corridors, select 300 meters on either side of stream and intersect with forest layer to see if adequate forest buffer to provide a protected corridor. If protecting headwater streams, use steep slopes and elevations to select upland streams for protection.	National hydrography data set for stream locations and augment with additional local data. See forest canopy above. In Virginia, a new modeling tool InFOREST can be used to map land cover and get N, P, Sediment loadings by watershed. State 305B Reports contain water quality ratings and the 303D lists contains impaired waters.

EXAMPLE GOALS AND DATA - CONTINUED			
GOAL	DATA TYPE TO MEET GOAL	DEFINITION/APPLICATION	SOURCE
Protect settings of cultural resources.	Historic Sites (in rural areas), battlefields, cemeteries, tribal lands, etc.	Historic sites are often dependent on the context of the surrounding landscape. Buffer each point (building) by 300 meters. You may also want to protect the views from this site for visitors.	Obtain historic data from State Division of Historic Resources. Some sensitive data, such as Indian burial sites, may not be available. Viewsheds can be mapped using the ArcMap Viewshed tool. It uses point data and Digital Elevation Models to calculate the visible area. Moderate to advanced GIS skill necessary.
Promote vibrant business districts.	Tree Canopy Street Trees Parks/Other green spaces	Trees provide aesthetics, shelter, and stormwater management. Treed business districts see higher revenues per shopper. Parks, river greenways and trails also attract business to downtowns. Offices are more likely to locate in greener downtowns.	See forest canopy. Also, use local data for trail and park locations.
Promote healthy lifestyles and nature based-recreation.	Parks Trails State Forests Wildlife Management Areas	Parks whose primary or majority of uses requires natural areas. Existing regional trails, rail trails, wildlife viewing areas. Select areas that are close to existing or proposed trails, to either buffer the users' experience or provide for potential new connections in the future.	State or locality park data. Wildlife and Birding Trails. State Parks. Open space lands. State Forests (if open for visitors). Rail to Trail Routes/regional trails. Important Birding Areas (publicly accessible).

STEP 4. ASSESS RISKS: WHAT ASSETS ARE MOST AT RISK AND WHAT COULD BE LOST IF NO ACTION IS TAKEN?

Making a map of your assets is just the first step to conserving those resources. While it is important to know what your organization or community values and to be able to represent those values spatially on a map, these mapped assets must be evaluated to determine if they are at risk from roads, redevelopment, dams, or other factors.

'Risk' refers to whether a natural asset is likely to remain intact or not and will help to prioritize which areas to conserve, how to rank them, and what actions may or may not be needed to protect them.

Remember that a map of natural resources is a snapshot in time. Land uses can change and land may be converted from one use to another. It is important to conduct even a cursory analysis of which resources are likely to remain and which may change or disappear.

To do this, we need to ask such questions as:

- Which areas are zoned for development and do they overlap key natural assets?
- Which forests and other key natural areas are threatened with fragmentation by roads or subdivisions?

- Are there areas threatened by natural enemies, such as pests or diseases?
- Are there areas at risk from natural disasters, such as extreme floods or wildfires?
- Which streams are likely to be impaired in the future?
- Are there impaired areas where habitat can be restored?
- What viewsheds are threatened?
- Which assets are most threatened by present zoning and currently planned developments?

In the future, zoning can be reviewed, land may change ownership, natural events such as floods or tornadoes can alter landscape conditions, populations may increase or decrease, and localities may have more or less money to spend on roads, land acquisition and conservation easements. Thus, it will be important to update maps and data along the way.

The chart of risks and associated actions provides a checklist of possible actions to forestall potential or unforeseen risks to natural assets. For each threat to an asset ask, "How can we change our plans to better protect it?"

EXAMPLES OF RISKS AND ASSOCIATED ACTIONS

RISK FACTOR	HOW TO EVALUATE	OPTIONS AND CONSIDERATIONS FOR WHAT TO DO
Incompatible Zoning	Overlay existing zoning with current natural resource priorities. Identify areas where uses are incompatible, such as industrial or residential zoning overlain with large intact forests or wetlands.	Zoning can be changed if a comprehensive evaluation is conducted. Zoning can also be changed if a 'mistake' is shown to have been made, such as information that was unknown or incorrect when the zoning was determined. Consider a rezoning effort to channel new development into other areas or build more densely and consider infill options. Even within areas zoned for development, is there room to include wildlife/recreation corridors to keep the landscape connected?
Future Land Use Changes	Review future land use maps to see where the community plans to grow in the future. Where are proposed service districts? Consider if people will encroach into forested areas. This can cause problems for wildlife as well as increase the risk of wildfire impacts to people. Invasive species may also be introduced by new residents.	Is the map still current? Is it based on actual/accurate population projections? Should it be changed? And when is the next update scheduled? Does the community need more education about the risks of living within these forested zones (also known as the wildland urban interface).
Impaired Waters	Waterways, lakes and bays can be designated as impaired and placed on the 303 list as required under the federal Clean Water Act. Overlay this list with those water features you consider to be important, in order to see which waters are polluted. For example, are impaired waters a threat to drinking water or trout fishing? Consider whether more waters could become polluted in the future: Are currently pristine areas zoned for more growth?	Determine why the surface water is impaired. If the impairment is caused by land runoff, you could help meet the regulatory requirements under the Total Maximum Daily Loading (TMDL) requirements by conserving more land in the watershed. When reviewing impaired waters, consider which are harmed by a cause that can be addressed through habitat or land-use mitigation. For example, if a stream suffers from excessive sediment or habitat destruction, your strategy could address needs for reforestation or enhanced stream buffers. If a cleanup plan has not yet been created, determine whether setting aside land for conservation could help to restore the water quality. Protecting key habitat cores for wildlife could also benefit a stream's health, depending on its location in the watershed.
Population Growth	If the area is likely to grow at a fast rate, where will people live? Evaluate whether there are currently enough housing units in the right places to meet this growth.	Where are designated growth areas relative to key natural assets? Do people have opportunities for recreation near to where they will be living? Consider whether land could be set aside to accommodate future recreation needs. Also consider whether waterway impairments could increase the costs of cleanup requirements, or if additional environmental regulations and incentives (such as density bonuses to encourage infill that also provide for low-impact development measures, such as rain gardens to mitigate stormwater runoff) could help modify development patterns.
Transportation Plans	Will planned roads bisect natural features? Will new roads lead to increased development that may also impact natural features?	Can other, less impactful routes be considered? Are the roads needed? Are transportation demand models based on up-to-date population projections? Can alternative transportation models solve some of the demand to move people? If road projects need to purchase land to mitigate impacts, such as wetlands or open space, can the natural asset map be used to prioritize which land to acquire? Also consider new approaches to green highway design that are less impactful to wildlife.
Impaired Landscapes	Are there areas that have a high degree of pavement causing excessive runoff and high urban temperatures? Are there old industrial sites? In rural areas are there overgrazed fields or streams without forest buffers? Are there restoration opportunities to reconnect core wildlife habitats?	Which areas could be reforested? Which streams could be planted with forested buffers? Could impervious areas be demolished and re-greened? Can brownfields be remediated through state and federal grant programs?

But first, before taking action, it is best to evaluate how great the actual threat is. For example, if a highly ecologically sensitive area has been zoned for development, it may be worth finding out just how likely the land is to be developed, and how soon. If it turns out that there are already plans in process, then prioritize the area and search for alternative ways to protect it.

Just because a parcel or tract is currently zoned for development does not mean that it will be developed. A developer may be willing to swap land that is desirable to a locality in exchange for land closer to existing roads or transportation, or that offers him other benefits.

Remember that green infrastructure asset planning does not try to halt development *per se*; rather, GI planners should evaluate and map their natural assets to be as strategic as possible in using land for its best functions, so communities can achieve a balance of ecological, economic and health goals.

The risk chart includes examples of common resources to evaluate for risk and what to address. This list will likely need to be informed by local planners. Other risks within the community, such as abandoned mines, Superfund sites and large paved areas lacking adequate stormwater controls, will need to be evaluated as well to determine their risk and what actions, if any, can and should be taken.

It is important to evaluate the potential that any identified risk has to affect your natural assets and what you can do, if anything, to remediate that threat. For example, a risk can exist, but its impact could be low, even though you could easily remedy the situation. Alternatively, it could have a high impact but not be changeable at all. Consult with local planners, the development community, land trusts and conservation groups and others to evaluate whether the potential risk actually exists and if the development plan has already been proposed. You can also use this process to determine whether or not it is too late to propose an alternative land development scenario that leaves some of the area as open space.

Sometimes, land can be swapped or traded so that areas more valuable for natural resource conservation or hazard mitigation can be protected in exchange for moving development to places more suitable for new growth. In an example from Albemarle County, Virginia, a nonprofit housing agency, Habitat for Humanity of Greater Charlottesville, owned land that is surrounded by the borders of newly designated state park land. Working with the county and state, the nonprofit

housing provider proposed to swap some acreage of land inside the park for land outside the park, thus preventing interior land uses incompatible with a state park. This allows Habitat for Humanity to create habitat for people and land for the county to construct an active-use recreational area. All sides – the park agency, the nonprofit housing agency and the county – thus get a better deal. Both habitat for animals and for people can now be in their appropriate locations.

A challenge can arise in trying to plan for your locality when an adjacent or nearby locality has created plans that conflict with your goals. Frederick County, Maryland has a border with Pennsylvania. It has designated this area as its agricultural preservation area, but Pennsylvania is allowing development to amass on its side of the border.

Such conflicts are also found between cities and counties. While it makes sense from a 'smart growth' perspective for counties to encourage development near urban areas, tall buildings and encroachment into once-forested areas are troubling for some city residents in low residential density areas, who are now faced with buildings and denser development just across the county boundary.

Your evaluation of risk should also consider the quality or health of the natural asset in question. For example, an area that seems to be worth preserving because it is covered by forest canopy and seems to provide good habitat for many species may, on closer examination, reveal that the trees are second or third growth, mainly pines and scrub oaks, and are suffering from diseases or pest infestations. If this is the case, additional management or forest restoration would be needed to help bring the forest back to a state that would be found naturally, had not past land clearing, invasive species or pests altered it.

STEP 5. DETERMINE OPPORTUNITIES: BASED ON THOSE ASSETS AND RISKS IDENTIFIED; WHICH ONES SHOULD BE RESTORED OR IMPROVED? AND WHICH NEED THE ATTENTION SOONEST?

Based on assets and risks, determine what land can or should be conserved or restored. This may also point to areas that are more appropriate for development, either because they do not contain rare or unique natural assets, or because they could provide recreation and other benefits to residents.

Once assets most at risk have been identified, rank them – to prioritize those natural assets that should be preserved or restored. Engage your community in ranking the key areas of importance. Map opportunities and draft strategies to conserve them.

Be sure to indicate *why* each asset is of greater significance. *Also, how assets are ranked should conform to pre-established goals.* If one of the goals is to avoid impacts from new development on existing forests and woodlands, then prioritize those parcels of forest and woodland most at risk from new development.

Basically, there are two things to consider here: Which assets meet your community's goals for conservation? And which are most threatened? It is those that fall into both categories that should have the highest ranking to protect first.

Here are some things to consider:

- Which are the top five/ten areas of forest or woodland that are most threatened, or that offer the most value for forestry, recreation and wildlife habitat? Specify why.
- Which are the top waterways to preserve, and why?
- What are the top geological features and viewsheds that need to be preserved, and why?
- Which historical landscapes are most important and most under threat?
- What recreational areas are of most value and are most threatened?

Your map can also include desired future assets:

- Where should future parks and recreational areas be located?
- Suitable locations and routes for future agritourism businesses (such as pick-your-own fruit orchards, wineries, honey producers, local beef, pork and chicken farms, and vegetable stands).
- Scenic views or routes through historic or cultural assets that should be protected and enhanced.
- The best areas for future industrial parks and housing developments.

Consider areas that will not be preserved or which may require extra care:

- Growth areas already set aside for new development.

- Industrial zones that may be incompatible with conservation.
- Areas that are currently contaminated, such as brownfield sites, and which may be reclaimable in the future.

Ranking Data

Ranking is another way to assign human values to data. Everything that is included on a green infrastructure map is based on a value. A specific value may be more objective or more subjective, but each resource included on a natural assets map is there because a value has been assigned to it.

An example of an objective approach would be: "Put all third-order or higher-order streams on the map." The parameter that the streams should be "third order" is objective, in that it was chosen to provide a specific size stream. Another example is to select all forested corridors at least 300 meters wide that connect large intact forest cores, to help facilitate wildlife movement.

Both parameters for mapping listed above are objective because they provide specific decision metrics for their selection and inclusion on a green infrastructure map. However, the *reason* for choosing them is more subjective. You may have selected large streams because they are more likely to serve as significant corridors for wildlife. Large forested corridors may have been selected because of a value placed on the importance of wildlife movement and enhanced opportunities for biodiversity from a connected landscape.

If you are planning a green infrastructure network without the aid of an existing state model, you may need to create your own data layers and overlay them to create your green infrastructure network. This will still require making a determination of what is most important. If you are following a community consensus-based project then you may have to resolve diverse or conflicting values for what is most important. People will value things differently and the values assigned may depend on their purpose.

Following clear scientific principles for how much habitat species need to survive and thrive can help to create more objective mapping guidelines. If you do not know this information, create a technical advisory committee of qualified scientists.

Assuming that clear goals have been established for why you are mapping the natural resources of your landscape, you may want to rank those resources. One way to do this is to incorporate *weighted overlays* to establish your conservation network.

Weighted overlay is a standard technique used with rasterized GIS data to determine the suitability of a landscape to meet existing objective criteria. Weighting allows an area that has a higher value to be selected.

Weighted Overlay

Weighted overlay is a standard technique used with rasterized GIS data to determine the suitability of a landscape to meet existing objective criteria (determined previously). Each raster is a matrix of cells containing data, such as aerial images (captured in a grid and made up of individual cells).

Cells can be selected based on their values (e.g. they have a certain color denoting tree cover) and these values can be weighted. This allows you to select an area that has a higher value. You can create a technical committee to assign weights and help in ranking.

Certain values could be added to a green infrastructure map to give some areas more points (weights) for human values, such as a watershed area that supports drinking water uses (+3 points), known endangered species (+4 points), and so on. When Virginia created its Natural Landscape Assessment, it assigned values (points) to different attributes that were used to rank forest cores. So areas that were larger received more points, as did areas that had more surface waters, unique geology and other factors. As a result, it came up with five different levels of ranking. In order to assign values, a science review panel is recommended to ensure that values relate to known importance.

What Can Be Restored?

Remember that many natural landscape elements can be restored. A successful green infrastructure strategy often includes, not only protecting existing natural assets, but improving their quality and extent.

When reviewing a map of existing natural assets, you may find areas that are disconnected or degraded. If two habitat cores lack a connection, a new corridor could be planted. Similarly, a forest or wetland core could be expanded by planting more trees or removing invasive vegetation. You may also need to manage specific rare habitats if they support a particular species that has been deemed important. An example of this are bogs that might need to be cleared of trees periodically to ensure that water elevations remain high enough to support rare amphibians.

Landscape Features as Key Corridors

Landscape features that tend to remain in place, such as streams, can be selected as corridors for a green infrastructure network. Their permanence in the landscape makes them well suited to serve as long-term corridors. However, to provide an adequate passage for wildlife, native vegetation may need to be re-established. This is especially true in livestock areas, where farmers may have cleared land right down to the stream edge.

If your goal is to provide a buffer to protect a stream's water quality, then a minimum width of 100 feet is recommended (for more on buffer design, see Bibliography). However, if you wish to encourage wildlife passage and protect the buffer from invasive species, a wider strip is recommended, say 300 meters (approximately 1000 feet) on both sides of the watercourse.

Ridges can also serve as key corridors. They are often undeveloped because of their elevation and steeply sided slopes. They are important because many species, such as bears, migrating butterflies, bats and raptors, rely upon high elevations to survive or migrate. They use them as corridors.

For other species, such as bighorn mountain sheep or the north American pika, these higher elevation ridges and meadows are their special habitat niches – places with the unique conditions necessary for their survival.

Pika can only live at colder, high elevation ranges.

Urban Restoration

In most urban areas, green spaces have become disconnected. City parks and waterways can serve as the core resources of a revitalized urban green infrastructure network. Your city may also have large vacant lots that have become overgrown as people moved to the suburbs and businesses relocated. Some of these can be quite large – if a foundry or steelworks closed, a paper mill or a car factory, there can be hundreds of acres of land available.

These vacant, abandoned spaces can become part of a restored green infrastructure network, though they will almost certainly need to be replanted, cleared of invasives and pollutants, or otherwise regenerated. If it is a brownfield site, there may have been past industrial uses that need to be remediated, if you want the public to be able to access it.

In cities, even paved areas can become part of a green infrastructure network. There may be large areas of concrete or asphalt that are no longer occupied or utilized. Abandoned car lots. Derelict factories. Demolished warehouses. Such areas are not uncommon in cities that are going through a post-industrial reorientation of their employment base.

Such areas can be nothing more than large expanses of cracked, trash-strewn, scrubby pavement that lack any respectable urban trees. However, even these old paved areas can be regreened by removing the pavement, regrading, bringing in good quality topsoil, opening up culverts to recover streams, and replanting them. On the other hand, if left alone, vacant areas can sometimes regenerate themselves, and over time, come to possess significant natural habitats or even rare species.

This abandoned parcel can become part of a new green network.

Vacant lots and large paved areas can also be connected to form new corridors and urban greenway trails. In its Richmond Project, the GIC created a database of all vacant and underutilized parcels by combining several city databases into one master, sortable data source. This resulted in a list of 9000 vacant and underutilized parcels! This was then overlain with the city's green infrastructure network to determine where vacant parcels could support a wider green infrastructure's existing natural assets. It further identified those lots that were vegetated and those that needed to be re-greened if they were to become part of a connected network. In fact, several key parcels needed to complete the network were found to already be owned by the city, thus facilitating creation of an integrated network!

"There is often enough vacant land in an urban landscape that a green corridor or 'green finger' could stretch across the back of several parcels."

When you consider which vacant or abandoned parcels could be targeted for re-greening, you can rank them according to their ability to contribute to a wider green infrastructure network. By developing a series of questions and scoring each question by importance (weighting the answers), you can develop a systematic approach to determine which parcels to acquire, where to obtain an easement, where to conduct a restoration project, and so on.

There is often enough vacant land in an urban landscape that a green corridor or 'green finger' could stretch across the back of several parcels. Planners may want to consider whether to request additional protections for parcels that contain unique natural assets or offer an opportunity to create a connected network.

The Relinking Illustration on the following page depicts an approach for recognizing regreening potential. Note that adding new green spaces and corridors does not necessarily preclude new development or redevelopment.

Urban Tree Canopies

In urban areas, when evaluating natural assets at smaller scales (fractions of acres instead of hundreds of acres), minor landscape resources become important to consider and can make a large cumulative difference. Smaller

FINDING URBAN RESTORATION OPPORTUNITIES

These maps show opportunities for re-greening Richmond Va. The top map shows vacant parcels and the bottom map intersects those parcels with water features. This helps to show which vacant parcels could provide water quality benefits if re-greened.

LEGEND

Vacant Parcels

- Vacant Lots
- Vacant Structures
- Other Vacant Properties

General Features

- Parcels
- City Boundary
- Planning District Boundaries
- James River

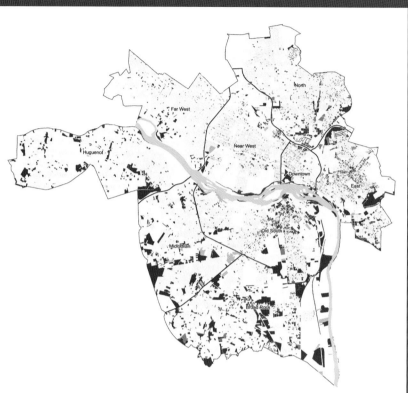

Vacant and under-utilized parcels in Richmond that could be re-greened.

City of Richmond

All Vacant Parcels Intersecting the Green Infrastructure Network

- Vacant Parcels Meeting Selection Criteria

Other Urban Features

- Primary Road
- Interstate Highway
- Parcels
- Planning District

Green Infrastructure Features

- Streams
- James River
- 100-year Floodplain
- Wetland
- All Conserved Lands
- Unconserved Lands of Ecological Value

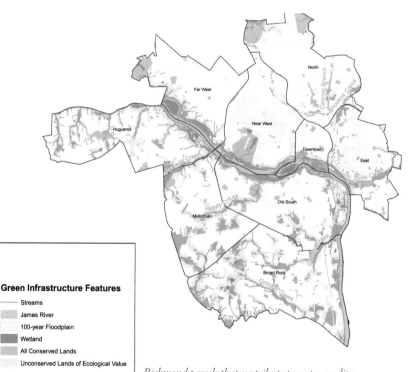

Richmond parcels that contribute to water quality.

RELINKING URBAN GREEN SPACES

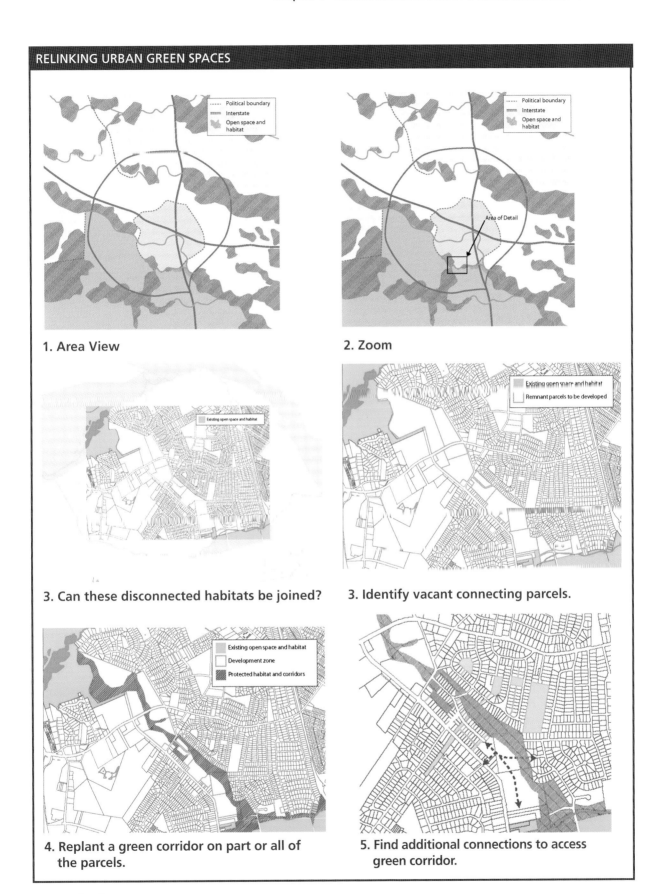

1. Area View

2. Zoom

3. Can these disconnected habitats be joined?

3. Identify vacant connecting parcels.

4. Replant a green corridor on part or all of the parcels.

5. Find additional connections to access green corridor.

Courtesy of Catherine Brown

urban spaces, such as linear stream valleys, or even pocket parks, can add to a connected green landscape. When evaluating the ecological health of an urban area, urban tree canopy is a key green asset.

An urban tree canopy (UTC) does not constitute a forest *per se,* but taken city-wide, can serve a vital role in keeping built-up areas cool and can provide many other benefits. New York City's street trees are a valuable asset, providing approximately $100.2 million, or $1,723 per tree ($15 per capita), in net annual benefits to the community (Peper et al. 2007).

Urban Forests for Stormwater Mitigation

Urban forests also intercept stormwater, which many cities need to reduce or better control. Studies have shown that the urban canopy can reduce a city's stormwater runoff by anywhere from two to seven percent (Fazio 2010). Many cities and towns now have to manage their urban stormwater and must make improvements in preventing excess stormwater runoff in order to comply with requirements to clean up impaired waters or to meet program mandates under Municipal Separate Storm Sewer Systems programs.

Even one tree can play an important role in stormwater management. For example, estimates for the amount of water a typical street tree can intercept in its crown range from 760 gallons to 4000 gallons per tree per year, depending on the species and age. A study by the USFS found the average street tree in New York City intercepted 1,525 gallons of rainfall annually, while larger trees, such as the London plane tree captured almost 2,875 gallons (Peper et al. 2007).

Cities are beginning to recognize these benefits and are paying to support their urban trees because they reap tremendous dividends. In Vancouver, Washington, the city allocated 100 percent of its stormwater utility fee funds to support the city's urban forestry program. They calculated that the services provided by the city's existing tree canopy saves $12.9 million per year in cost savings to city residents for not having to manage that stormwater with constructed systems (Vancouver Urban Forestry Management Plan 2007).

Assessing Tree Loss

Cities may have information on their tree canopies, but it's important to ensure that the information is current enough to be accurate. Following the extreme storms of Sandy in the Northeast and Katrina in the South, many urban tree canopies were devastated. In New York City, at least 8,000 street trees were destroyed, along with thousands more in parks and on private lots (*New York Times* 2012). This means not only a loss to the city's natural assets, but also a tremendous loss in capacity to intercept rainfall and evapotranspire excess stormwater.

Of course, trees are not only lost in storms. Land conversion is perhaps the greatest threat to tree loss. Even already developed areas, when redeveloped, may not replace as many trees when the site is rebuilt. Conversion of forested land to pavement has serious consequences for cities, leading to increased flooding, which harms property values and threatens public safety. During a rainfall event of one inch, one acre of forest will release 750 gallons of runoff, while a parking lot will release 27,000 gallons; 36 times more runoff (PennState Extension).

In addition to land conversion, trees are also lost to attrition. Even if no land conversions occur, failure to replant trees as they age and die will lead to canopy loss over time. Trees planted poorly (wrong site), not well managed (inadequate care), or trees planted inappropriately (wrong tree) can also lead to tree canopy losses. While there have been studies of urban tree survival rates, results vary greatly due to differences in planting conditions, species and other factors, such as susceptibility to storms. In the 1980s, and still continuing today, many US cities planted the pretty flowering Bradford pear tree. This non-native tree is highly susceptible to wind damage and tends to be short-lived because of its brittle branches. It is commonly planted along entire boulevards, and unfortunately, as these trees decline and die, often nothing is replanted in their place.

Bradford Pears are a poor choice for urban planting.

How Many Trees Are Enough?

If you have access to an UTC assessment, you will see that, while your town, city or urbanized county may have an acceptable city-wide percentage of trees (American Forests recommends at least a 40 percent canopy for urban areas east of the Mississippi), certain areas will have far fewer trees than others. For example, In Virginia, Richmond City's canopy is 42 percent overall, but some downtown areas are as low as 9 percent.

Tree canopy assessments can be used to target priorities for reforestation of those areas most in need. In New York, Los Angeles and elsewhere, Million Tree Initiatives have created ambitious goals for re-greening cities. These programs emphasize planting goals that most often target street tree sites, but also include reforestation efforts on vacant land.

Notwithstanding these ambitious programs, America's cities are losing their trees. A study of tree canopies in major cities found that tree cover is declining at an average rate of 0.27 percent/year, while impervious surfaces are increasing at an average rate of about 0.31 percent per year. This translates to a loss of about 4 million trees per year (Nowak 2012).

A review of tree survival studies found that urban trees often do not make it to their full potential life span. Factors such as lack of watering or insufficient soil volume put stresses on urban trees, stunt their growth or reduce their lifespans. For every 100 street trees planted, only 50 will survive 13 20 years (Roman 2014). This means that, when establishing urban canopy goals (e.g. your city has 15 percent trees and you want to raise it to 25 percent), you will need to account for tree mortality when calculating how many trees to plant. Also, different species have different canopy spreads, which you will

Poor tree planting; not enough room to grow

Good tree planting: Pavers allow water and air to enter and may be removed as the tree grows

need to consider when assessing how many trees to plant, and at which sites. A dogwood has far less canopy spread than an oak, for example.

Even No Net Loss Requires Management

In some cities, such as Denver, the primary focus is on managing and sustaining the existing canopy and addressing future pressures from urban development, climate change and pests, such as the emerald ash borer. Active management is required simply to maintain existing trees and to replace trees lost to development, disease, storms or just old age. This requires proper inventory, pruning, soil conditioning and watering; all of which require investments of time and money. Cities such as Seattle, Austin and Pittsburgh have exemplary urban forest programs, often because they work in partnership with nonprofit and community groups to care for their urban forests, and are supported by city agencies with knowledgeable staff.

Urban trees especially should be selected for the right conditions, such as for tolerance to drought or pollution. If they are planted in rain gardens or along streams, they should be able to thrive under periodic inundation. Also, trees should not be planted under power lines or in

White Oak

Kentucky Coffee

Redbud

Shown above are trees with canopies ranging from large (top) to small (bottom), and they should be located where they best fit.

POSSIBLE PLANTING AREA (PPA)

When assessing the PPA for Jersey City, the GIC included three types of land cover. These land cover types were included in the PPA, while all other types were removed from consideration

- non-tree vegetation
- bare earth
- non-building impervious

The process involved two distinct steps:

1. A 1-meter land cover dataset was queried to map the three land cover types.
2. A series of exclusionary factors were used to eliminate certain areas in order to develop a more realistic estimate of plantable area. Obvious barriers, such as buildings, railroad tracks, athletic fields, golf course fairways, footpaths and roads were excluded.

Note: This map did not represent areas of potential tree canopy, but rather identified those areas in which trees could possibly be planted (as tree canopy can overhang a street or building). See page 73 for a graphic illustration of the difference.

places where their roots will interfere with underground utilities (there are tools and materials to reduce this likelihood) or where they will push up sidewalks and cause danger to pedestrians – or traffic. Large canopy trees will do best in open areas, whereas smaller spreading trees can often thrive in tight spaces. The simple rule is right tree, right place.

Modeling Tree Planting Potential

Determining how many trees are possible can be modeled in GIS to hypothesize how many trees might be fitted into an urban landscape. In Jersey City, the GIC mapped the city's tree canopy and then used exclusion factors to determine how much of the non-treed area would be suitable for planting in the future. A Possible Planting Area (PPA) analysis was created to show areas in which it is possible to plant trees.

A PPA map estimates areas that are *feasible* to plant trees – it is not a suitability map. For example, a wide sidewalk may be initially identified as a feasible place to

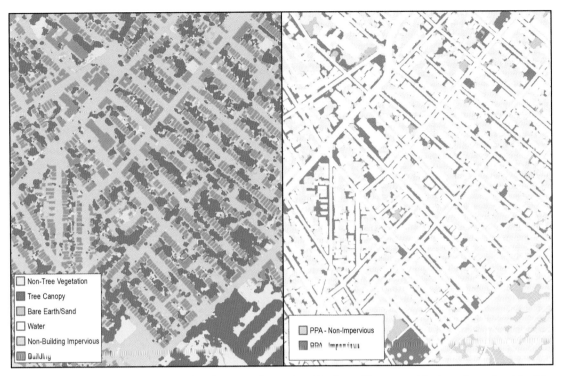

Non-Tree Vegetation
Tree Canopy
Bare Earth/Sand
Water
Non-Building Impervious
Building

PPA - Non-Impervious
PPA - Impervious

The map at left shows Urban Tree Canopy data for a part of Jersey City, New Jersey. The map at right shows the predicted Possible Planting Area for the same geographic area. Note that two types of Possible Planting Area are distinguished: Impervious (e.g. parking lots, sidewalks) and Non-Impervious (e.g. grass, bare earth).

This series of images highlights the difference between possible planting area and possible tree canopy. Possible planting area (highlighted yellow in the center image) estimates area in which a tree could be planted. This is different than potential tree canopy (highlighted orange in the image on the right), which can overhang areas in which it is not possible to plant a tree (like a road).

plant a tree, but may not turn out to be suitable if there are low power lines or an abundance of underground utilities. Thus, any PPA still needs to be field checked and compared against unseen barriers, such as underground utilities, and against city development plans: you might not want to plant trees alongside an avenue that is due to be widened.

A PPA map is a tool that can be created using GIS, in order to hypothesize how many areas might be re-planted. The next steps include calculating how many trees that would take and how much funding is available.

For more ideas on how to address urban canopy and canopy gaps, see Chapter Seven.

Urban Agriculture

You can use small-scale raised beds and greenhouses to locate agriculture in areas where it would not naturally occur, or where contaminated soils on brownfield sites require you to do so for health reasons. While raised beds are not dependent on locations of good agricultural soils, you can use GIS to map areas where community gardens exist and where they are lacking and could be added.

Cities, such as Cleveland, OH, have begun using their large vacant parcels to create urban farms, thus creating a more livable city with a future that includes abundant local food. This also creates a new urban economy for residents who can now sell produce to their neighbors. Urban agriculture can be done on rooftops, on school grounds, on vacant lots and many places where there is open land and people need access to healthy food. These garden spaces (or potential sites) can be included on an urban green infrastructure plan. See the community gardens map on page 75, created for Southside Richmond. In this map, existing gardens were mapped as well as vacant parcels to determine options to add more gardens to the area.

A CHECKLIST FOR URBAN GREEN INFRASTRUCTURE OPPORTUNITIES

Once land has been prioritized for its importance in a green infrastructure network, the question needs to be asked, "What is the best way to include it?"

Should it be acquired, or would a partnership or management agreement with the landowner ensure that it is managed in a way that contributes to the locality's ecological health or to other goals, such as stormwater infiltration and attractive views?

Sometimes, a parcel is already under government ownership and simply requires a joint management arrangement with the appropriate agency. Or only part of the parcel may be needed to meet conservation goals. A large parcel might be improved to contain an office building in the front half and a restored stream buffer on the back half.

This checklist is intended to help planners prioritize the land they want to conserve in urban areas at the parcel scale. Add additional questions that meet your own specific goals.

- [ ] Does the parcel help maintain an existing goal for the city, such as infiltrating water or providing recreation?
- [ ] Does the parcel contain natural features, such as mature trees, a meadow or a waterway?
- [ ] Is the parcel adjacent to a stream, such that its conservation can contribute to good water quality?
- [ ] Does the parcel contain a wetland?
- [ ] Does the parcel contain any rare, threatened or endangered species?

- [ ] Does the parcel contribute to a larger natural network?
- [ ] Does the parcel provide a key recreation opportunity?
- [ ] Does the parcel offer an opportunity to change a noxious use into a productive one?
- [ ] Does the parcel provide an environmental educational opportunity, such as open space next to a school, community center, or other community facility?
- [ ] Would the parcel help form a corridor between two or more key landscape features?
- [ ] Is the parcel near to another significant natural area? For example, in urban areas, wildlife, bees, butterflies and birds can utilize a stepping stone approach to movement, so that even areas that are close, but not touching, can create a connected habitat network and support biodiversity.
- [ ] Does the parcel present a restoration opportunity? For example, are the trees invasive, non-native species that could be removed and the area replanted with native species?
- [ ] Does the parcel provide a buffer to an existing priority feature? For example, does it abut a Civil War or Revolutionary War site? Is it part of the viewshed for a key cultural asset? Does it shelter a sensitive area, such as a bog?
- [ ] What are the quality of the existing trees/vegetation on the neighboring properties? Are there re-development plans that could impact the site?

The Urban Farm, a nonprofit farm in Denver, Colorado is growing crops and livestock in the city and providing education for residents of the mile high city to learn about and cultivate healthy food. The provide farm plots for anyone to grow their own food. Urban farms help bring nature into cities and provide an opportunity to conserve open spaces.

Urban agriculture can also entail growing native plants for city projects. The Presidio of San Francisco, California, formerly a military park for 218 years, is now being adaptively re-used. It includes open spaces, nature trails and land for tenants who enjoy its rich cultural and natural landscape. The Presidio's plant nursery provides training for hundreds of volunteers. In 2012 it grew 120,000 plants used for restoration work as well as hundreds of trees, including native species such as, Coast live oak, Wax myrtle and California buckeye.

Urban farms are also green infrastructure.

COMMUNITY GARDENS AND POTENTIAL LOTS FOR GARDENING IN SOUTHSIDE RICHMOND, VIRGINIA

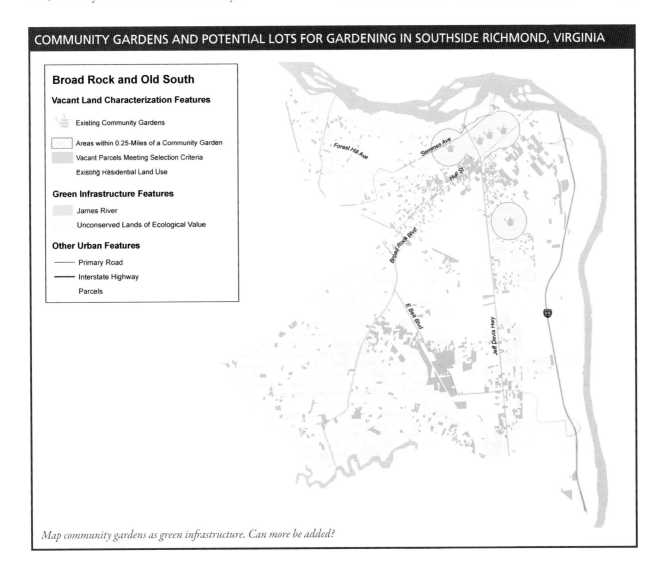

Broad Rock and Old South

Vacant Land Characterization Features

Existing Community Gardens

Areas within 0.25-Miles of a Community Garden

Vacant Parcels Meeting Selection Criteria

Existing Residential Land Use

Green Infrastructure Features

James River

Unconserved Lands of Ecological Value

Other Urban Features

—— Primary Road

—— Interstate Highway

Parcels

Map community gardens as green infrastructure. Can more be added?

Some Assets Cannot Be Restored

Restoration is not always feasible from a practical or a financial standpoint. For example, high-quality agricultural soils cannot be relocated. Similarly, areas that have a unique geology, or contain old-growth forests or other rare habitats should be protected wherever they are found, and whenever possible. Wetlands also may have unique hydrology, plant assemblages and amphibians,

GREEN INFRASTRUCTURE APPLICATIONS

Green infrastructure plans can fit into existing city and county planning efforts and can compliment already-identified conservation goals. The following are examples of how green infrastructure assessments may be utilized to inform planning:

- Environmental chapters in comprehensive plans, or to implement existing comprehensive plan goals for resource assessments and conservation.

- Park, open space and recreational planning or strategic land acquisition.

- Strategies for determining where to zone land for conservation or growth.

- Lands for the purchase, or transfer, of development rights.

- Heritage tourism strategies and viewshed protection.

- Urban tree canopy surveys and management.

- Transportation planning for roads and multi-modal planning.

- Targeting land for conservation easement programs.

- New ordinance development, (stream buffers, watershed protection, historic landscape or other conservation district overlays, codification of requirements for landscaping within developments).

- A rezoning decision for more or less dense development (upzoning or downzoning).

- Conserving forest cover to protect surface water quality and supply, mitigate stormwater runoff and facilitate the infiltration of water into groundwater aquifers.

- The identification of areas where conservation is appropriate or needed.

along with recharge processes that cannot be fully replicated when moving (recreating) the wetland elsewhere. Once a unique species has become extinct, it can't be brought back.

STEP 6. IMPLEMENT OPPORTUNITIES: INCLUDE YOUR NATURAL ASSET MAPS IN BOTH DAILY AND LONG-RANGE PLANNING

This section includes examples of how to ensure that your maps are utilized for informing daily land-use decision-making: what is meant by 'implementation.' However, it does not cover all aspects of planning regulations and practices, as it assumes some familiarity by the reader.

Of course, natural asset planning is not limited to 'natural' or pristine areas. It is often needed because of the challenges posed to those remaining green areas in suburbs and towns when more and more gray infrastructure is being built. In already developed areas, green assets can be reconnected through new corridors. They can also be restored by revitalizing a brownfield site with trees and shrubs.

Planning to conserve natural assets involves more than identifying what to protect. The converse is also true. Once you have identified areas to conserve, you can identify areas where development may be more appropriate. If an area does not contain rare species, key water features or does not meet other conservation objectives, it may meet development goals such as, proximity to an existing urban development area, access to a primary road, or lies in a service district for urban wastewater and drinking water treatment. Thus your map can also be used to point to areas less suited for conservation and more suited to development.

Of course, all developed land should also have some 'green resources' (parks, open spaces, tree canopy). The key is to think at multiple scales, of how resources connect, and to ensure that the best use is envisioned for each parcel and region based on its actual landscape features and infrastructure conditions.

Utilizing Green Infrastructure Data in Day-To-Day Planning

Once you have evaluated and mapped your community's natural and cultural assets, it is time to utilize this information as part of everyday planning and conservation work. It is likely that, unless you take some action, your assets will decrease over time. For example, fragmentation caused by roads, buildings and other disturbances is the single greatest threat to forests in the southern U.S. (USDA Southern Research Station). And, left uncontrolled, it will get worse. But this fragmentation could be avoided by careful planning to prevent bisecting critical natural areas that may be serving key purposes that should be recognized.

Of course, you can also *increase* your natural assets by setting new areas aside for restoration, such as replanting forests, restoring stream buffers and habitat and removing invasive species. You may also suggest additional measures to buffer a high-value asset from adjacent or potential disturbances.

Since decisions affecting land uses occur within many different branches of government, you may need to hold briefings and workshops for other agency staff, as well as local conservation groups, in order to explain your project's goals, outcomes and priorities. Hopefully, some of this already occurred during your stakeholder engagement and outreach efforts, but it is common for people to prefer to engage with a process at the end, when there is a product (maps) to work with.

The following are examples of how to use GI information in your planning efforts. In addition, the GIC's website has project case examples on implementation ideas and examples:

http://www.gicinc.org/projects.htm

Turning Asset Maps Into Policy – Prioritizing Opportunities

We have discussed two concepts: first, the notion of risk assessment – determining which assets will be lost if no action is taken; and second, the notion of opportunity mapping – figuring out where there are opportunities to achieve community goals. Prioritizing opportunities, however, is key to ensure you can move from ideas to implementation.

Consider which opportunities are the most timely. For example, you may already have a mandate to create a new water supply plan in the next twelve months, in which case it will be key for you to identify and conserve the watershed around any new reservoirs you are planning. Similarly, if the new reservoir's construction will require mitigation actions, consider which landscape

elements are highest priority to restore. Also, consider whether there are some objectives that can be achieved more easily than others, or right away. For example, have your community work to reforest a stream buffer as part of Earth Day activities. Or incorporate your natural asset maps into a current update process for the local comprehensive plan.

You may decide you want to have a formal strategy just to implement the conservation of your natural assets. However, consider how to make use of your natural asset evaluation as part of everyday planning to ensure that your maps are consistently applied to planning activities.

The following are examples of how green infrastructure information can be implemented in specific fields.

Park and Open Space Planning

Could an area that is already large and has intact habitat be acquired as a park to ensure its long-term conservation?

If your community is currently developing plans for future parks, consider adding a natural asset criteria for location selection: Does the location support a key natural asset identified on your community's natural asset map?

You may also want to co-locate parks with features that provide other community benefits. For example, would placing a park in a particular location also protect an area around a reservoir? Could existing parks be better protected and buffered by conserving large landscape blocks adjacent to them? Current and potential trails and tourism routes can be overlaid with natural asset maps to show how they support the locality's tourism. In addition, they can be used to lure new businesses to the area.

Make sure your parks department or open space committee is aware of and using your natural asset maps.

Identify Lands for PDR or TDR Programs

Purchase of Development Rights (PDR) programs allow local governments to purchase these rights from willing landowners. Ensure that your state allows PDR programs. These programs allow landowners to reap some of their land's financial development potential without having to sell it. They also help local government agencies conserve land they do not want to develop because

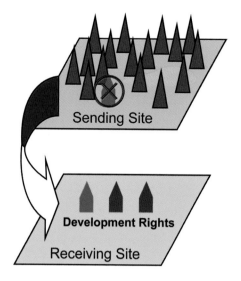

Sending Site

Development Rights

Receiving Site

it provides other, more important values, such as watershed protection. Localities usually have ranking criteria to allow them to objectively determine which lands are most strategic to conserve through PDRs.

The Transfer of Development Rights (TDR) program has similar aims. It allows a local government to adopt an ordinance that enables existing development rights to be transferred from a *sending zone* to a *receiving zone*. Sending zones are those areas where development should be limited because the area will not support it (e.g. the area lacks the necessary infrastructure, such as roads, rescue facilities and schools, or the local government is trying to keep development density low there). A receiving zone is an area that is more desirable for development.

Sending and receiving zones must be ascertained in advance by local governments as part of their ordinances. Their natural asset maps can inform decisions about which zones to allocate by highlighting high-priority natural asset areas for their sending zones and, similarly, avoiding them when establishing receiving zones. If your state allows TDR programs, your local government will probably require an implementing ordinance.

Comprehensive Plans and Zoning

As noted earlier in this guide, comprehensive plans provide goals and data about how a community should grow and develop in the future. When zoning is changed from its original designated use, it generally requires a demonstration that there is new information – a substantial change – that warrants a new zoning class.

Or, if a comprehensive analysis has been completed, this can also be a basis for rezoning. A natural asset evaluation and map can form the basis for why new zoning is needed. Overlay future land use and zoning maps to see where natural assets may conflict with existing zoning. Then decide, should zoning and land use be changed? Should we try to work with landowners to conserve a buffer or corridor through the area? If these areas will be lost, does other land need to be set aside to make up for these losses in the future?

Species Protection

Use natural asset maps to set aside areas for conservation of key species.

Are there areas where rare, threatened or endangered species are known to exist? Local governments can usually obtain this information from their state's natural heritage program. Also, consult the state wildlife action plan for key strategies. Areas containing rare species can be ranked higher or given greater priority for conservation. It is easier to protect species than to try to restore populations later on. Also, ensure that areas are linked by corridors to allow species movement and repopulation. Of course, protecting species ahead of time to avoid having to list them not only save the species but also saves valuable staff time and money later. It is much more expensive (and sometimes ineffective) to seek to restore something once it has been lost.

Heritage Tourism and Viewsheds

Work with the tourism director to explain how to use natural asset maps to bolster your visitor's experience and conserve key natural assets. Create a map that overlays key recreation areas, trails and activities with natural assets. Which activities do these assets support? For example, a connected network may support cross-country horseback riding, or a large lake may require a forested watershed to adequately protect water quality and support fishing.

One tourism director from a very rural county recently used their natural asset maps to show a business why they should locate its outdoor adventure camp in their county. They were able to search their digital maps of natural assets to find parcels with intact forests, water features, views and access to meet the client's demands.

Also consider whether there are special routes and key heritage features that should be added to your asset maps, in order to be better protected. Consider partnerships with state and local land trusts to seek permanent protection for key heritage assets and viewsheds that support local businesses and tourism.

Agricultural and Forestal Districts

Agricultural and forestal districts provide a way to recognize and foster agriculture and forestry operations. Most states require parcels to be contiguous, but some distance gap is usually allowed, to account for roads or other intersections. These districts allow member parcels to pay lower taxes based on their use for agriculture or forestry. Some localities offer both ag and forestal districts and use value assessments or present use value. These use values allow for lowered tax rates based on the actual use, such as a farm use which is operating in an area zoned for commercial development. In localities with use value assessment this is less helpful, but having a district can also signal to landowners and decision-makers where agriculture is desired.

A natural asset map can be used to inform where there are key agricultural soils for row crops, or you can utilize other data from your state department of forestry to determine which areas are most conducive to timber management. Overlay your green asset maps with existing districts or areas which have use value assessments in place. Should forestal districts be expanded to include natural assets or should new districts be created?

Transportation Planning

Most localities follow multi-year plans for transportation. Incorporate natural asset awareness and review of natural asset maps as part of this planning. Use your natural asset maps to inform environmental impact assessments. Mitigating road impacts could mean conserving a key natural asset somewhere else. The key is to have an already-prioritized map for what should be protected next.

Similarly, think about trails as part of transportation plans. They are not just for bird watching; people use them to commute by foot or bike. In Charlottesville, VA, the GIC helped the city identify trails and new routes to create a multi-modal plan for transportation that included off road routes – even through the woods! Similarly Lynchburg VA found people commuted to

work on their trail network following creation of a convenient trail that linked city neighborhoods to the business district. Cities such as Portland Oregon or Arlington Virginia have also had long standing trails that serve as commuting routes for bikers and walkers.

In the Richmond project, the GIC combined the themes of watersheds and healthy water with community walkability – the Walkable Watersheds Project linked healthy people to healthy landscapes. It created new green routes though the community and to key sites, such as schools, community centers and parks. For more information visit the Project at http://www.gicinc.org/Bellemeade_Report.pdf

Regulatory Mandates

Total maximum daily loadings (TMDL) assessments and implementation plans are required for waters that have not met state standards and are listed as impaired. Natural asset maps can be used to prioritize which lands to set aside to buffer impaired waters and to avoid future risks. For example, if your locality has a TMDL based on bacteria and human fecal coliform, is this occurring in an area that is already mapped as having poor soils for septic systems? Consider evaluating areas where septic function is poor and making them off limits to development, in order to avoid future TMDLs. In Virginia, you can use tools such as InFOREST to model current and future loadings of nitrogen, phosphorus and sediment based on various future development scenarios.

Watershed Improvement Plans (WIP) affect states in the Chesapeake Bay Drainage. Consider how they can help you conserve areas of natural assets and help your state or local governments achieve credits for pollution reduction. Conversely, since restoration of natural assets will be important in many WIPs, conserving the existing natural assets can serve as an insurance policy to protect investments in restoration. For example, large amounts of money have been spent on restoration, only to have these projects literally washed away because of a lack of conservation planning upstream.

As noted earlier, natural asset maps can show where land should be conserved to meet mandates for water supply plans. Will current and future zoning allow enough forested land cover to adequately protect drinking water supplies? Will current drinking water intakes be affected by changes in land use that may degrade the quality of intake water? Although water can be treated, it is much cheaper to keep water clean to begin with by maintaining the drainage's buffering potential with natural land cover.

Hazard mitigation is another planning need that is often mandated and can be met by identifying areas that are more likely to be subject to problems such as floods, landslides or wildfire. These areas may be set aside as places to conserve or avoid developing to protect future property damage and loss of life. They may also meet other goals for conservation. And if you live in a coastal or tidal area, you may need to consider future threats such as sea level rise and plan on how to protect your low-lying areas now or make plans to move inland.

Some groups are already addressing climate change. They are mapping current and predicted future water levels in 25, 50 and 75 years. They are asking whether communities at risk will need to be moved and if they will need financial assistance to do so. And they are wondering if their public parks will soon be underwater, necessitating the acquisition of new areas that will be waterside in the future, as lakes, bays and rivers migrate inland.

Long-Term Financing

A major, and too often overlooked, part of developing your implementation strategy is figuring out how you will finance it over the long term. This necessitates that you develop a strategy to ensure you have the fiscal resources to implement, monitor and manage your strategy over many years. It requires financial resources to be available for individual projects over their entire lifespan. The University of Maryland's Environmental Finance Center has some good information on these approaches, and the distinction between funding and financing.

IDEAS FOR FUNDING LAND CONSERVATION

Ideas for funding land conservation are listed below:

- Conservation Easements: Partner with local land trusts (*you may be* the land trust) to seek easements for those lands assessed at the highest conservation value. Many land trusts have used green infrastructure maps to prioritize their efforts and create a connected landscape.

- Ask landowners to donate the highest-value lands. For example, both North Carolina and Virginia, have a conservation tax credit that can reimburse developers for loss of development value if they put land under easement. Development rights can also be purchased if the locality has such a program.

- Work with developers to create schemes that develop homes in new patterns and possibly on smaller lots to conserve open land as part of their development. Publish maps of key resources and examples of how landscapes could be connected. (Contact GIC for permission to use illustrations from this guide.)

- If your locality has *proffers,* let the development community know which land resources, viewsheds or trails you want to acquire or protect. In states that accept proffers in exchange for new zoning or variances, it is perfectly okay to have a wish list of items; it helps developers know exactly what you want and have available.

- Transportation programs will fund viewshed protection. Showing how a GI network gives added value to viewsheds from designated scenic roads has been used to secure funds to conserve land within the viewshed.

Note: A *proffer* offsets the impacts from new development by conserving land or providing walking access and can be seen as offsetting the impact of new residents on existing parks and infrastructure. As noted before, apply natural assets to criteria for PDR or TDR programs.

If you foresaw that your project would need funds for both its implementation and long-term viability, hopefully you included members of the funding community early on. If you did not, and you need implementation funds, it is time to engage them now!

If you already have a strategy for land conservation and natural asset/green infrastructure priority maps in place, they can be very effective fundraising tools. They demonstrate to funders that you have engaged in a strategic and science-based process to determine your priorities and that you are serious about them. You are not just full of empty idealism. You have a plan in hand.

If you establish clear goals based on your priorities, it will show funders that your effort is worthy of funding because it has used a logical and defensible approach and (assuming you engaged the community in your process) that it represents and meets real community needs.

You may want to seek planning grants to provide funding for more staff time for a local government or nonprofit agency to develop maps and conduct community engagement. If a local government is not eligible for grants, partner with a nonprofit that is. The GIC has partnered with local governments to help fund projects. In addition, urban and community forestry grants are available at the state level to conserve forests in developed and developing areas. Similarly, NOAA's Sea Grant program has funds available for coastal work.

Most importantly, consider how much of this work can be done with existing resources. If the staff planner, GIS expert and parks and tourism staff each spent a few hours a week creating and reviewing maps and strategies,

Additional data may be needed to help create priorities. These college students are analyzing stream organisms to determine the health of local streams.

a new set of asset maps and action steps could be created in fairly short order.

Also consider the tremendous resources available from local universities. Students have provided free mapping, model building and implementation assistance to local governments. Students who do this work receive valuable work experience and often college credit if the work is part of a class.

In this chapter, we presented the steps to create a green infrastructure strategy along with myriad ways to implement long term stewardship. In the next chapter, we revisit the steps in an actual project to help you envision how to utilize maps to create your priorities.

5

MAPPING STEPS

- Step 1: Set Goals
- Step 2: Review Data
- Step 3: Make Maps
- Step 4: Assess Risks
- Step 5: Opportunities
- Step 6: Implement

CHAPTER 5 - Case Studies: From Region to Site

This case study chapter provides examples of green infrastructure planning at multiple scales, beginning with a region, scaling down to a county, a city, and ending with a local watershed. Full case study booklets are available on GIC's website. The New Kent County example also demonstrates how to use the six-step process we have just discussed.

REGIONAL SCALE: RICHMOND REGION, VIRGINIA

Between September 2008 and April 2009, the Richmond Regional Planning District Commission (RRPDC), the Green Infrastructure Center (GIC) and the Capital Regional Land Conservancy undertook a cooperative project to document the Richmond Region's green infrastructure assets. Located in central Virginia, the Richmond Region encompasses 1,165 square miles inhabited by more than one million people. It includes the City of Richmond and several surrounding counties. The RRPDC provides planning support to member counties, cities and towns, such as transportation and comprehensive planning.

Since many green infrastructure resources are shared across county and regional boundaries, the RRPDC enlisted GIC's help to create a Regional Priority Map. Using the Virginia Natural Landscape Assessment of habitat cores and corridors, a base map was created and then updated to determine which areas had undergone significant change. This required reviewing new building permits and subdivision plans along with aerial photos to identify those structures that had been built since the landscape model was first run in 2000. These areas were buffered and clipped from the maps to determine if a core had retained enough significant interior habitat to be still considered a core. For a diagrammatic representation of this process, see the images on page 87. From that, the highest-ranked priority habitats were selected to show which areas remained the most important to consider at a regional scale.

The process was advised by a committee made up of representatives from each locality which met several times to review and prioritize the network. The project culminated in a March 2009 workshop that brought together local governments, state and federal agencies, as well as a selection of diverse stakeholder organizations to discuss the region's green infrastructure assets and priorities. Workshop participants also received training in what is green infrastructure planning and why it matters.

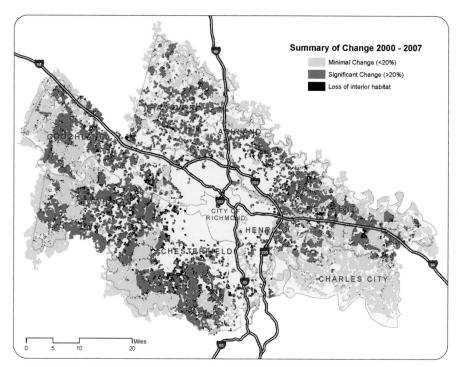

Before and After: seven years in a changing landscape

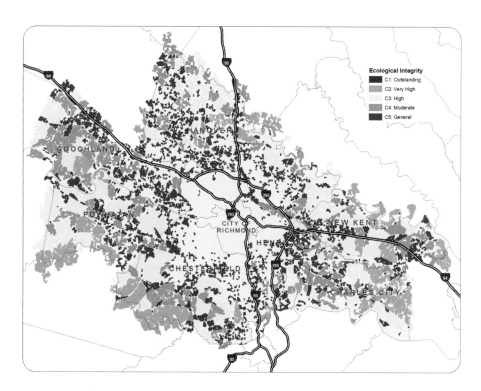

Remaining Habitat Cores After Update

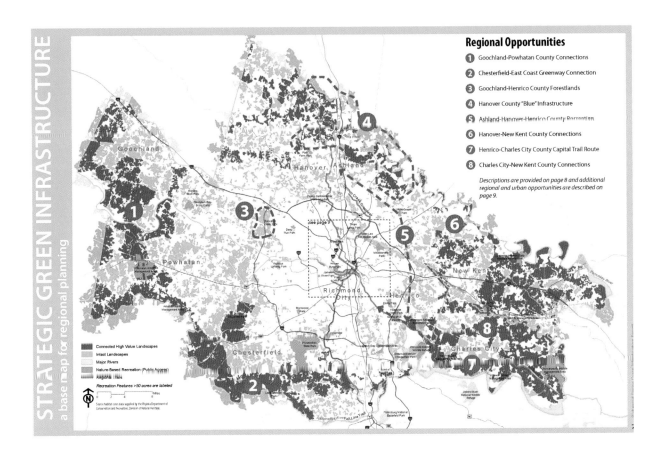

STRATEGIC GREEN INFRASTRUCTURE
a base map for regional planning

Regional Opportunities

1. Goochland-Powhatan County Connections
2. Chesterfield-East Coast Greenway Connection
3. Goochland-Henrico County Forestlands
4. Hanover County "Blue" Infrastructure
5. Ashland-Hanover-Henrico County Recreation
6. Hanover-New Kent County Connections
7. Henrico-Charles City County Capital Trail Route
8. Charles City-New Kent County Connections

Descriptions are provided on page 8 and additional regional and urban opportunities are described on page 9.

Connected High Value Landscapes
Intact Landscapes
Major Rivers
Nature-Based Recreation (Public Access)
Regional Trails
Recreation Features >50 acres are labeled

Source: Habitat cores data supplied by the Virginia Department of Conservation and Recreation, Division of Natural Heritage.

Participants acknowledged the region's riparian network as a major asset and identified cores along the Appomattox River, James River, Pamunkey River, South Anna River and Chickahominy River as primary areas of focus for the future. These river buffers supported several significant green infrastructure values. They provided natural corridors for wildlife and plant species and were important for water quality and leisure activities. In addition, they choose connections which allowed riparian areas to be joined to other high-value areas, ensured the retention of healthy landscapes and abundant recreation.

With the Regional Priority Map now in place, as each locality works on its individual plans, they can consult the regional map to ensure cross-boundary resources are protected. Furthermore, the RRPDC provides ongoing regional advice and guidance to localities so they can determine how to keep the landscape connected. The Capital Region Land Conservancy adopted the maps as their framework for seeking conservation easements, prioritizing easements on those landscapes that are the highest ranked in the model.

COUNTY SCALE: NEW KENT COUNTY, VIRGINIA

Following on from the region, the GIC next partnered with a local county to demonstrate how to create a green infrastructure map at the county scale. The GIC worked with New Kent County, Virginia from 2008-2009, to demonstrate the process for green infrastructure planning, a process that involved the incorporation of local data and resources, such as local parks, favorite fishing spots, scenic drives and historic features, into the model to create locally relevant priorities.

New Kent County initiated its green infrastructure project as a community-based effort built on a foundation of stakeholder engagement, partnership and comprehensive information gathering. Community input and input from county staff and elected officials shaped the project from its outset through to the development of the final asset maps. The GIC conducted several field visits in the county and conducted detailed interviews with residents, business owners, community organizations, county staff, elected officials and other resource users throughout the project. The county worked with

THEMED MAPS

A themed map is a map which highlights a particular issue or resources. As noted in earlier chapters, everything cannot go on one map because it becomes unreadable. Selecting themes to focus on allows the map team to highlight and focus on certain key topics of interest. So for example, a themed map about forested lands and agricultural soils can be used to show where there are good lands for agriculture (not currently covered by forests and containing high quality ag soils).

This agricultural themed map can then be used by the extension service, local planners and citizens to determine the areas best suited for agriculture. It also can be used to ask questions about risk and opportunities. For example, zoning can be overlaid on this map to determine if lands most suited for agriculture are zoned for agricultural use or whether they have already been zoned for development. Then you can ask, should this zoning be changed or will we have less land for a rural economy in the future?

the GIC to convene a twenty-member focus group that met three times and provided feedback throughout the project. Draft findings from the project were shared with the board of supervisors and planning commission, and with the community at a June 2009 open house held at the New Kent County Visitors and Commerce Center, to solicit input and refine final map output. The following sections detail how the six steps were followed to create the county's natural asset maps.

Step 1. Set Goals

In order to set goals for the project, we formed a mapping team with county staff and determined the key focal areas to overlay on the base map. This included a review of past county planning documents, such as the comprehensive plan, to determine and ground truth existing goals.

A focus group was formed, comprising a multitude of stakeholder groups from interests such as the extension service, department of economic development, board of supervisors, a local developer, a land trust and a conservation group, to horseback riders, hunters and

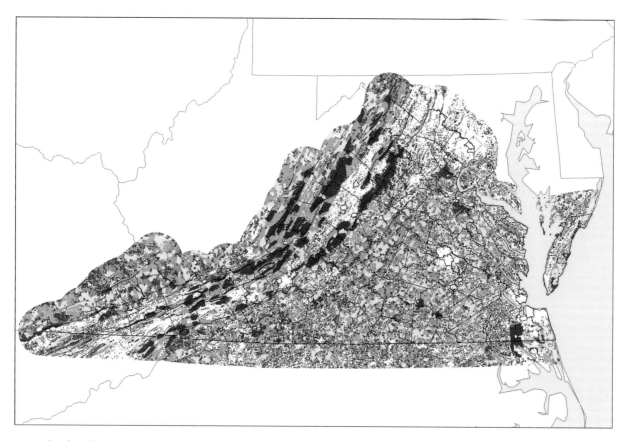

Virginia's ecological integrity cores.

Photo courtesy Virginia Division of Natural Heritage

landowners. Members were appointed by the county to validate and review the themes and associated maps.

Based on the county's review and meetings with staff, several themes by which to group information were determined as important to the county:

- Ecological Cores for Habitat
- Forested Lands and Agricultural Soils
- Water Resources and Riparian Habitat
- Natural Resource-Based Recreation
- Heritage Resources and Rural Character

Step 2. Review Data

The team decided to utilize Virginia's model of cores and corridors alongside local data. The data used to create the base map were from the Virginia Natural Landscape Assessment (VaNLA). This is a landscape-scale, geospatial analysis used for identifying, prioritizing and linking Virginia's natural lands. Using land cover data derived from satellite imagery, the VaNLA identifies large patches of natural land, such as forests, wetlands or dune systems, with at least one hundred acres of interior habitat. Interior land, or the ecological core, begins thee hundred feet from a forested area's edge. The area without edge is the 'interior' and needs to contain at least 100 acres to be considered substantial enough to support a diversity of species.

The model also includes habitat fragments -- small parcels with between ten and ninety-nine acres of interior cover that support landscape corridors. These fragments can also serve as stepping stones across the landscape.

The model scores and ranks each ecological core based on several parameters, such as overall size, depth of interior, amount of surface water (streams and wetlands), the presence of rare species and important habitats.

Basically, the larger an area, the higher its overall ecological integrity score. Scores may also be higher for areas that contribute to good water quality or are part of a complex of natural lands or contain rare threatened or endangered species.

The resulting scores were classified into five categories of ecological integrity:

C1 - Outstanding (red)
C2 - Very High (orange)
C3 - High (yellow)
C4 – Moderate (light green)
C5 - General (dark green)

The model also showed key corridors that linked cores of the two highest ranks (C1 and C2).

This core has had development since the first model run in 2000.

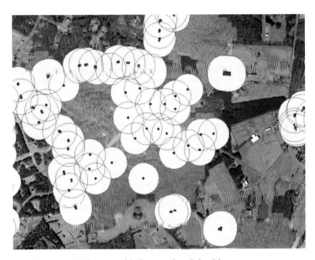

A 100-meter buffer was added around each building to account for the area of impact (driveways, lawns, edge).

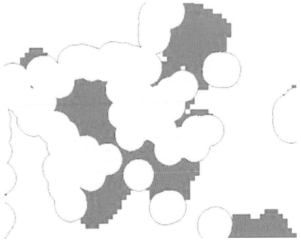

Once removed, these areas of impact show this core is no longer intact and should be deleted.

Step 3. Make Maps

These VaNLA ecological cores were then included as the base map. However this land cover data was from a dataset compiled in 2000 and it needed to be updated to reflect habitats lost since then. In the seven years since 2000, a great deal of development had occurred in the region. We used aerial photography and new-building location data to identify all the new development that had occurred within the cores.

The image on page 87 shows a core that experienced new development since the year 2000. Buffers were added using GIS to indicate all the areas impacted by the new structures (middle). Finally, the image on the bottom right shows the areas that now had to be excluded from this single VaNLA core because of the fragmenting impacts of recent development. As a result, this core was removed from the model, as it was clearly no longer intact and viable.

Those cores that lost at least 20 percent of their interior habitat as a result of this process were dropped one rank for every 20 percent of loss.

A new map was generated of all the updated cores in the study area. To the left are the before (Figure 1) and after (Figure 2) maps. Development to the east along Interstate 64, which bisects the county, occurred closest to Richmond and caused both pockmarks (habitat core loss) and a change in ranking for a large swath of the county. Note color changes and loss of large yellow (high) cores especially to the west. Cores have disappeared or dropped a rank.

Other data were also utilized to map the other themes, including parcels, zoning, agricultural and forestal districts, rivers, topography, future land use and agricultural soils. Finally, once all the data were compiled the cores were evaluated to determine their viability.

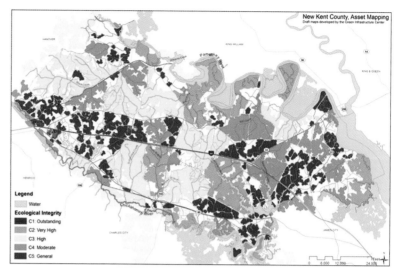

Figure 1: New Kent County before update.

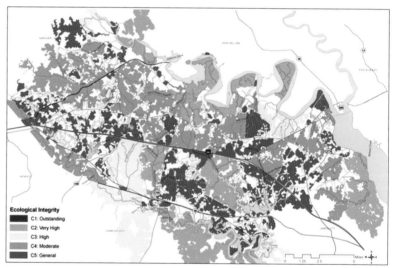

Figure 2: New Kent County after update.

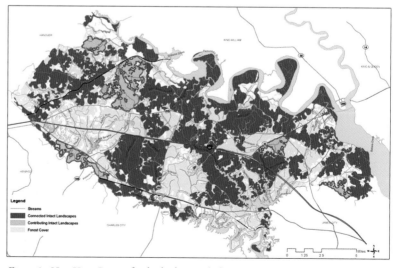

Figure 3: New Kent County final – highest ranked cores.

To select the highest value cores, we selected those ranked high-to-outstanding quality, in order to choose the highest value landscapes for our conservation focus. Note that it was a committee decision to focus efforts on those areas most important for wildlife.

All these highest-ranking cores were then turned to the same color to make the connected landscape of high-value assets easier to see (Figure 3). An additional, lower-ranked core was also added because it protected water quality. It is in light green in the upper left corner.

We also selected cores which formed a connecting corridor between highly ranked cores. We can now clearly see the overall connections between all the key core areas.

Step 4. Assess Risks

In this step, parcels and zoning were overlaid on the network to determine areas where habitats might be at risk.

In Figure 4, to the right, parcels show how some of the larger tracts have been subdivided along the reservoir to the southeast. Tan color shows parcels of between 25 to 100 acres and maroon shows parcels greater than 100 acres. As a general rule, the larger the parcel, the easier it is to work with the landowner on conservation actions to preserve large blocks of habitat.

The next map (Figure 5) shows where lands zoned for development overlap key habitat cores (cross-hatched). For example, note the large industrial and economic opportunity zoning (purple) that intersects with key cores.

This information was then used to ask several questions: Are these cores likely to be conserved or more likely to be developed? Should zoning be changed to a less intensive use to protect

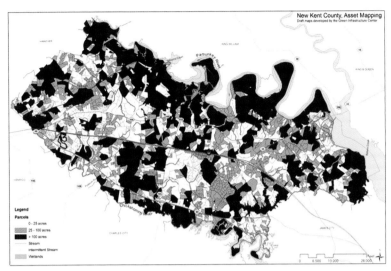

Figure 4: New Kent County parcels sorted by size.

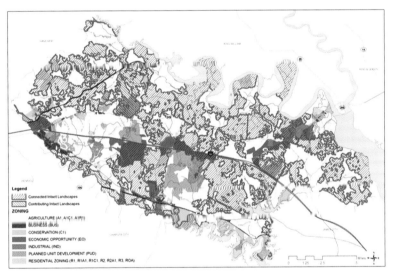

Figure 5: New Kent County zoning overlaid to show conflicts.

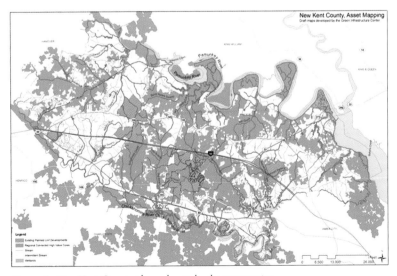

Figure 6: New Kent County planned unit development zoning.

these cores? Should they be removed from the map? Can these landowners still develop their land using conservation approaches that leave cores connected and reduce their development footprint?

Step 5. Determine Opportunities

Zoning can be changed, of course, and land uses are not set in stone. In the map to the right, *planned unit developments* (PUDs) were evaluated. These are zoning designations that are usually mixed use (e.g. residential and business) and allow for exceptions to lot arrangement, in order to avoid sensitive areas – such as wetlands or steep slopes – and to conserve areas that may hold special value.

The map in Figure 6 shows several PUDs in pink. The large PUD in the lower center had a core trapped in the middle that was actually an ag forestal district and was actively being logged. Surrounding an active logging operation with homes and golf courses is not the safest and wisest approach to land planning. However, the PUD was not completely built out. Could a corridor be left to keep the central core from being isolated? Could less of the PUD be developed?

A similar situation occurred with the easternmost PUD. This landowner was unable to afford to develop it. Could that development be changed to conserve more land? Could development rights be purchased and a park be created?

These are examples of how the maps can be used to showcase potential opportunities.

To determine risk and opportunity, areas protected by easement or another protected designation (such as a national park or wildlife management area) were overlain to see where this

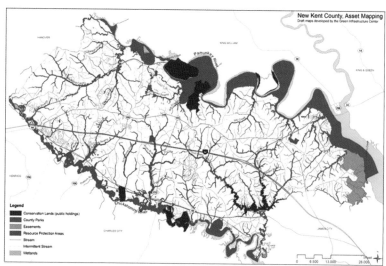

Figure 7: New Kent County protected areas.

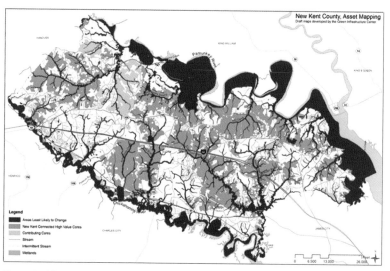

Figure 8: New Kent County protected areas and cores.

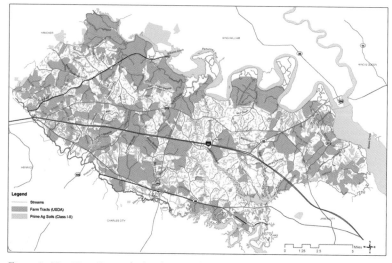

Figure 9: New Kent County high value ag soils and farms.

core land remained unprotected and may need focus. In the map in Figure 7 the blue areas are restricted from development because they border streams (riparian protection areas) and those in yellow and orange are protected by easements.

Step 6. Implement Opportunities

Once you have created your natural asset maps, it is time to include them in daily and long-range planning, such as park planning, comprehensive planning, zoning, tourism and economic development. These maps also can be adopted into the comprehensive plan to help guide future growth and development decisions.

The map in Figure 8 shows the high-priority green infrastructure network, with those areas that are protected shown in maroon. Remaining cores (green) may need additional protection.

Themed maps can also be used to show other natural assets of importance and to determine how the natural asset network supports other cultural values. In Figure 9 agricultural soils were added to the map to show where they support farming. Similarly, data showing areas important for forestry were mapped (Figure 10). Areas greater than 25 acres could better support sustained silviculture than smaller parcels.

These maps can be used by county extension agents, foresters and staff to help zone areas appropriately and allow these 'working land uses' to continue, if desired.

The map to the right, Figure 11, shows those key cultural assets and places for nature-based recreation that utilize and are supported by the natural asset network. As future parks are created, areas that include key resources can be selected. Furthermore, historic

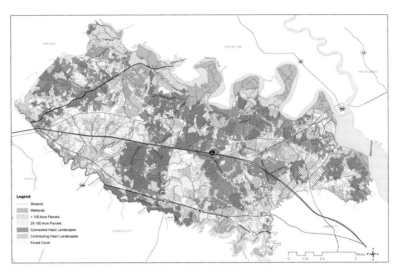

Figure 10: New Kent County high value forest lands.

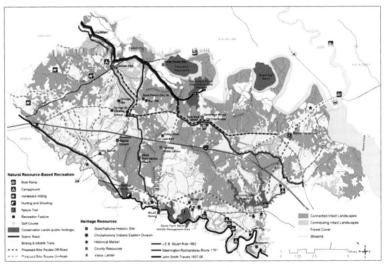

Figure 11: New Kent County recreation and cultural uses.

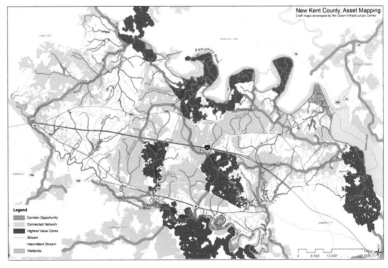

Figure 12: New Kent County green infrastructure network with key corridors.

Sunset over Cumberland Marsh in New Kent County.

and cultural resources, such as old mills and churches, scenic roads, tourist and cycle routes, and key vistas can be supported by the green infrastructure network.

Lastly, we ensured a connected landscape by including key conservation corridors — dark green lines (Figure 12). The maps were adopted into the county's comprehensive plan and used to guide future growth and conservation.

These maps can all be used to guide growth and development by planning staff, inform developers about conservation priorities and options, help land trusts seek out those parcels of greatest importance that are also at greatest risk, and inform other key decisions about what to protect and where and how to grow.

MAP USES SUMMARY

Map uses:

- To identify where future parks are needed and select key cores.
- To identify lands for PDR or TDR programs and give more points to lands in the network.
- To create new ordinances to zone land and development appropriately.
- To protect key species at risk and promote abundant wildlife.
- To attract new heritage tourism and identify and protect viewsheds.
- To protect existing and select new ag and forestal districts.
- To review all transportation planning to avoid sensitive areas.
- To select future trails and utilize corridors.
- To prevent economic loss by avoiding hazard areas.

CITY SCALE: RICHMOND, VIRGINIA

To demonstrate this work at the city-scale, the GIC next partnered with the City of Richmond, located in the heart of the RRPDC region. This case example shows how to work at a city scale, where smaller watersheds, streets and pocket parks can become important landscape features. The City is Richmond is home to more than 200,000 people within a land area of $62mi^2$, of which $2.7mi^2$ is water. The James River flows through the heart of the city on its way to the Chesapeake Bay.

The project followed on from the creation of the regional map featured at the beginning of this chapter. Since an urban area requires more fine-grained details – such as parcels, pocket parks and tree canopy – the inclusion of local data and smaller landscape features becomes significantly more important at this scale.

In 2010, the GIC advised the RRPDC how to create a green infrastructure map called the Green Print for the City of Richmond. This map included data from the landscape priorities found to be significant at a regional scale, as well as key city environmental and cultural features, such as community gardens or historic sites. The Green Print not only showed key green features but also discussed the need for restoration of the city's vacant landscape in order to enhance the environmental quality of the city.

In 2010, the GIC, together with consultants from the firm of E^2, produced a Green Infrastructure Assessment that considered restoration potential for the city. The City of Richmond provided guidance and oversight throughout the assessment process to ensure it was consistent with current and future city programs and priorities. The purpose of the assessment was to evaluate the suitability of vacant and underutilized parcels to contribute to a city-wide green infrastructure network and to explore strategies for the reuse of vacant land with the goal of making Richmond a cleaner, healthier, more beautiful and economically sound city.

It was found that traditional patterns of sprawl had left gaps where disinvestment in urban neighborhoods had diminished community life. The city grew and then shrank as industry left the city and residents moved out to the suburbs, leaving many vacant sites. It was decided that these vacant sites could be viewed as opportunities to retrofit a green infrastructure network into the urban landscape, thereby providing recreational venues,

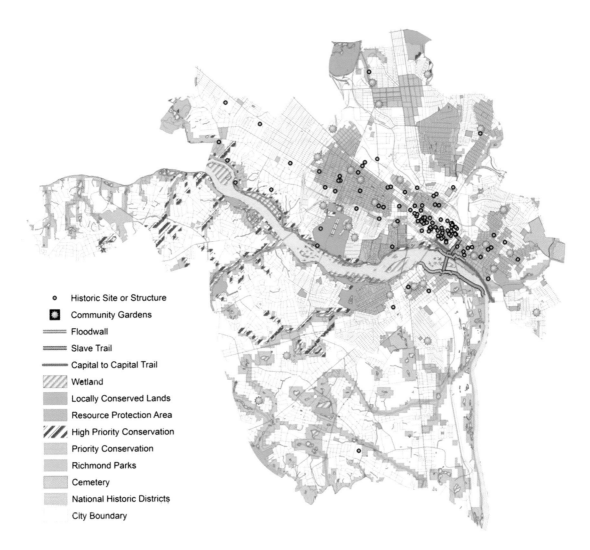

○ Historic Site or Structure

▣ Community Gardens

▬ Floodwall

▬ Slave Trail

▬ Capital to Capital Trail

▨ Wetland

▨ Locally Conserved Lands

▨ Resource Protection Area

▨ High Priority Conservation

▨ Priority Conservation

▨ Richmond Parks

▨ Cemetery

▨ National Historic Districts

▫ City Boundary

community gardens, outdoor classrooms and much -needed wildlife habitat. There were also opportunities to re-create and relink a green infrastructure network. The following diagram shows how this might be done.

As part of the Richmond Green Infrastructure Assessment, the pilot project sought to evaluate and expand the city's green infrastructure by identifying the strategic reuse opportunities of underutilized properties. It aimed to demonstrate how an assessment of vacant and underutilized properties could be applied to select priority areas for development and green infrastructure investment. This project included an evaluation of the city's vacant and underutilized parcels to identify existing green resources and opportunities for re-greening and reconnection. A Richmond Vacant Parcel Inventory Database was created to capture the entire city's known vacant parcels in a comprehensive dataset. It found more than 9,000 vacant and under-utilized parcels, many of

Richmond City was small, it grew bigger, industry and residents left to the suburbs, green spaces can now be put in the vacant parcels!

Many vacant parcels have become green.

which contained natural features such as trees and wetlands that have re-emerged on the abandoned urban sites over time.

Once these 9,000 parcels had been identified, opportunities to improve the city's natural systems and green space network became evident. Many vacant sites were viewed as natural assets for the city – an unexpected resource that would allow the city to expand its green infrastructure network while enhancing its city neighborhoods, especially those where local residents sought alternatives to traditional development patterns. As a result, some of those vacant and underutilized parcels were earmarked for recreation, community gardens, outdoor classrooms and habitat that would benefit residents and help attract economic re-investment.

The vacant parcel inventory integrated a number of datasets submitted by several city departments and entities into a single GIS database founded on parcel identification numbers. Departments and agencies that contributed data included:

- The City Assessor's Office
- The Department of Parks and Recreation
- The Department of Planning and Development Review
- The Department of Economic and Community Development
- The Richmond Redevelopment and Housing Authority

Existing Urban Tree Canopy Analysis

Tree canopy is an important component of the existing green infrastructure network. The figure on page 95 shows the urban tree canopy analysis conducted by the Virginia Department of Forestry for the city. The analysis was derived from high-resolution aerial imagery (1 meter) acquired from the National Agriculture Imagery Program in the summer of 2008, combined with remote sensing techniques. The analysis determined that 42 percent of the total land area within the city was covered by existing tree canopy. It was not evenly distributed throughout the city, however, and certain planning districts and neighborhoods had significantly less existing tree canopy than others. For example, some areas in the downtown had only 9 percent canopy. This map was then used by the city's arborists to prioritize where to plant trees. Prior to creation of the canopy assessment, trees were planted without consideration to where they were needed most.

In addition to seeking restoration options, other key assets were mapped, such as community gardens, access to open spaces including parks and trails, water resources, and more. These maps can be used to inform local transportation plans, community food networks, recreation and fitness planning and watershed planning.

Setting Priorities

At a city scale, deciding where to focus your efforts should be based on where you have identified the greatest need. For the City of Richmond, the GIC created an analysis of conservation lands, parks and vacant lots and then a list of priority questions to help determine where

Urban Tree Canopy Analysis - Richmond, VA

Legend:
- Water
- Non-Building Impervious
- Non-Tree Vegetation
- Tree Canopy
- Building Impervious

0   0.5   1   2 Miles

Canopy analysis completed 09/27/2010 JKM

City tree canopy is 42 percent except in the urban center.

to focus priorities. The vacant parcels were characterized according to the following goals:

1. To protect priority conservation areas
2. To improve water quality and stormwater management
3. To increase park access
4. To support greenway development
5. To identify green infrastructure network opportunities

Each vacant parcel in the inventory was evaluated based on whether it met the most important criteria, as identified through a series of public meetings and other consultations with city staff. The vacant parcels identified as meeting these priorities then provided an opportunity

Community gardens such as this one can provide an urban oasis for inner city residents, along with stormwater infiltration, cleaner air, natural beauty and air and food!

SUMMARY OF PRIORITY CONSERVATION AREAS, PARK LAND AND VACANT PROPERTY ACREAGE BY PLANNING DISTRICT							
	Total Area (acres)	Priority Conservation Areas		Park Land		Vacant Lots	
		Total Area (acres)	Percent	Total Area (acres)	Percent	Total Area (acres)	Percent
Broad Rock	7939	2891	36%	154	2%	1087	14%
Downtown	1128	396	35%	98	9%	76	7%
East	3434	492	14%	215	6%	457	13%
Far West	3989	852	21%	246	6%	108	3%
Huguenot	5342	1897	36%	301	6%	465	9%
Midlothian	4369	1369	31%	128	3%	569	13%
Near West	4267	68	2%	472	11%	154	4%
North	4684	531	11%	538	11%	263	6%
Old South	5257	1797	34%	351	7%	552	11%
Downtown Master Plan Area	2201	739	34%	106	5%	229	10%

to enhance desired green infrastructure function and features, such as improving water and air quality, walkability, equal access to recreational activities, community safety and health, and surrounding market value.

Another significant aspect of the local project was the use of Priority Conservation Area (PCA) data. PCAs are landscapes of significant conservation value and the dataset evaluates conservation sites, natural landscape

PLANNING DISTRICT SELECTION CONSIDERATIONS										
	Broad Rock	Downtown	East	Far West	Huguenot	Midlothian	Near West	North	Old South	Downtown Master Plan
Which districts have significant Priority Conservation Areas?	✓				✓				✓	
Which districts contain high-priority watersheds?	✓								✓	
Which districts are lacking existing parkland (by percent of area)?	✓	✓				✓				✓
Which districts offer a critical mass of vacant parcels that could offer network opportunities?	✓		✓		✓	✓			✓	✓
Which districts offer greenway leadership capacity?*	✓							✓	✓	
Which districts have other city initiatives to consider?	✓									
How might neighborhood equity factor into district selection?	✓								✓	

networks, wildlife diversity conservation areas and the integrity of water resources. The PCA data were modeled by the state, but had not previously been applied to city-wide planning.

The Selection Chart was used to highlight which districts within the city need attention the soonest was based on their high percentage of conservation priorities and the lack of public open space. This showed that the Broad Rock and Old South Districts had the greatest potential and the greatest need.

Parcels Can Be Selected for Many Purposes

Watershed Health: Parcels with potential to decrease stormwater flow or improve water quality in the city. The vacant parcels identified on the map on page 67 are either in a designated Resource Protection Area (RPA), which limits development along streams, or are located within 30 meters (100 feet) of a stream.

Community Spaces: Parcels with potential for public school programming and to increase access to local food were analyzed.

Creating Outdoor Classrooms: Hands-on learning activities related to ecology, gardening and green infrastructure can engage students in active learning and lead to improved test scores. Vacant parcels with green features were selected based on whether they were within a quarter mile of a public school.

Growing Community Gardens: Community gardens can provide a catalyst for neighborhood and community development and opportunities for improved water infiltration. It was determined whether vacant parcels were located outside unprotected areas of high ecological value and more than one quarter mile from existing community gardens. This indicated a possibility for new use as a garden site. Note that urban parcels will need to be evaluated to determine if the soil is safe for agriculture and if permission can be obtained to use or lease the land for a garden.

Conserved Lands and Existing and Planned Urban Trails and Greenways: Parcels with potential to connect conserved lands and support or expand urban trails were analyzed. Urban trails and greenways can provide opportunities for recreation, as well as for multimodal transit between destinations.

LOCAL SCALE: UPPER GOODE'S CREEK WATERSHED, RICHMOND, VIRGINIA

Following on from working with the City of Richmond as a whole, the next question of scale was where to focus local efforts. The city was embarking on a major new stormwater master plan, to provide a watershed framework for local planning and to comply with the city's orders to clean up combined sewer overflows and reduce runoff pollution. This was undertaken as part of the city's stormwater permit. The Upper Goode's Creek Sub -watershed was selected as a good demonstration watershed. It spanned an area of warehousing and old industrial sites, as well as older inner-city neighborhoods, and included plans for a new LEED-certified green school to

be built, which could provide a prime catalyst to excite the community about other green potentials within the watershed. It was also located in the priority area of the city mentioned earlier. Furthermore, the vacant lots assessment showed that there were vacant lands adjacent to the planned school.

Upper Goode's Creek is a tributary of the James River located in south side Richmond, Virginia. A master plan was created for the park and a more organized community process was initiated to create a forum for other ideas to be created and implemented at the community scale.

As part of this effort, the GIC developed a community planning process known as the Walkable Watersheds Project. Walkability was part of a wider interest in community fitness and had been identified in a survey of local residents carried out by a consortium of local churches within the area. The top priority identified in the survey was the need for safe places to walk and for children to play outside.

As a result, walkability to local schools was analyzed and areas along streets and through parks were identified where it would be useful to install new permeable

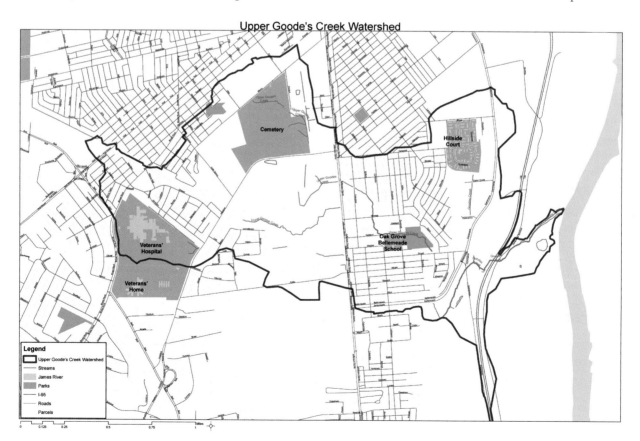

Upper Goode's Creek Watershed

Legend
- Upper Goode's Creek Watershed
- Streams
- James River
- Parks
- I-95
- Roads
- Parcels

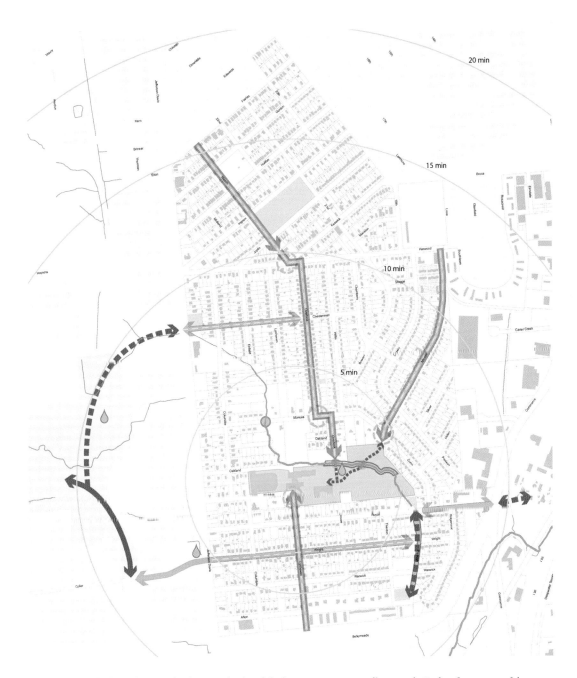

The green rectangle shows the space for the new school and the lines are 5 minute walk intervals. Eighty-five percent of the children live within a 5 minute walk. Arrows show the children's preferred routes.

sidewalks. In addition, plans were drawn up for green streets and to implement new projects to restore the stream, reforest the stream buffer and build nature trails.

Next, the Upper Goode's Creek Watershed Coalition was formed by the City of Richmond with funding from the Environmental Protection Agency's Urban Waters Program to create a forum in which to discuss implementation of goals and priorities. It was coordinated by the GIC, who in turn trained community residents to manage the project work. Coalition members represented key constituencies in the watershed and included partners from government and the private sector.

The Coalition planned and sponsored a community open house in June 2013 to share ideas and get input on strategies, which it followed up with a festival on October 19, 2013, to enlist community residents as volunteers and partners in on-going stewardship. It determined that its priorities should be to restore the watershed and creek, as well as to increase environmental awareness and community health. From the fall of 2012-2013 it developed key strategies to help infiltrate and clean stormwater, restore habitats, provide access to outdoor recreation, reconnect pathways through the watershed, end blight and beautify the community.

Since its inception, the Coalition has fostered many other projects to green the community. Coalition partners, including the James River Association and the Alliance for the Chesapeake Bay, have worked with residents to plant greener yards and to hold use rain barrels to reduce storm flows. Residents have become tree stewards, youth have been trained to take care of the green landscape and new curriculum in the schools is under development. Raingardens have also been added to the land adjacent to the school to filter and clean roof runoff. This is an example of how low impact development strategies were included in the project.

In addition, as part of restoring the Upper Goode's Greek landscape, in 2012, the GIC added the McGuire Veterans Hospital to its restoration efforts. It employed local residents and disabled veterans to create a forest

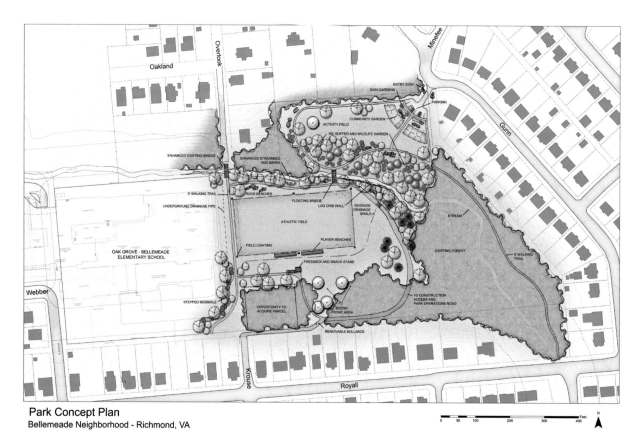

Park Concept Plan
Bellemeade Neighborhood - Richmond, VA

This concept plan depicts the community's vision for the park. Most of these elements, such as trails, stream buffers and natural habitats, are now built.

Children and adults learned their watershed address at the Coalition's Fall Festival.

Planting a new arboretum at McGuire Veterans Hospital

Volunteers planted trees and built a new trail along the creek.

arboretum and healing tools up to replace a barren area where the old hospital had once stood. A healing flower garden was added in the spring of 2015. As noted in Chapter Six, people heal faster when they can see or access natural green spaces. Engaging disabled veterans in healing the land helps them heal too.

The work of the GIC in association with the Upper Goode's Creek Watershed Coalition is a prime example of how to implement local, site-scale green infrastructure. It evolved as the final, culminating step in a process that began with a regional assessment, a city-wide needs and resources study, then implementation at a watershed and then a site level. In this way, the mapping green infrastructure can be used to inform protecting and healing the landscape from a variety of impacts, whether urban or rural, can restore forests, streams and other natural landscapes and provide safe drinking water, cool our cities, and provide recreation and healthful lifestyles for our communities.

These case studies described how the green infrastructure network was created by selecting the highest value habitats and connecting corridors; how the network was updated to reflect new development; potential risks from parcelization; and, how other green infrastructure services for working lands such as farming and forestry were analyzed. In the next chapter, we provide options for making the case to decision makers and building community support for this work.

Thanks

The GIC would like to acknowledge the many funders who contributed to these field tests highlighted in Chapter Five. They include the Virginia Department of Forestry's Urban and Community Forestry Program and the U.S. Forest Service, the U.S. Environmental Protection Agency's Urban Waters Program, the Altria Group, the Virginia Environmental Endowment, the Robins Foundation, Dominion Virginia Power, Wells Fargo and the Luck Companies. Many thousands of volunteer hours were also donated by city residents and companies. These funders and volunteers allowed GIC to provide all of the mapping and analysis pro bono for the participating localities.

6

- Building Support
- Outreach
- Key Messages

CHAPTER 6 - Building Community Support

This chapter provides a number of options for gaining community support for a green infrastructure plan. As described earlier in this guide, citizens will usually work to help implement ideas that they had a hand in creating. Similarly, elected and appointed officials should feel some ownership of ideas if they are expected to carry the implementation torch. In this chapter we describe options and ideas on how to build broader community support for your green infrastructure plan along with examples of 'key messages' you may want to use to build community support for conserving natural assets.

OPPORTUNITIES AND OPTIONS FOR OUTREACH

There are many ways to engage people. However, you are not likely to have unlimited funds for public engagement or to build community support, so whatever methods you pick should be those that are most likely to engage key stakeholders. Note that not every member of a community will be interested in your project.

Assuming that you have developed some clear target groups to reach out to, the following are some options, both traditional and non-traditional, for community engagement.

There are many methods of engagement. We discussed committee formation and consensus building in Chapter Three. In this chapter we discuss:

- targeted presentations
- online surveys and maps
- open houses
- engaging with decision makers

Targeted Presentations

We recommend that you make presentations to your appointed and elected officials about your project at least three times: at the beginning; during the middle; and near the end. This will ensure that people are not caught off guard – or that they worry the process was hidden intentionally from public view.

In addition to government officials, key groups to target for presentations include conservation groups, land trusts, hunt clubs, cross country horse clubs, or nature groups. Many people will not attend committee meetings, public meetings, open houses or other civic events, but they may be very active in other civic groups, such as the Lions Club, the Rotary or their church. Make plans to reach out to those groups as well.

Consult with community leaders and local planners to learn which groups are key to engage. If the locality is not yet on board with the need to evaluate its assets, it may be necessary to conduct your own research to obtain community input. Contact agencies that interact with key stakeholders, such as your forestry division, soil and water district, or watershed council for suggestions on whom to reach out to. If possible, find out if there are meetings at which several groups will be present, such as a community faith day in which multiple churches participate, an Earth Day event or a county fair.

Next, plan how to target your message to the group's interests. For example, if you are speaking to a chapter of the National Wildlife Federation, focus your message on wildlife habitat and access to nature. If you are addressing a hunt club or the local equestrian club, discuss the importance of a protected landscape for wildlife movement and uninterrupted cross country rides.

More ideas about targeting your messages are found later in this chapter.

Online Surveys and Maps

One option for reaching more people is to create an online survey, where you can ask people to comment on your goals or rank areas as top priorities for conservation. Off-the-shelf online survey tools, such as *Survey Monkey*, allow you to make a short, simple online survey for free or a more complex and longer survey for a small fee.

To ensure that you collect objective information, enlist help from a local university or survey research firm to review your questions and ensure they are not misleading. One caveat is to determine first whether your community has access to adequate computer resources and the requisite computer skills; some rural areas or areas with high poverty rates may not be able to access online resources. In these cases, if possible, project information and surveys can be deposited at local libraries or other public places to be filled in and picked up later.

You could also have people mark up a map through programs like *Green Maps* or your own custom software application. You can make your online map more interactive by setting it up so that people can click to turn layers on and off. While this will require some engineering on your part (and possibly the use of GIS add-on software, such as ArcEditor), it allows members of the public to see relationships easily. Keep in mind that if people add information or factual comments to your map, you will

need to ground truth and fact check them before adding them. You may want to ask for their emails or phone numbers, so you can follow up with questions, if needed.

Open Houses

You may recall from Chapter Three that 'no committee' was an option. It is quite possible that you prefer to simply conduct expert consultations and then hold a public 'open house' to invite review of the work. An open house may or may not involve an introductory presentation but remember that the central notion of an open house is that it has an informal setting, allowing people to drop in when it's convenient for them. Perhaps you can videotape a presentation or provide an automated introductory slide show for people to watch when they do drop in.

An open house allows participants to interact with project staff in small groups or one-on-one. Engaging people in this way can be much more interactive and meaningful than the traditional public meeting, where people sit in an audience and offer short comments into a microphone. In addition, if you are seeking input on maps of natural and cultural assets, it is important that people can see the maps up close, ask questions and offer corrections or suggestions.

Engaging with Decision Makers

Most localities have comprehensive plans that describe community goals, as well as future land-use plans that depict where and how they plan to grow in the future. However, these plans may not include key green infrastructure information, such as soils data, which can designate the best areas for agriculture.

If your board of supervisors, planning board, planning commission or other elected or appointed officials are unfamiliar with the new green infrastructure information you are presenting, they will need to understand the system you used to prioritize key natural assets. They will need to know what values led to your decision to select certain areas as high value. Make your decision process as transparent as possible by writing down your process. And be sure to carefully document the methods you used for prioritization, as well as special considerations for features added to your map (e.g. a natural area which supports outdoor learning for a nearby school).

Despite your efforts, decision makers may still decide to replace or impact the highest-quality natural area with

TIPS FOR AN ENGAGING OPEN HOUSE

- To maximize options for public participation, offer flexible hours to drop in, such as from 3pm to 8pm, to allow people to arrive when it suits their schedules.

- Avoid meeting conflicts by checking calendars for other related or popular community events.

- Allow more families to participate by offering child-sitting services, kid-friendly activities, and advertise that families are welcome.

- Advertise the event through public service announcements on radio and television and post flyers in places where people will see them, such as at schools, libraries or grocery stores.

- Offer refreshments. Seek corporate or community sponsorship for snacks or a light meal – food is a great magnet for busy families and singles.

- Use separate areas for commenting, to avoid overcrowding. If you are using themed overlay maps, begin with a base asset map and have a table for each of the themed overlays. For fun, use a train motif and emphasize that people should visit each 'station.'

- If you forgo a formal presentation, have an orientation 'station' where a team member ('conductor') explains the project and the purpose of each map before the participants chug around the stations.

- To avoid overcrowding by too many people at one station, stagger participants as they enter. Begin with an orientation at the base map for everyone, but change which map each participant visits next. If adopting the train motif, provide each participant with a numbered ticket and stagger the starting location so the first person starts at station one and moves to station two, while the next person begins at station two, then goes to three, and so on. This avoids participants overcrowding each station as they move around the room.

- At each 'station,' provide introductory information concerning the themed map's purpose and graphics. Prepare a series of questions, such as, "Does this look accurate to you?," "Is the map easy to understand?," and "Are the map symbols and graphics easy or difficult to interpret?" You may also have specific data-related questions, such as, "Does this map include all the key areas for natural resource-based recreation?"

- Provide a map for people to contribute their own data or favorite places, to validate or correct assumptions about community priorities. However, try to avoid non-uniform or inconsistent methods of adding data to maps. Consider asking key questions such as 'Where is your favorite place to view nature?'

- Avoid overcrowding maps with notes by using numbered sticky dots that reference corresponding numbers on a flip chart. For example, dot #1 = favorite bird watching area; dot #2 = best area for a forested buffer; dot#3 = best fishing spot. Alternatively, heavy clear plastic sheeting (available from art supply stores) can be overlaid on maps to allow people to mark key areas with permanent markers. Once a sheet gets overly congested with illustrations, save it and lay down a new sheet. Once comments have been reviewed, the favorite places and priorities data can be digitized to provide common symbology and phraseology, such as fishing, hunting, best views, and then included as a reference map.

- Let people know where information will be posted and how they can follow the process to completion. Be sure to have a sign-in sheet for people's contact information so they can be included in future updates.

a new industrial park or school, but if they have a map of key natural and cultural resources, at least it allows them to make their decision with a fuller understanding of what may be lost.

Acknowledging that something will be given up to permit development could also lead to conserving other areas through acquisition or zoning changes to compensate for the loss of a key area. They may decide to compensate for that loss by adding better protection to another high-value area or taking on a habitat restoration project to mitigate the loss.

MESSAGING: HOW TO MARKET NATURAL ASSET CONSERVATION

In Chapter Two, we made the case for why mapping and evaluating natural assets makes good sense for the economy, public health, safety and aesthetic reasons. In this section, we provide some of the facts and studies that we have used to best communicate key messages. Feel free to utilize these arguments and create your own local examples. Much of the advice in this section is based on the GIC's experience in effectively targeting messages to multiple audiences across the U.S.

Messaging is shorthand for how you communicate your project's purpose and goals. How and what you communicate is critical to your project's success and could make the difference between a project that is widely accepted or one that is turned down before it begins. The way you describe or frame your project's aim can affect whether it appeals to a wide range of interests or whether it is seen as overly narrow or something to be stopped.

Politics in the United States has been growing more acrimonious by the day. The poor state of the economy has led to a great deal of worry, concern and fear about the future. Related to this, many environmental efforts and institutions are under attack or suffering from excessive criticism. Anything labeled as 'green' may be attacked and accused of trying to take property rights away, or of adding to regulation and red tape. In addition, the accusations that regulations stifle industry and prevent 'progress' have been levied against the environmental movement, although there exists much

Messaging is shorthand for how you communicate your project's purpose and goals in a way that people can understand and find meaningful to them.

evidence to support the claim that having clean water, clean air, healthy communities and safe and productive workers actually benefits the economy and can reduce future costs for environmental cleanup and public health.

One central point you can make to answer these concerns is a cost-benefit analysis: If we identify and protect resources before they are damaged, we can avoid future cleanup costs of polluted waters and soils. And prevention of air quality impacts will save money in the long run. You will not face the costly expenses of establishing a Total Maximum Daily Loading of Pollutants (TMDL) for an impaired water or preventing your area being listed as a Non-attainment Area under the federal Clean Air Act. You can also protect public safety and future loss of both life and property by conserving sensitive areas and identifying areas that are at high risk from impacts of storms or sea level rise.

Know Your Audience

The first step in developing a key message is to know your audience. So you may want to conduct a pre-assessment of stakeholder interests and values before you begin your project, in order to learn what are the hot-button issues and to get different community perspectives on the key issues involved with your project.

You can also utilize a focus group to test your ideas, review the effectiveness of your message and map graphics before presenting them to the public or to decision makers. The worst time to find out that you have created an unintentional controversy is in the middle of a public meeting. It is best to anticipate and address potential conflicts before they come to a head. However, it is likely that you will still need to actively respond to tough questions throughout the duration of a project. Having well-informed answers at the ready can help you to navigate the pitfalls and firestorms inherent in most land planning efforts.

Tailor Your Message

Assuming you know who your audience is and what are its main concerns, you can tailor your message to pre-address many of them. When possible, it is better to answer the question that has not yet been asked and allay concerns and fears during your presentation, as opposed to afterwards. Develop a set of key messages and put them

Seeing is believing. This group decided to visit the wetlands they were discussing to 'ground truth' their knowledge of conditions.

on your web pages, in project brochures, in presentations, in a Frequently Asked Questions (FAQ) document, or in other written, filmed or online communications.

Which topics are most relevant to your audience will vary depending on your community and the specific setting. One evening you might be presenting your project to the chamber of commerce, on another it might be to the biodiversity council. You should not actually change your project's mission and purpose, but you may utilize arguments and descriptions that most resonate with your intended audience. You may also modify the format (making it more formal or informal), depending on the setting and timing of your presentations.

You will also have to decide if your audience will resonate more with one of the following types of information:

- evidence based on studies (e.g. academic journals)
- stories and anecdotes (especially local or familiar)
- pictures and evidence they can see for themselves (take a field trip)
- support from key community members and respected community representatives (testimonials)

State the Benefits of Natural Assets

Your central message needs to share the benefits of protecting and restoring key natural assets as part of your green infrastructure strategy. Whichever arguments you decide to use, remember that positive points resonate more effectively. In addition, many psychological studies have shown that people respond best when told what they can do, rather than what they can't. Studies

of signage in national parks saying do not do X, Y, or Z have sometimes made it more likely people will do those things. Similarly, we tend to copy what our peers do. Peer pressure originates not just from verbal communications from your peers, but also your own tendency to copy your colleagues' and neighbors' behavior.

Much of the academic literature about peer pressure influences stems from studies of recycling or littering behavior, which examined people's motivations. Recycling studies found that the most effective way to gain participation in recycling programs was not to tell people to avoid making excessive waste, but rather to place recycling bins strategically at several homes and watch people ask to join once they saw their neighbors recycling. Similarly, programs that tried to reduce littering by posting negative signage (Don't litter, big fines!) were not as effective as ensuring that places were kept clean, since people would throw trash in areas where there was trash already, but tended not to litter in cleaned areas (Reiter and Samuel 2006).

The tone and approach of your message is relevant because you want to make evaluating and mapping your community's assets the 'normal' thing to do. So, instead of discussing what you will lose if you do not evaluate and map your assets, present the many benefits of doing this work and point out how many other communities are doing it already, and with what success (try to pick communities similar to your own to model exemplary behaviors with which people can resonate).

Key messages are short statements (stated directly or implied) that get to the heart of the argument you wish to make.

Economic reasons are probably the most important benefits to highlight in the early 21st century, when most of the world's economies are struggling. They also provide a way to use economic analogies to which most people can relate.

Earlier, we introduced several of these ideas. Here, we will show how these concepts can be structured as arguments for why it's important to map and evaluate natural assets. Each sub-section has a 'key message' that you may wish to utilize when making your case for natural asset planning; it is then followed, either by scientific evidence or by examples that you can use to back up the message's claim.

The Personal Finance Analogy

MESSAGE: You Make Informed Decisions About Managing Your Own Financial Assets, So Make Sure You Are Also Well Informed About the Values of Your Natural Assets!

Do you hand out blank checks to the cashier at the grocery store or sell your home or stocks for just a dollar? Of course not! That is because we sell or buy things based on some understanding of their economic value. So, just as we know the value of our financial assets, we should know the value of our natural assets before we decide what to do with them. By mapping our natural assets, we can determine which land features are the most valuable and make wise, informed decisions about their management.

Green Areas Spur Investment

MESSAGE: Mapping Green Assets Saves Both Kinds of "Green"!

Utilize the argument that restoring green spaces attracts redevelopment. For example, "By converting an old levee on the Savannah River to a riverwalk, the town's investment of $8 million in the trail has attracted $198 million in new commercial investments" (Benedict and McMahon 2006).

The creation of a new riverfront park in downtown Hartford Connecticut led to $1 billion in new reinvestment within walking distance of the park, according to the nonprofit group Riverfront Recapture, which developed and runs the park (Riverfront Recapture 2012).

MESSAGE: Creating or Restoring Natural Areas Protects and Increases Property Values!

Property values and real estate revenues rise 10 to 30 percent when green spaces are preserved, raising property values without raising tax rates. Properties near green spaces sell faster and for more money.

For example: "The National Association of Realtors found that 57 percent of voters would be more likely to purchase a home close to green space, and 50 percent said they would be willing to pay 10 percent more for a home located near a park or other protected area" (Benedict

and McMahon 2006.) And, "a developer who donated a forty-foot-wide, seven-mile-long easement along a popular trail in Front Royal, Virginia, sold all fifty parcels bordering the trail in just 4 months" (Benedict and McMahon 2006).

There are many studies of the benefits of parks and natural areas on property values and some make a distinction concerning the size and type of green space. One of the evaluation methods used in a study of home sales in Portland, Oregon, found that the 193 public parks analyzed had a significant, positive impact on nearby property values. The existence of a park within 1,500 feet of a home increased its sale price between $845 and $2,262 (in 2000 dollars) (The Economic Benefits of Recreation, Open Space, Recreation Facilities and Walkable Community Design 2010).

MESSAGE: Size and Quality of Natural Areas Matter for Benefitting Property Values (and Quality of Life).

The size of natural areas matters not only for wildlife but also real estate values. The Portland study also showed that the larger the park, the more significant the property value increase.

Another study found that large natural forest areas have a greater positive impact on nearby property prices than small urban parks or developed parks, such as playgrounds, skate parks and even golf courses. Homes located within 1,500 feet of natural forest areas enjoy statistically significant property premiums, on average $10,648, compared to $1,214 for urban parks, $5,657 for specialty parks and $8,849 for golf courses (in 1990 dollars).

Similar studies in Howard County, Maryland, Washington County, Oregon, Austin, Texas, Minneapolis-St. Paul, Minnesota, and other areas used data from residential sales, the census and GIS to examine marginal values of different types of parks. They too found that the type of open space affects the benefits for property values (The Economic Benefits of Recreation, Open Space, Recreation Facilities and Walkable Community Design 2010).

MESSAGE: Protect Natural Areas – Especially Trails – To Attract Home Buyers.

When citing sources for economic studies, the National Association of Realtors (NAR) proves very useful since it is in the business of selling homes and is considered to be an avid supporter of economic growth. It compiles many useful statistics, such as the NAR national study, which has found that, of all homebuyers polled about what they were looking for in recreational amenities, "1-2 percent golf, 5-6 percent swim and more than 50 percent use paths." This shows that creating trails in a development is a very appealing investment.

Green Assets and Jobs

MESSAGE: To Attract a Well-Paid Workforce, Offer Abundant Green Areas and Outdoor Recreation.

The goal of attracting companies with well-paid jobs is shared by most localities. However, well-paid positions are often harder to come by than low-paid service jobs. To attract good paying jobs, the focus should not be on 'industrial parks,' but actual parks.

Small companies, especially those that have a well paid and skilled workforce, place a strong importance on the 'green' of the local environment (Crompton Love and Moore 1997). Also, the creative class of artists, media personnel, lawyers, analysts, and so on, tend to reflect a better paid workforce. They make up 30 percent of the U.S. workforce and place a premium on outdoor recreation and access to nature (Florida 2002). So, to attract

The Hartford River Park includes may wild areas downtown for urban residents to enjoy.

a skilled, creative workforce (and thereby the companies that employ them), it is key to provide them with green areas and outdoor recreation.

MESSAGE: Clean and Abundant Natural Resources Support the Economy

Many businesses depend on clean water for their production process. For example, computer chip manufacturers require a great volume of water that is as pristine as possible. Of, course, bottled water plants require clean water, but so do beer and spirits companies. In addition, those type of businesses that depend on a healthful environment tend to be good stewards of the earth.

In addition to clean water and recreation, remember that green infrastructure includes natural resources that we depend on for agriculture, timber, honey and other non-extractive and regenerative assets. These resources support a large economy. For example, in Virginia, forests and associated forest products bring the state $27.5 billion in annual revenue while agriculture brings in $55 billion annually and provides more than 357,000 jobs. Similarly in North Carolina, the state's top grossing industries are agriculture (farms and forestland) and tourism; both highly dependent on existing natural resources and the quality of those resources.

In rural areas, these numbers can be used to justify a focus on conserving those landscapes that contribute to the rural economy – they are both economic and ecological assets!

Green Assets and Tourism

MESSAGE: Nature-Based Recreation Spurs New Businesses!

While service jobs are usually low paid, those that require some skill, such as guides for hunting, fisheries and whitewater rafting, depend on a green and well-connected landscape. These types of businesses bring in hotels, bed and breakfast inns, restaurants, craft and boutique stores, and all the other services needed, such as gas stations, groceries and outdoor gear shops.

The Creeper Trail in Virginia has lured $2.5 million in new tourism dollars to Virginia and $1.5 million to Grayson County, along with 27 new jobs in new businesses near the trail (Bowker and Bergstrom 2004). These include everything from trail-side cafes to bike and equipment rentals and lodging.

MESSAGE: Nature and Heritage Resources Attract Tourists Who Will Spend More Money.

Green assets tend to attract tourists who are high spenders. Those people whose outdoor sport requires the purchase of expensive gear, such as ATVs, snowmobiles, powerboats, mountain bikes and fishing equipment, will often shop locally and get their equipment serviced locally as well. They will spend money on boats, camping gear, high-powered cameras, camouflaged survival gear and other equipment.

Some tourists also tend to spend more on amenities. Even birders, who may appear to need nothing more than a pair of binoculars, a chewed pencil and a notebook, spend more than other types of tourists. This is due, in part, to the type of recreation, as well as the type of individual who engages in that sport. In addition, they tend to stay in bed and breakfast inns (which cost more and generate more revenue in taxes than budget inns) and eat out at finer restaurants (e.g. a nice bistro, not fast food), which results in higher bills and greater tax revenue per person. They will also buy better binoculars, more bird guides and more expensive scopes. Those sales add up.

Similarly, heritage tourists, those who like history and culture as part of their tourism experience, spend, on average, two and half times more per person than all other types of tourists (Thomas Jefferson Planning District Heritage Tourism Project). However, they also are choosy about the areas they visit – therefore protecting scenic vistas, conserving viewsheds along scenic roadways and preventing the encroachment of development into historic landscapes are important to lure them and keep them visiting as long as possible. They will not want to travel through multiple blighted areas simply to reach a historic site.

As noted earlier, people shop longer and spend more money per item in shopping areas with trees, so providing and restoring the tree canopy in business districts and downtowns is critical to getting and keeping dollars from residents and tourists alike. Charlottesville, Virginia, bricked its main street in the 1970s. Today, this pedestrian, mall with many trees planted where there was once a street offers a unique outdoor and green café scene, with which modern malls are not able to compete.

Ecological Reasons

MESSAGE: Bigger Is Better – Especially for Wildlife!

A general rule of thumb is that the larger the natural area, the greater the diversity of habitat types that are possible. A minimum size for forested cores is 100 acres, but most models assign higher points for larger areas. Seek to conserve as large an intact area as possible.

MESSAGE: Connections Count!

A connected landscape helps with species diversity by providing multiple pathways for plants, pollinators and animals to live and travel. If a species is reduced in one area (due to disturbance or disease), connections facilitate colonization. They also ensure that, if one pathway is lost or broken, there will be other ways to cross the landscape.

An analogy that is easy to relate to and that the GIC has used in college towns is, if you are hungry when the

big football game is on and game day traffic has closed down the roadways, you'll be out of luck if you only have one route to the grocery store. But if you know a favorite shortcut, or where there's an alternative store, you have more chance of getting what you require. In nature, we also need to have multiple routes and pathways to ensure we don't get stuck, go hungry – or go extinct!

Existence value or *intrinsic value*, is a human value that something should exist and possesses its own independent value in and of itself, whether or not the person perceiving that value has ever experienced it directly.

Social Benefits

MESSAGE: People Value Natural Assets for Their Own Sake!

Many people appreciate nature and wild things just because they exist. Known as *existence value* or *intrinsic value*, many people take heart in knowing something exists, even if they have never, or will never, see it in real life – the Emperor penguin is an exotic example, but think of how many people get excited by the possibility of a mountain lion in the nearby hills? As famous naturalist

TREES PROVIDE MANY VALUES – AND THEY WORK FOR FREE!

Trees:

- Provide habitat and food for wildlife.
- Provide oxygen.
- Remove particulate pollution, sequester carbon and mitigate global climate change.
- Absorb and filter runoff, and protect water quality.
- Conserve land by preventing soil erosion.
- Mitigate urban heat islands and reduce energy demand.
- Increase property values.
- Improve children's performance in school.
- Reduce levels of domestic violence.
- Attract shoppers and tourists who stay longer and spend more.
- Reduce mental fatigue and stress.

Urban Forestry News, Spring 2004.

Aldo Leopold once said in his *Sand County Almanac,* "There are some who can live without wild things and some who cannot. I am one of those who cannot."

One theory posited about why people relate to and care about nature is known as *biophilia*. First proposed by Erich Fromm and later popularized by noted ecologist E.O. Wilson, it is described as "the connections that human beings subconsciously seek with the rest of life." These connections are thought to be deeply rooted within our own biology as animals. Whether or not one subscribes to this notion, it is true that simply looking at something natural or 'green' improves our attitude and state of mind.

MESSAGE: Natural Assets Make You Nicer and Smarter!

Simply looking at pictures of natural objects can improve your attitude and make you more altruistic. In a recent study, participants immersed in natural environments reported a higher valuing of intrinsic aspirations and a lower valuing of extrinsic aspirations. In essence, seeing nature made people more caring (Weinstein, Przybylski, Ryan 2009). It might seem incredible to link them, but occurrences of both attention deficit disorder and domestic violence are significantly reduced around trees, while people's IQs actually increase (Southern Forest Research Station).

MESSAGE: Natural Assets Make You Healthier!

Increasingly, green infrastructure planning is being linked to the field of public health. According to the US Centers for Disease Control, as of 2010, 25.6 million, or

"The last word in ignorance is the man who says of an animal or plant, "What good is it?" If the land mechanism as a whole is good, then every part is good, whether we understand it or not. If the biota, in the course of eons, has built something we like but do not understand, then who but a fool would discard seemingly useless parts? To keep every cog and wheel is the first precaution of intelligent tinkering."

— Aldo Leopold, in *Round River: From the Journals of Aldo Leopold.*

11.3 percent of all people over the age of 20 have diabetes and it rose to the seventh leading cause of death in 2007. Twice that number of Americans are at risk of contracting diabetes. However, many studies show that diabetes can be prevented by weight loss and exercise. Green infrastructure planning can help communities link people to trails and parks that reduce stress while getting them fit and healthy.

Doctors are beginning to prescribe walking to lower the risk of heart disease, obesity and diabetes from lack of fitness and weight gain by ordering trail walks for their patients (*Washington Post* 2009). Walking just 30 minutes a day significantly increases your health, avoiding metabolic syndrome – the cluster of risk factors that raise the odds of developing heart disease, diabetes and stroke (*American Journal of Cardiology* 2007).

Most articles also find that having access to recreation opportunities makes it more likely that people will exercise. The fitter employees are, the lower the health care costs for businesses. That is why businesses are attracted to areas that offer abundant recreation and opportunities for people to walk near to where they work.

Even having a view of green spaces can reduce illness. One study found that employees without views of green spaces, in response to questions concerning 11 different ailments, reported 23 percent more incidences of illness in the prior six months (Kaplan 1989). Less illness means more productive workers.

Similarly, studies of hospital patients by the Center for Health Systems and Design at Texas A&M University found that physical or visual contact with natural spaces leads to faster recovery. Dr. Ulrich measured patient's alpha rates, which are associated with stress and levels of relaxation. He found that those patients who could experience natural scenery were more relaxed than those who had urban views and, as a result, those experiencing nature views had "shorter post-operative stays, fewer negative comments from nurses, took less pain medication and experienced minor post-operative complications" (Ulrich 1984). Many hospitals are beginning to provide views from their rooms. Since it is likely that most hospitals do not own those views, they depend on local planners and developers to maintain the green space that is helping their patients heal faster. They are also incorporating 'healing gardens' and outdoor trails for their more ambulatory patients, as well as for the enjoyment of staff and visitors, who also experience their own forms of stress.

A great deal of research shows that residents within lower-income urban neighborhoods have higher rates of health problems. While less income and lack of access to health care are certainly factors, the surrounding environment also plays a role in a community's emotional and physical health.

Dense urban areas often lack trees and vegetation. Trees' role in improving air quality is fairly well-known. They absorb volatile organic compounds and other contaminants from the air while also providing oxygen. However, what may be less well known is that they influence our propensity to walk and exercise. The green of our environment exerts a positive influence on our desire to walk outdoors. Downtown urban areas often have less trees. For example, the GIC's urban canopy maps of Richmond, Charlottesville and Staunton show less trees in these cities' downtowns. The closer one gets to the urban core, the less trees are found. In the case of Charlottesville and Richmond, these less-treed areas correlate to areas suffering from greater poverty.

Studies concerning factors that motivate people to walk show that, while having opportunities to stroll on sidewalks and other pathways is important, it is also important, if not equally so, to have trees to walk under and alongside. Research has shown that residents in neighborhoods with abundant green spaces have better health than those in areas without green space. People are more likely to walk in areas with green space, a correlation that is strongest for the elderly, homemakers, and lower socio-economic groups.

Destinations that must be reached through areas without trees and vegetation are perceived to be farther away, perhaps influencing people's reluctance to walk through them (Wolf 2008). Thus, residents of inner city urban areas with less trees have greater poverty, poorer health and less desire to walk and exercise outside. This demonstrates why urban green spaces, the tree canopy, a connected landscape and other natural assets are key factors to include in any green infrastructure plan.

People's lack of access to outside spaces, as well as their reluctance to venture outside, have received new attention in recent years. The term *nature deficit disorder* refers to the effects that occur when children do not have access to outdoor natural areas. The popular book *Last Child in the Woods* by Richard Louve synthesized literature concerning the importance of nature to reduce

attention deficit disorder and create healthier kids. It also stressed why we need to actively ensure that our kids are out in nature as part of their emotional, physical and cognitive development.

In this chapter, we have covered opportunities for building public support and examples of key messages that can be tailored and utilized to appeal to your community. In Chapter Seven, we provide detailed information about data sources and models.

MAPPING NATURAL ASSETS

- Building a Habitat Model
- Identifying Cores
- Connecting the Network
- Ranking Cores
- Updating Data

CHAPTER 7 - Using Models and Spatial Data to Create Natural Asset Maps
by R. Andrew Walker

This chapter presents guidance on using state and local data to create natural asset maps. Before embarking on the steps presented in this chapter, read prior chapters to understand why it is beneficial to create a green infrastructure network and how to set clear goals and priorities that will guide the mapping process. Chapter Five presents case studies of how natural asset mapping was applied from regional to site scales.

Asset mapping is an invaluable tool in planning for healthy and resilient communities. In order to set priorities and develop strategies, it is necessary to know what your assets are, as well as their condition and location. Creating a program to protect water quality by preserving and restoring forests can be far more effective if the location of land that has the greatest impact on water quality is known. This allows the source of the problem to be addressed. Mapping and understanding your assets in a geographic context takes time and resources up front, but ultimately sets you up for successful implementation.

The most unique and high-quality natural assets can be identified through a mapping process. The term 'assets' is used here because natural features can fulfill one or more community goals, and can be prioritized and ranked using objective and consistent criteria. Assets can be natural features, such as forests and wetlands, or constructed features, such as a hiking trail or historic building. In the case of constructed features, the common theme that connects them is that their value is partially derived from the natural landscape that surrounds them. For example, the area visible (or 'viewshed') from an historic plantation home influences its character and historic integrity.

Mapping can be done at any scale, and ideally should be done at multiple scales. For example, some details that may be hard to see at a regional level might be obvious at a county level. However, some larger patterns and connections might be missed at a county scale that would be clear at a regional level.

You should also be aware that mapping across administrative boundaries can be a challenge, largely because data may have to be collected for a number of different localities and merged into a consistent database. If this is not done, trans-boundary assets can easily be overlooked. When recognized at a regional scale, they can be managed cooperatively. Rivers and large waterbodies are examples of features that frequently cross administrative boundaries. However, large tracts of intact forests and wetland complexes also need to be assessed at a regional view to better understand the benefits they provide and their level of risk.

This chapter should be used as a starting point for those interested in building a landscape-scale habitat model and creating natural-resource-based asset maps as part of strategic green infrastructure planning. If this is beyond your capabilities, read this chapter to understand the principles involved and consider hiring a firm, such as the GIC, or partner with a university to assist you in building a local habitat model.

USING THE RIGHT TOOLS

At a minimum, GIS software is required to make asset maps and to map intact habitat. This chapter will therefore assume that you are using ESRI's ArcGIS software, although there are other options available.

Before we begin, let's note several features that are important when using GIS analysis to identify habitat core and corridors (the Base Map):

- The **Spatial Analyst** extension to the ArcGIS suite is an invaluable tool for conducting landscape analysis. It allows you to manipulate raster data in more complex ways. As this methodology relies on land cover data in raster format, this extension is necessary to complete the model.
- The **ModelBuilder** tool inside ArcGIS is a useful way to document your steps, as well to quickly re-run a series of GIS operations (ie automate a workflow). For example, you might finish building your model, but want to go back and change one parameter that was used in the middle of the analysis. Instead of redoing the analysis step-by-step, you can simply change the parameter and let the computer redo the entire process while keeping all other parameters the same.
- The use of **Python scripting**, while not necessary to identify intact habitat, can provide additional flexibility not achievable with ModelBuilder. Python can be used to build custom tools that use conditional logic, which makes it much easier to reuse models.

If you do not have access to these tools, the GIC recommends you partner with a non-profit organization, an educational institution or a regional planning authority that does have these capabilities.

DEFINING A STUDY AREA

Defining a study area is a critical step to achieve quality results. Note that the methodology presented here is most appropriate for relatively large areas, such as a city, state or ecoregion. For ideas about how to work at smaller scales, such as urban neighborhoods, or to link parcels, refer to earlier chapters.

Study areas will vary depending on the goals of the asset mapping program. For example, a study area could be a county, a watershed or a city district. To include natural features that cross its outer boundary, *you will need to decide on a buffer to apply to your study area.* For a county, a good rule of thumb is to apply a 10 kilometer (6 mile) buffer around its external boundary. For a city or a watershed, this buffer may be smaller since you are working at a finer-grained scale. There will also be times when you will want to have a much larger buffer – if, say, you are studying an area that is part of a much larger ecoregion.

Looking outside of political boundaries ensures that features spanning across the study area boundary are not misconstrued as smaller than they really are and will help you see wider connections across the landscape. Correct ranking of habitat areas requires that their full extend is considered. Note any special geographic features (large forests, reservoirs, wetland complexes, etc.) that cross the boundary of your study area and make sure to that your buffer size allows them to be fully captured in the analysis.

Regarding data collection, make sure you collect data for your entire study area, *including the buffer you defined*. If your study area is a county, you will most likely need to collect information from neighboring counties. If your study area is a watershed, you will mostly likely have to collect some types of information from all the counties and incorporated places within the watershed, as many datasets are maintained at the local level.

BUILDING A HABITAT MODEL

Identifying high-quality habitat should be the first step in an asset mapping process. Since the network of intact natural landscapes forms the backbone from which the benefits of green infrastructure are derived, it is important to understand, build and rank the network before overlaying related data, such as water resources or historic sites.

The habitat network should serve as your Base Map, and will help address questions such as:

- What are the largest and best-quality tracts of habitat?
- Which areas have the most intact habitat?
- Which areas are the most fragmented by development?
- Which habitats are the most connected?
- Which habitats are the most isolated?

A handful of states have created statewide models to identify and rank their green infrastructure networks. For example, one of the earliest statewide green infrastructure network models in the country was created in Florida in 1994. The GIC has created models for South Carolina, New York State, and Arkansas. It is worth investigating whether a model has been created in your state and, if so, if it can be used to support your planning process. However, you will still need to add local data to refine it and local priorities when deciding what to include in your final network.

Necessary Data

There are two major parts to mapping intact habitat cores:

1. Identifying the location and shape of the habitat cores.
2. Ranking the cores based on their ecological integrity by using the best available data and science.

It is ideal to perform both steps, but completing only the first step is preferable to not completing either. Part 2 requires the completion of Part 1.

Below, we discuss several major data types that are useful in this process and the parts of the process necessary to build the base map. See the "Relevant Data" table for a list of the most relevant data for identifying, ranking and assessing green infrastructure assets.

Part 1: Identifying the Location and Shape of Habitat Cores

The first map you should create is your Base Map, which will depict intact habitat in your study area. Before creating this map, it is necessary to identify the *location* of high-quality habitat. This requires some analysis using GIS to calculate key aspects such as intactness, water richness (the amount of water resources and their diversity), or area to determine the likelihood for supporting high biodiversity. As explained earlier, it is also important to use the most up-to-date information possible to ensure its reliability.

As explained in Chapter One, *habitat cores* are the main building blocks of green infrastructure networks. In this book, a habitat core is a 'natural landscape.' For example, even though crop lands can provide habitat for some species, they are not eligible to be part of a core as they are not natural landscapes. Keep in mind that 'natural' does not mean 'never modified.' Many landscapes in the United States have been cleared, regrown, cleared again, or otherwise altered, such as wetlands drained to create farmland.

Some lands, such as those managed for forestry, can either be very similar to natural habitat or very dissimilar. The decision on whether or not to include them will have to be made on a case by case basis depending first on the quality of the data available (e.g. Is it possible to identify these areas and to ground truth their habitat quality?),

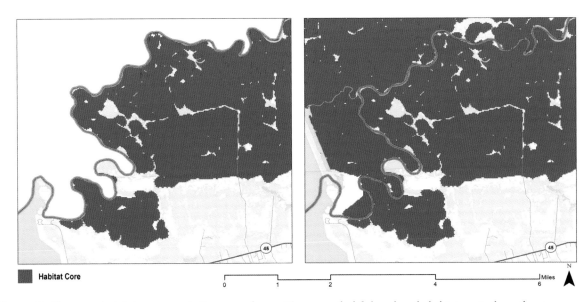

Habitat Core

0   1   2   4   6 Miles   N

This graphic illustrates why it is important to buffer your study area. The map on the left shows how the habitat core in the southwest corner appears isolated from the larger core to the northeast. In the map on the right, land on both sides of a county boundary (in orange) is shown, and it can be seen that the core to the southwest is actually part of an interconnected system. In the map on the left, if the cross-boundary landscape had not been considered, the core would have been ranked lower, since it would have been assessed as a much smaller area than it actually is.

MOST RELEVANT DATA FOR MAPPING NATURAL INFRASTRUCTURE

CHECK*	DATA	PURPOSE	SOURCE
Base Information			
	Habitat Cores and Corridors Model	Habitat Cores and Corridors; i.e. interior forests, dunes, wetlands that provide wildlife habitat blocks and connections. Check with your state or regional agencies to see if a model has been built. Otherwise, see Chapter Seven for guindance on how to begin the process	Division of Natural Heritage, Department of Natural Resources, or similar.
	Roads (inter-state/primary)	Reference for locations.	County/Local GIS, or State Department of Transportation.
	Parcel Information	Parcel size and ownership are helpful for evaluating long-term conservation potentials (e.g. are they large enough to manage for habitat or working lands?). For urban areas, knowing where vacant parcels are located can help identify opportunities for restoration and creating new green space.	County/Local GIS. For working lands, you may want to sort by ownership and adjacency, as farms and forests are often made up of several parcels under one owner.
	Building Location	Used to determine exact locations of occupied dwellings to determine if any new fragmentation of cores has occurred.	County/Local GIS – E911 Point Data
	Service District Boundaries	For orientation and management plans and to show areas most likely to develop.	County/Local GIS
	Land Cover	Shows types of land coverage.	Various sources (Federal, State, County). Select the most recent and highest resolution data.
	Major Federal and State Land Ownerships	Shows land protected or managed by another entity that may affect the degree of protection for current use.	County/Local GIS, state, federal
	Digital Elevation Models (DEM)	Stitch downloaded 'tiles' together to show elevation. Slopes may be important in thinking about runoff potential or lands that are more or less attractive for others (development, farming, grazing). Can also help with map graphic quality by using 'hillshade.'	http://www.ngdc.noaa.gov/mgg/dem/demportal.html
Land Use			
	Zoning	To evaluate allowed land uses and potential risk or compatibility with priority habitat cores.	County/Local GIS
	Future Land Use	To evaluate future risk or compatibility.	County/Local GIS
	Conservation Easements (county, state and nonprofit / private)	To determine what is protected and least likely to change. Overlay with priority habitats to determine their level of protection.	County/Local GIS, Land Trusts, State Division of Natural Heritage (confirm with county data to ensure it is up-to-date),
	Other public facilities	City golf courses, city landfill, city compost yard, etc.	County/Local GIS
Water Resources			
	Watershed Boundaries and major streams	To manage by watershed and also to determine boundaries for land cover types and potential runoff issues.	National Hydrography Dataset. Use blue lines for most streams (line data) and polygons for large water bodies or very large rivers.
	Floodplains and Floodway Fringe	To determine areas of risk that may be best left undeveloped for public safety while also providing wildlife corridors. Overlay with forest cover to determine buffer capacity.	County/Local GIS
	Healthy Streams	It is important to flag streams of exceptional quality. These can be included on a map of best water resources. Also consider adding naturally reproducing trout waters (not stocked but self-sustaining) and waters with exceptional or rare species.	Environmental Protection Agency, Department of Fish and Game, Department of Environmental Quality, or similar.
	Impaired Streams	Useful in determining risk and where additional forest cover or stream buffers needed. Also to evaluate risk of new impairments that may occur.	County/Local GIS, Department of Environmental Quality, or similar.

*Check box if you have data

	Wetlands	Provides sensitive landscape and key hydrology.	National Wetlands Inventory. (note this is not very precise, especially for small and forested wetlands.) County/Local GIS.
	Wetland Banks	Land that is protected.	County/Local GIS
	Fisheries	Includes known natural trout waters and streams that support other key species.	Department of Fish and Game, or similar.
	Public Wells	These serve 20 or more people. Correlate wells to land cover to determine the level of protection. Public wells within corridors and cores provide another reason for conservation prioritization.	County/Local GIS, Department of Health, Department of Environmental Quality, or similar.
	Public Reservoirs	Areas draining into reservoirs should be as forested as possible. A forested buffer around a reservoir is also important. While water will be treated, treatment costs increase if water is not clean to begin with.	County GIS should also include drainage area.
	Water Monitoring Stations	Can be used to obtain stream data and current water quality. Also use impaired waters list to determine level and source for impairment. Consider whether impairment type can be addressed by land conservation measures.	State Department of Environmental Quality, or similar. 305B Report for Water Quality. May also review the 303D list from the DEQ for impaired waters.
	LID/BMP Features	Best Management Practices for low impact development (rain gardens, green rooftops, pervious pavement, rain barrels, etc.)	County/Local GIS
Recreation			
	Federal Parkland	Use to determine the levels of protection for natural assets and who are the management entities.	County/Local GIS
	State Parkland	Use to determine the levels of protection for natural assets and who are the management entities.	State or County/Local GIS
	County Parkland	Use to determine the levels of protection for natural assets and who are the management entities.	County/Local GIS
	County Trails (Future and existing)	Determine trails that intersect and utilize natural assets and areas of natural assets that support views from trails. Include water trails, if any.	County/Local GIS
	Federal Trails	Determine trails that intersect and utilize natural assets and areas of natural assets that support views from trails. Federal ownership denotes a higher level of protection from change.	Various federal agencies and state GIS
	Other Regional Trails	Same as above, and may show areas where inter-jurisdictional cooperation is needed.	Varies.
	Hunting Lands	Almost always privately owned and leased to hunt clubs. Leases are usually for set periods of time. May show preferred land use and importance of ensuring a connected network of land.	Can be difficult to find one data source. May need to ground truth or contact hunt clubs individually to learn which tracts are leased for hunting.
	Wildlife Management Areas	Shows level of protection and use. Pay particular attention to lands outside areas that may also need protection since they are a magnet for adjacent development and adjacent land uses may impair WMA.	Department of Fish and Game, or similar.

*Check box if you have data

MOST RELEVANT DATA FOR MAPPING NATURAL INFRASTRUCTURE

	State Forests	Use to determine the level of protection for natural assets.	Department of Forestry
	Birding and Wildlife Trails	Often privately owned and not formally protected. May provide greater priority for conservation of land underneath or adjacent to it.	Department of Fish and Game, or similar.
	Boat Ramps and Launches	Denotes public put in access area that may need protection. Consider different symbols on map for motorboat launches versus canoe only.	Department of Fish and Game, or similar.
	Scenic Rivers	Denotes areas that may offer special recreation and views. *Also consider this for the water map and heritage map.*	Department of Natural Resources, or similar.
Historic and Cultural Assets			
	Historic Register Sites	Particularly sites in rural areas influenced by landscape setting. May also include suburban areas. Consider placing a buffer around these. How do the natural assets you have mapped support these historic sites?	County GIS (federal, state and local) and State Division of Historic Resources.
	Potentially Eligible Historic Sites	Ditto *re* above; also protection of adjacent land may protect these sites.	CountyLocal GIS
	Historic Districts and Rural Historic Districts	You may want to include all districts. What are significant for natural asset maps are those districts supported by natural landscape features (viewsheds and buffering adjacent land uses).	County/Local GIS and State Division of Historic Resources
	Battlefield Areas (National Register and Eligible)	You may want to maintain sites for historic reasons and determine whether, and how, natural assets include and buffer these sites.	County or state GIS
	Scenic Roads (byways)	Overlay with natural assets and determine whether, and how, assets support viewsheds of these routes.	Dept of Transportation
	Rural Historic Districts	While not a protected landscape, designation shows historic significance. You may want to prioritize natural assets within the district.	County GIS and State Division of Historic Resources
	Boat/Kayak Paddling Trails	Shows routes for non-motorized recreational paddling.	Department of Conservation/ Recreation, Department of Fish and Game, or similar.
	Century Farms	These are farms at least 100 years old. Based on nominations, not comprehensive. *May also include on working lands map.*	County GIS and State Division of Historic Resources
Working Lands (Ag & Forest)			
	Forest Cover/Tree Canopy	Use to show forest cover relative to habitat cores and corridors. Also can be used to determine forest cover for a watershed to consider runoff potential and impacts to water quality. Can often be derived from land cover data.	Various sources (Federal, State, County). Select the most recent and highest resolution data. Check if an urban tree canopy (UTC) assessment has been conducted for your study area.

*Check box if you have data

MOST RELEVANT DATA FOR MAPPING NATURAL INFRASTRUCTURE

	Parcels >25–<100 Acres	Useful to determine areas less or more suitable for commercial farming or forestry.	County/Local GIS
	Parcels >100 Acres	Ditto *re* above; also consult with your county forester to determine the ideal minimum size for sustained forestry. Contact the extension service about farm size for fruit and row crops.	County/Local GIS
	Prime Agricultural Soils	Useful to determine areas suitable for row crops. Overlay with zoning and development to take out soils with incompatible land uses.	County and NRCS Soil Data Gateway. Spatial data is available for most (but not all) counties. http://datagateway. nrcs.usda.gov/
	Ag. and Forestal District Lands	Shows land intended for agriculture and land with some temporary level of protection. Compare to adjacent and possibly incompatible land uses.	County/Local GIS
	Farms with PDR Acquisition	Shows land with permanent protection from development. You may also use it to compare farms with nearby and adjacent incompatible land uses.	County/Local GIS
	Active Forestry Lands	Shows lands that are actively being managed for forestry, such as plantation forests. Can be used to distinguish different types of forest.	Department of Forestry
	Orchards and Vineyards	Identifies orchards, vineyards, or similar land uses that contribute to a region's economy.	County GIS
	Active Farms	This is difficult to define and usually not a layer within county GIS, but it can potentially be derived.	USDA has data by commodity type available for download by government agencies at: http://www.fsa.usda.gov/FSA/ apfoapp? area=home&subject=prod&top- ic=clu Some counties also have use-value assessment and if the size minimum is realistic (at least 10 acres), can reflect actual farms.
	Areas of Steep Slopes	Can be used to determine areas unsuited for development that may be most appropriate to conserve, especially if they contain key natural assets.	Steep slope must be defined. Use of Spatial Analyst can help you generate slope data from a DEM.
Wildlife			
	Essential Wildlife Habitat	Selected based on land cover and acreage.	Division of Natural Heritage, Department of Natural Resources, Department of Fish and Game, or similar.
	Important Bird Areas	This is useful if data are spatially recorded and discreet. Flyways and known nesting areas can be protected or used to add reasons for protecting a particular region.	Typically too large to be meaningful for local planning and these areas may move across the landscape (they are often not static).
	Species (rare, threatened, endangered)	This data is not usually made available publically. States often have a subscription service for counties to look up species by area.	Contact Division of Natural Heritage, or similar.
	Rookeries or other unique habitat areas	Shows key habitat areas and useful to know, in order to protect. You should mask data (buffer) to prevent the public from disturbing the area.	Local knowledge (location can change). Also contact Division of Natural Heritage, or similar.

*Check box if you have data

as well as the specific goals of the study (e.g. Does your community desire very specific strategies related to land management (forestry) operations?).

As explained more fully in Chapter One, the main thing that differentiates a core from a mere patch of trees is the size of its *interior habitat*. The area that qualifies as a core will vary depending on ecoregion.

Land cover data are then used to create a *natural land cover data layer*. This methodology is intended for landscape-scale applications, such as a county or region, and not for site-scale applications, such as locating amphibian habitat on an individual parcel. However, it can be used to show whether development on one site is likely to influence the quality of an overall habitat network positively or negatively.

As explained in Chapter One, the more fragmented the landscape, the more edge it has and the less habitat intactness it supports. To determine *habitat intactness* and assess the *fragmentation* of the natural landscape, you will need to overlay and analyze fragmenting features, such as buildings, roads, rail lines and power lines, in relation to the natural land cover data layer.

Once you subtract areas that are fragmented, you need to look at what is left and ask, "Is the remaining area large enough to constitute a core?" This is done by applying a buffer around each fragmenting feature to account for its impact zone. Natural land that is within this buffer is considered to be *edge habitat*, or the transitional zone between a fragmenting feature and interior habitat. After distinguishing between edge habitat and interior habitat, unique habitat cores can be identified.

To summarize, the rules for identifying habitat cores are:

1. Locate the natural land cover.
2. Add fragmenting features.
3. Clip out all that is fragmented from the natural land cover.
4. Subtract edge habitat (the buffer around fragmenting features) from the remaining natural land area. This is the *interior forest* (unfragmented habitat).
5. How large are the remaining areas? Is the unfragmented land cover ≥ the minimum size necessary to qualify as a core? If yes, it is a core. If no, it is deemed to be a *habitat fragment* or *patch*.

The minimum size of the cores in your study area will depend somewhat on ecoregion, as well as the data available.

Useful Datasets For Identifying Cores and Corridors

Land Cover. Land cover data show the geography of different cover types in the area of interest, such as forest, cultivated land, open water or fields. Some datasets use more refined land cover classes than others. For example, instead of simply showing 'Forest,' a land cover dataset may distinguish between deciduous and evergreen forests.

Popular land cover datasets that cover the entire United States include the National Land Cover Database (NLCD) and the Cropland Data Layer (CDL). Both use a resolution of 30 meters and are free to download. Some regions have high-resolution land cover datasets available but if you consider using them in your analysis, make sure they meet the guidelines outlined in this chapter.

The most important question to keep in mind when building the habitat model is: Can I distinguish between natural and highly-modified areas? For example, you may know that the 'Forest' type represents natural forests, whereas the 'Urban' type represents urbanized land. However, you may also find that 'Barren' land cover is included in the land cover classes. Does this type represent areas that have been cleared in preparation for development, natural sandy areas that encompass coastal ecosystems, or both? Again, the goal is to be able to differentiate between what is natural land cover and what is non-natural, or modified cover, and then to determine the intactness of the landscape.

It is important to fully understand what type of data you need, or that you can obtain. For example, if you are using moderate resolution (30 meter) data from a federal source, it is likely that areas designated as 'Shrubland' in the data represent either natural shrubland or artificially created shrubland (fallow agriculture, cleared land, etc.). This is a problem since the former is eligible to be part of a habitat core, while the latter is not. For example, 'Shrubland' inside a national park may be assumed to be natural, while elsewhere it is more likely to be non-natural.

Remember that *land use* is not the same as *land cover*. For example, a GIS layer identifying a parcel as having a 'Vacant' land use might either be naturally forested or a cleared parcel with abandoned buildings on it. One way to solve this question is to use local knowledge to verify the land cover data.

The best way to present land cover is in grid cells of the same size, for instance 30 x 30 meters (roughly 100 x

100 feet). This is referred to as *raster* data. Consider the following example: A county has a GIS layer of parcels, each of which has been assigned a type of land use/land cover. One particular parcel is identified as 'Industrial' because of the presence of a large factory. But since the factory requires a large buffer area, either due to safety concerns or buffer requirements, most of the parcel is actually forested. Since the parcel-based land use/land cover data would show the entire parcel as 'Industrial,' this forest would be missed. This is why raster data will typically provide more accurate results when identifying habitat cores.

Infrastructure. These data will usually comprise multiple GIS layers and will include roads, bridges, rail lines, pipelines, electrical transmission lines and any other above-ground infrastructure that divides the landscape. In your model, these should be treated as fragmenting features. Natural lands near these features are considered to be 'edge habitat.' The depth of this edge habitat will vary by ecoregion.

Location information for development and infrastructure helps identify how the landscape has been fragmented into smaller tracts. Data layers for fragmenting features, such as roads, are often available in GIS format. Land cover can often be used to identify impervious surfaces and urbanized areas, but depending on the resolution of that data, bringing in additional information can provide a more refined picture of development.

When considering road data, it is important to know additional information about each road, such as surface type or the number of lanes. Using such additional information will help you assess the road's actual impact on the landscape. For example, rural, unpaved logging roads that experience very low levels of traffic typically do not significantly impede wildlife movement. Therefore, it may not be appropriate to consider them as fragmenting features.

Development. This refers to land that has been 'developed' or 'urbanized.' It can usually be approximated by using the land cover layer (e.g. 'urban' or 'impervious' may be land cover classes in your dataset). Another very useful set of information identifies building locations. These data are not necessary to identify habitat cores, as long as you can distinguish developed land from your land cover layer, but will make the results much more accurate. Often, these data are not collected or maintained at the state level, but are available at a county or city level. Data on new buildings can show where landscapes have been impacted since the most recent land cover data were created, making this a useful way to mitigate the effects of outdated land cover data. Similar to the type of infrastructure mentioned previously, these will be treated as fragmenting features. Building locations can be buffered in GIS to approximate the area of impact and resultant edge effects.

Water Quality Information. Intact natural landscapes help protect water resources. Depending upon internal land cover, cores can filter pollutants, allow for groundwater recharge, cool streams and provide habitat and food for a variety of species (Weber 2003). Surface waters within cores add value by providing habitat for aquatic and semi-aquatic species, as well as water sources for terrestrial creatures. Both the extent (stream miles, wetland acreage) and the condition (water quality) are important to collect.

Biodiversity and Species Data. Biodiversity and rare species data can take many forms, but generally will fall into one of two categories:

1. Modeled Data: A dataset created by a computer model that *estimates* biodiversity across a landscape. An example is a GIS-based Species Richness model that estimates the number of species likely to be

supported in any given area. The advantage of these data is that they can uniformly cover a landscape, and therefore are not geographically biased. A disadvantage is that it is usually impossible to ground verify these models across a large landscape. Therefore, they represent a 'best guess' using GIS.

2. Field-collected Data: A dataset that represents actual observations of wildlife, typically rare, threatened or endangered species. An example is the data collected and maintained by the Natural Heritage Division in many states. The species and communities tracked are often referred to as *elements of biodiversity* and their individual locations are referred to as *element occurrences* (EOs). Due to the sensitive aspect of these data, it may be necessary to buffer the specific points to keep the exact locations confidential. An advantage of these data is that they represent actual observations (not modeled). However, be careful that your data are not geographically biased towards areas that are more accessible or more heavily studied. A field survey that only covers a portion of your study area may overinflate that area's importance simply because no data exist for the other parts of your study area.

Urban Tree Canopy Data

In urban areas, tree canopy data are one of the most important pieces of information for mapping and planning for green infrastructure conservation and restoration. These data identify which areas of a city are covered by trees and often distinguish other types of land cover, such as impervious surfaces or turf. As noted in Chapters Four, Five and Six, trees provide many benefits and are a key feature in maps of urban and developing areas.

There are several common ways that cities or developing areas assess their trees; canopy, subsamples or street tree/open space inventories. There are different reasons to choose one or all of these approaches. Whichever approach you choose, make sure the method is based on the decisions you will need to make. For example, do you need to be strategic in where to plant new trees, calculate ecosystem services, evaluate diversity, estimate management costs, flag areas for future protection, or everything just listed? While there are budget considerations, the data and method chosen need to be based upon what you plan to do with the results.

Tree canopy refers to mapping the actual location of the tree coverage (a bird's eye view). Knowing the location of your tree canopy is necessary when using spatial strategies to manage urban forests. Tree canopy data are created by interpreting aerial or satellite images using software packages designed to differentiate types of land cover. This process of 'classifying' a remotely-sensed image requires the use of special software and GIS skills, as well as high resolution imagery (1 meter resolution or better). Compared to other methods, this is often the fastest and cheapest way to generate data for a large area, such as an entire city. The resulting data can help prioritize where to plant trees for the best social, environmental and economic outcomes. Ecosystem services, such as stormwater runoff reductions or cooling effects, can also be estimated using tree canopy data. However, to get more precise results based on tree species and size, you may need to conduct sub-sampling.

Sample plots are used as a way to estimate tree canopy and diversity without evaluating every tree in the locality. These sample plots are used to provide data for statistical methods to estimate the total amount of canopy coverage and other values. This requires you to use software to generate locations for sample plots and then determine the coverage of those sample plots. These tools often also require an expert to identify such attributes as tree species, size and age within the sample area.

Based on these sample plots, the software tools provide citywide estimates for tree coverage, diversity and the ecosystem services provided, such as uptake of carbon or stormwater. Keep in mind, however, that sample plots do not identify the location of a city's complete tree canopy. For example, if you use the subsampling approach to estimate tree coverage, you will not know whether a parcel slated for development or rezoning has important tree resources, nor can you determine areas of the city where trees are lacking. For more examples of using urban tree maps, see Chapter Five.

Street tree inventories are usually conducted by cities to help them evaluate and manage their public trees. This requires a knowledgeable expert to complete an on-the-ground inventory. Data collected usually include species, diameter, general condition and sometimes age estimates. It is also helpful to include information on planting conditions, how large the open space is and other issues, such as whether a tree is buckling the sidewalk or if it is leaning and posing a hazard. For example, an inventory may reveal that the street contains large oak trees but that they are nearing the end of their life-span and that a replanting plan may be required in the near future. Similarly, inventories can be conducted for park lands and other open spaces to identify tree diversity, conditions and planting needs.

The GIC recommends that, at a minimum, a city, urban county or developing area evaluate its tree canopy. This will provide the most useful information for understanding where trees are abundant and where they are lacking (and may be needed). If a park and street tree inventory are affordable, it will prove a valuable addition to your plan for public trees. Lastly, if your locality has the expertise, resources and time, sample plots may be obtained to generate data about tree benefits citywide. GIS also can be used to estimate areas where trees might be planted.

Contact your city or state to learn if there is already a tree canopy data layer for your area of interest. Also consider the age of the canopy data. Is it too old to use? Has there been a major natural change since it was collected, such as a hurricane or flood? Or have there been significant development changes, such as the completion of a new shopping mall? Any of these may have removed a high percentage of the trees. If you need a new tree canopy assessment, there are several new tools available to help with this, but you will still need technical skills and GIS to evaluate the data and use it for planning.

Connecting the Cores

While cores form the main building blocks of a green infrastructure network, the ways in which they are connected are critical for its success. It is useful to think of these connections as *corridors* that connect the cores. Corridors can be existing, or they might need some restoration work. The appropriate size of a corridor will vary depending on ecoregion, but generally, corridors should be a minimum of 300 meters (1,000 feet) wide, to provide enough space to allow 100 meters (330 feet) of edge habitat on each side while still maintaining 100 meters or more of interior habitat.

There are various ways to identify corridors. One is simply to look for any obvious connections, or opportunities for connections, on a map. For example, rivers and their riparian zones often provide natural corridors across a landscape. You can also use GIS models to identify potential corridors. It is recommended to use both techniques; first, use a computer model to identify potential corridors and then view your results to identify actual (and potential) connections in the overall network.

To use GIS to identify corridors, first identify any *impedances* (blockages) to movement across the landscape. Impedances are factors that discourage the movement of plants and animals. Once you identify them you can model the path of least resistance between two areas. In ArcGIS, this is referred to as *least cost path* analysis. To run such an analysis, create a single layer in raster format that represents all impedances. To do this, you will need multiple data sources.

Note that these data will create a *general impedance layer*. In other words, it will not be species-specific.

The list below highlights some major features that encourage and discourage movement across a landscape. A plus sign indicates that the feature encourages movement, while a minus sign indicates that it impedes movement:

- Habitat cores (+)
- Interiors forest (+)
- Riparian forest (+)
- Land cover (+/-)
- Steep slopes (-)
- Proximity to major roads (-)
- Proximity to urban land (-)
- Proximity to building/address point (-)

To locate the best corridors, there are several questions to consider:

- Which corridors could potentially connect the largest and most important habitat cores?
- How could smaller cores be used to connect larger and more important cores? This is related to the *stepping stone* concept discussed in Chapter One. Are there smaller fragments of natural land that, while they cannot be considered habitat cores, could play a role in connecting those cores?
- Are there natural features – such as forests, wetlands, dunes or streams – in your study area that form connections between larger areas of natural land?
- Are there any *corridor barriers* that are effectively impassable, such as a very wide river or major interstate? Remember that many rivers cross under roads and large bridges may allow enough of a passage under them, so do not assume that roads are necessarily corridor barriers without first considering this.
- Does a future plan for land development, such as a new subdivision, render a potential corridor infeasible? If so, is there a possibility to work with the developer to maintain the natural connection in the master plan?

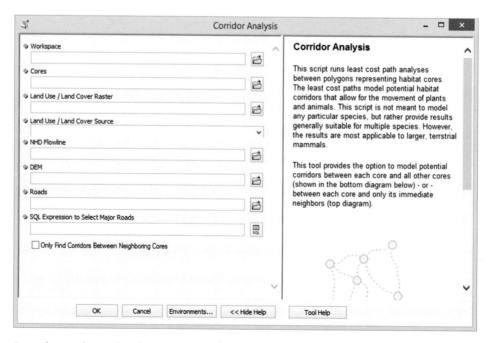

Image showing the interface of an automation tool built by the GIC to model corridors.

- How can currently protected lands serve as corridors? These areas are often great choices for corridors as their land cover is less likely to change.
- Are there areas that, if restored to their natural state, would provide a key connection between cores? Restoration work can be time- and resource-intensive, but a case for restoration can be made if an area would create key connections for important habitat.
- Remember to visit potential corridors in person! This is the best way to make a final determination of whether a corridor is viable.

Running a corridor analysis in ArcGIS can be a time-intensive process because of the amount of processing that needs to occur, and this is multiplied when performing corridor analyses between many cores. To automate the process of performing many least cost path analyses, scripting is required. The image on page 126 shows an example of an automation tool built by the GIC to model corridors.

Part 2: Ranking the Cores

The goal of the second part is to rank the identified habitat cores. It is an essential prerequisite when defining priority areas for conservation and uses additional datasets to learn more about those cores that have just been identified. The primary purpose of ranking is to summarize the estimated values that these lands provide, such as supporting wildlife and supporting clean water.

Since it is most often infeasible to conduct a complete physical survey of the cores, especially in a large study area, it is necessary to approximate their ecological significance by using available data. Metrics that are difficult or time-consuming to measure, such as biodiversity, can be approximated by using a series of other quantitative metrics. For instance, several metrics that can approximate biodiversity are soil diversity and topographic diversity, since more varied soils and topography provide more opportunities for a diversity of flora and fauna.

EXAMPLE METRICS FOR ESTIMATING CORE QUALITY

Metric Name	Data Input	Description	GIS Process
Area	Habitat Cores	The total area of each core, including both interior and edge habitat.	Calculate geometry.
Area Conserved	Protected and Conserved Areas	The area of protected/conserved land in each core. It is also possible to distinguish between difference levels/types of protection (easements, federal protection, state protection, etc.)	Intersect with cores, summarize area by core.
Area of Ground/Surface Water Protection Zones	Areas that contribute to ground/surface water quality/supply	The area/percentage of each core that has been identified as a priority protection zone.	Intersect with cores, summarize area by core.
Area of Steep Slopes	Digital Elevation Model or Slopes layer	The area/percentage of each core that is greater than, or equal to, a specified slope threshold (will depend on ecoregion).	Generate a polygon layer representing areas of steep slopes; intersect with cores; summarize area by core.
Area of Unmodified Wetlands	Wetlands (e.g. National Wetlands Inventory)	The total area/percentage of unmodified wetlands in each core. The wetlands data can be queried to eliminate human created/modified wetlands.	Intersect with cores; summarize area by core.
Area of Waterbodies	Waterbodies (e.g. National Hydrography Dataset)	The total area of waterbodies in each core. Can be subtracted from the total area to find the total land area.	Intersect with cores; summarize area by core.

Metric Name	Data Input	Description	GIS Process
Compactness Ratio	Habitat Cores	The ratio between the area of the core and the area of a circle with the same perimeter as the core. This is one measure of roundness. A circular core functions better than an elongated core because the depth to its interior is more consistent and it has a lower proportion of edge to interior habitat (all things being equal).	Calculated using the area and perimeter of the core (see description).
Core Depth/Thickness	Habitat Cores	Measures the radius of the largest circle that can be inscribed within each core. This estimates the depth of a core.	Convert cores data to raster format; calculate geometric statistics.
Interior Forest Area	Habitat Cores	Measures the area of the core, then subtracts edge habitat.	Calculated either before or after edge habitat has been accounted for, depending on methodology.
Isolation/Proximity Index	Habitat Cores	Measures how isolated a core is from other habitat cores or patches.	Many methods have been devised. A simple approach is to measure the distance from the edge of one core to the edge of the next core. For methods that account for multiple cores in proximity see Whitcomb, et al, 1981, and Gustafson and Parker, 1992.
Mean Elevation	Digital Elevation Model	The mean elevation in the core.	Calculate zonal statistics using cores as zones and DEM as the value raster.
Mean Species Richness	Species Richness raster (format and methodology will vary by location)	The average number of species that a core could potentially support. This is based on modeled data, not on field observations. Can also calculate the median, mode and other statistics.	Calculate zonal statistics using cores as zones and species richness as the value raster.
Number of Soil Types	Soil Associations	The number of soil associations in each core.	Intersect with cores; summarize soil types by core.
Perimeter	Habitat Cores	The length of the perimeter of each core.	Calculate geometry.
Perimeter-to-Area Ratio	Habitat Cores	The ratio of the perimeter length and the total area of the core.	Perimeter/Area.
Range of Elevation	Digital Elevation Model	The difference between the maximum and minimum elevation values in the core.	Calculate zonal statistics using the cores as zones and the DEM as the value raster.
RTE Abundance	Rare, Threatened and Endangered Species (Element Occurrences)	The number of observations of RTE species in each core.	Spatial join (RTE data to cores).
RTE Diversity	Rare, Threatened and Endangered Species (Element Occurrences)	The number unique RTE species observed in each core.	Intersect with cores, summarize species count by core.

Metric Name	Data Input	Description	GIS Process
Size Category	Habitat Cores	It is useful to categorize the cores into general size categories. The size thresholds will vary by ecoregion, but an example might be: cores > 10,000 acres, >1,000 – 10,000 acres, > 100 – 1,000 acres.	Query cores by size thresholds and populate a new attribute field.
Standard Deviation of Elevation	Digital Elevation Model	Also called the topographic diversity. This is a measure of the variation in elevation that occurs in the core.	Calculate zonal statistics using the cores as zones and the DEM as the value raster.
Stream Density	Streams	Calculate the total length of streams that intersect the core, and divide by the area of the core to normalize.	Intersect with cores; summarize length by core.
Buffer Suitability of Surrounding Land	Land Cover	Estimates the suitability of land adjacent to a core for serving as a buffer zone. Land cover types are assigned a value based on their suitability to serve as a buffer. This measure is an average value for all land cover types within a specified distance from the edge of the core. The distance will vary, depending on the optimal buffer distances in an ecoregion.	Create buffer around each core; reclassify land cover types to suitability scores; calculate zonal statistics using the buffer zone and the land cover suitability raster as the value raster (taking the mean value).

Note that this table is not an exhaustive list of the metrics that can be calculated. States often have their own unique data sets, such as wetlands of special significance or particular habitats of concern, which can also be used to rank habitat cores.

As alluded to above, the metrics that you will calculate for the cores in your study area will depend somewhat on the ecoregion, as well as data availability. The following table lists example metrics that you can consider calculating. Once metrics are calculated, you will use all or some of them to rank the cores. There are a variety of ways to do this, but a good idea is to combine the metrics to create a composite score that represents the overall quality and integrity of the core. This could be done, for example, by giving each core a score for each metric, and taking a weighted sum of these scores. The weights will represent the relative importance of each metric to the overall score.

It is also acceptable to incorporate specific or locally relevant metrics that are not on the list into your model (e.g. trout spawning waters), but make sure you have the data to do so (in this case, perhaps a countywide survey of trout spawning waters).

The locations of observed rare, threatened or endangered (RTE) species is one part of the data required to rank the habitat cores that will require special effort. Due to the sensitive nature of these data, it is necessary to formally request the dataset from your state's division of natural heritage. As mentioned above, the species and communities tracked by the heritage division are referred to as element occurrences (EOs).

Data on protected/conserved areas are also necessary for completing a Base Asset Map. It is likely that these data will have to be collected from several sources; for example, the most up-to-date conservation easement data are not always maintained by the same agency that maintains other information, such as park boundaries or designated wilderness areas. Calculating which core habitats are under a permanent state of conservation or in resource management use shows how protected a core is from fragmentation and degradation. This is also useful for identifying gaps in protected habitats, or where limited resources would be best spent to increase the network of protected lands. Contact your state department of conservation or natural resources to determine if they have a state database of easement lands. Also, contact local and regional land trusts and land conservancies to crosscheck that against the state data (or to provide data in the absence of any state data layer).

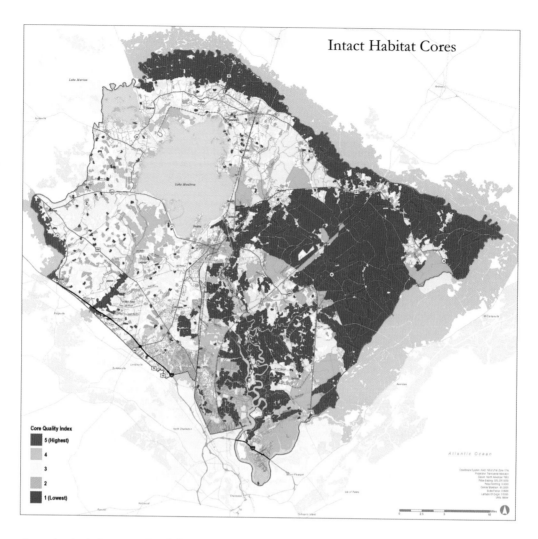

A map showing habitat cores identified in Berkeley County, South Carolina. This is an example of a 'Base Map' onto which additional layers can be overlaid to gain additional insights.

Note that the methodology presented here does not reflect site-scale issues such as deer browse or damage from invasive species. These issues require very fine resolution data that are usually not available for large areas. The model can, however, help prioritize where to expend effort on further field investigations.

Making Your Maps

Before beginning the map-making process, consider these three questions and design your maps accordingly:

1. *What is the purpose of the map?* Addressing this question will help you include relevant information and, perhaps more importantly, exclude information that does not contribute to the purpose of the map. It is easy to make maps cluttered and confusing, so remember Antoine de Saint-Exupéry's famous quote, "Perfection is achieved, not when there is nothing more to add, but when there is nothing left to take away."

2. *Who is the audience?* Will the people viewing your map be technical experts or members of the public? Maps are about communicating ideas and, as with any type of communication, are most effective when you know your audience.

3. *What will be the final format?* A good map designer will design his or her map according to a desired format. For example, a large map printed on

a three-by-four-foot poster can include more detail than a map in a PowerPoint presentation. If a map is to be projected, colors will need to be a bit bolder to be distinguishable, whereas colors on a printed map can be more subtle. Knowing whether or not the map will need to be printed in both color and black-and-white versions, and designing accordingly, is another common example.

If your maps are poorly designed, no matter how high-quality your data, their message will not be effectively communicated to the viewer. While it is outside the scope of this guide to review cartographic techniques (there are plenty of resources on this topic), it is worth noting several important points.

Visual hierarchy: Remember that the focus of the map should be on natural assets. These are the elements that the viewer's attention should be drawn to when they first look at the map. So, for example, if showing all local roads is visually distracting, it may be wise to only show major roads. The same could be done for streams, watershed boundaries, etc.

Common map elements: It is a best practice to include certain map elements on any map, such as a legend, scale bar and north arrow. If you rotate your map, perhaps to fit your area of interest inside a specific layout, the north arrow becomes even more important.

THEMED MAPS

A themed map highlights a particular land use or resource as it relates to the green infrastructure Base Map of intact habitats and locational information, such as towns and highways. As noted in earlier chapters, not everything can go on one map because it becomes unreadable and unusable. Selecting themes to focus on allows a map to highlight a key topic of interest. For example, a themed map about agricultural soils can show lands containing high-quality agricultural soils not currently covered by forests and that may be suitable for farming.

Themed maps can also show relationships. For example, you can place a recreational activity layer that highlights key areas for birding, hunting or hiking over a map of high-quality habitats to see how large intact landscapes also support human leisure activities that depend upon a connected landscape.

Base features: The main purpose of base features is to provide reference points for the viewer. Specific elements will vary according to the scale of the map, but major roads and rivers are common to maps of most

THEMATIC MAPS COULD INCLUDE THE FOLLOWING:

Surface Water Features	A map showing all wetlands, floodplains and habitat cores.
Agriculture Map	A map showing prime and important agricultural soils, agricultural districts and habitat cores. May also include farmers' markets or farm-related facilities.
Base Map	A map showing all habitat cores, displayed according to their overall core rank.
Birds Map	A map showing important reservoirs, reservoir catchments, aquifers, waters classified for drinking water use and habitat cores.
Favorite Places	A map created by a community during an open house which labels their favorite places. Create a large printed map that can be marked with the public's favorite places (that relate to green infrastructure). These points can then be digitized by GIS staff to make a final map.
Forestry	A map showing forestry tax use lands, forestry stewardship plans, potentially viable silvicultural lands and habitat cores.
Historic, Cultural and Scenic Resources	A map showing cultural trails, scenic roads, mountain peaks, wineries, breweries, distilleries, historic areas, agricultural tourism trails and locations, plus habitat cores.
Hunting and Fishing	A map showing public hunting lands, private hunting lands, trout waters, top fishing waters and habitat cores.
Protected Lands	A map showing conserved lands. This can include strong protection, such as land in a national park or under a conservation easement, as well as land under softer forms of protection, such as a Wildlife Management Area (WMA) managed by a non-governmental entity.
Recreation	A map showing publicly accessible recreational features, such as hiking, equestrian and bicycle trails, boat ramps and swimming areas.
Water Resources	A map showing state regulated wetlands, waters ranked for biodiversity, major watersheds and habitat cores. May also include public wells or impoundments.

scales. If your area of interest is mountainous or hilly, it might be useful to use a hillshade effect as the bottom layer, which can be created if you have a digital elevation model (DEM), and make the top layers semi-transparent to let it come through. Another good idea for your base is to leave no white space on the map, which tends to look 'empty' to the viewer. For example, on a map that shows where forests are located, it's relatively simple to include non-forest land as a light beige or gray to avoid that empty look. Beige may be used to represent open spaces, such as fields or lawns, while gray is commonly used for urban areas, green for forests, blue for water, and so on.

Creating Themed Map Overlays

Since trying to include all green infrastructure elements on a single map would be too complex and visually overwhelming, it's necessary to categorize your data layers by *theme*. The purpose of a themed map is to highlight a single, specific element in your study area so that its relationship to other factors becomes clear. Once completed, your collection of themed maps will inform your final green infrastructure network maps and strategies.

Themed maps can be used to highlight an issue of interest to the community and to target your natural asset Base Map towards different applications. For example, by overlaying recreational trails data on top of habitat cores (Base Map), you might notice an opportunity to extend an existing trail that would improve recreational opportunities while also linking two high-quality habitat cores. So, while the habitat map remains your Base Map, new data relating to your themes can be added to show the relationship of connected habitat and landscape protection to the themes you are seeking to enhance.

These maps are also useful across agencies and departments. For example, the parks and recreation department or tourism department may find the Recreation Map most useful for their needs, while the extension service agent or economic development director may want to utilize the Working Lands Map.

You can create a map with any theme to highlight particular land uses or applications of key interest in your study area.

Some theme maps, such as a Protected Lands Map or an Agriculture Map, tend to be important to most localities and are usually created as part of a series of natural asset maps. However, it is also beneficial (and fun!) to create special theme maps that highlight a unique or

MAP USES SUMMARY

Map Uses:

- To create new ordinances to zone land appropriately.
- To protect key species at risk and promote abundant wildlife.
- To attract new heritage tourism and identify and protect viewsheds.
- To determine areas where land management planning may be needed to protect critical resources.
- To inform transportation planning to avoid sensitive areas.
- To select future trails and utilize corridors for wildlife.
- To identify hazardous areas and avoid developing in those locations

idiosyncratic aspect of your study area. For example, you may want to highlight rare ecosystems that occur in your study area or key whitewater runs on a local river. Chapter Five includes examples of themed maps.

The most significant limiting factor in thematic mapping is the availability of data. However, you can potentially fill missing data gaps by engaging local organizations. Bird watching groups, historical societies, professional farming or forestry groups, outdoor recreation enthusiasts and tourism departments can all provide valuable information that can be included on your themed maps. Community workshops and open houses with relevant groups are also excellent opportunities to gather local knowledge (some of which can be mapped) and to determine local priorities.

Remember to have fun with the asset mapping process – you can combine seemingly disparate GIS layers to reveal new patterns or insights that no one had thought to investigate until now!

Creating the Final Green Infrastructure Map

The final green infrastructure map will illustrate the most important natural landscapes in your study area; in other words, *your community's priorities*. However, 'importance' is a relative term; what is important to one community may not be to another. Some factors, such as the size of a habitat core, are always important and will increase the overall significance of an area. Others may only be locally relevant. For example, a community that seeks to secure its future water supply may place more importance on habitat cores that protect their drinking water reservoirs while a community that wants to restore water quality to an impaired stream may place more importance on restoring small cores along the stream. These examples illustrate why creating the themed maps, and using them to inform your final green infrastructure network map, is such a critical step in the process.

As stated previously, your first map will be a Base Map that shows all the habitat cores you have identified in your study area, as well as their rank. In the final network, it is typically most effective to not show cores unless they are a priority and/or a critical part of the network. You will use the Base Map, which shows the core ranks, along with your theme maps, to determine which cores will be shown on your Final Green Infrastructure Network Map. In other words, while the Base Map showing cores can help inform land use planning on its own, it gains the most value when paired with thematic maps that represent local goals for natural resource use or cultural or heritage protection. So, while the Final Green Infrastructure Network Map may be the center-piece of your planning effort 'table', your themed maps are the legs that support it and link other local priorities to it. They also allow you to do more in depth analysis on particular issues, such as exploring how the natural asset (cores) network supports tourism or scenic roads.

Keeping Your Maps Current

The methodology presented here has mapped land use and land cover, which change on a daily basis. As a result, new and improved datasets will need to be regularly created for your study area. Accordingly, your asset maps should be treated as living documents that can be updated as needed. To achieve this, you should re-run your cores and corridors GIS models on a periodic basis. Having up-to-date maps that reflect the reality on the ground will improve their legitimacy, help gain support for them, and ensure they continue to be consulted during routine planning activities, such as the review of new development proposals.

The most important thing to do is integrate your maps into both everyday and long-range planning procedures. Ensure that your local government departments – planning, parks, public works, water, economic

development, tourism, and so on – have access to the maps and understand how to use them when making land use and land management decisions. Ensure that local conservation groups, land trusts and conservancies also have access to the maps for their strategic decision making processes. Also ensure that the development community knows about the maps and consults them when planning for new developments. And, finally, ensure that those who make management decisions, such as homeowner associations or local campgrounds, are aware of any open space connections they might impact and whether they own key landscapes requiring management. In short, use what you create as a living tool that will enable your entire community to make better informed decisions that represent community values based on real data.

BIBLIOGRAPHY

The following bibliography is not comprehensive but does provide a snapshot of the diversity and age of relevant titles. It includes technical references, exemplar plans, programs, web sites and technical assistance. There are many case studies that have been published individually and links to those are provided on the Green Infrastructure Center's website at: www.gicinc.org.

_____ Precious Heritage: *The Status of Biodiversity in the United States*. Washington, D.C.: The Nature Conservancy, 2000.

_____ Environmental Law Institute. *Planning for Biodiversity: Authorities in State Land Use Laws*. Washington, D.C.: Environmental Law Institute, 2003.

_____ Trust for Public Land, *Building Green Infrastructure: Land Conservation as a Watershed Protection Strategy*. San Francisco: Trust for Public Land, 2000.

_____ *Ecological: An Ecosystems Approach to Developing Infrastructure Projects* (FHWA, Brown, 2006). <http://www.environment.fhwa.dot.gov/ecological/eco_index.asp>

_____ *The Economic Benefits of Recreation, Open Space, Recreation Facilities and Walkable Community Design*. May 2010. Active Living Research

Adams, Jonathan S., *The Future of the Wild: Radical Conservation for a Crowded World*. Boston: Beacon Press, 2006.

Akbari, H., Kurn, D. et al. 1997. "Peak power and cooling energy savings of shade trees." *Energy and Buildings* 25 (1997): 139–148.

Barten, P.K., and C.E. Ernst., "Land Conservation and Watershed Management for Source Protection." *Journal of American Water Works Association* 96(4) (2004):121-135.

Benedict, Mark A. and McMahon, Edward T. *Green Infrastructure: Linking Landscapes and Communities*. Washington, D.C.: Island Press, 2006.

Benedict, Mark A. and McMahon. "*Green Infrastructure: Smart Conservation for the 21st Century*." Washington, D.C., Sprawl Watch Clearing House, May 2002. Accessed July 2010 http://www.sprawlwatch.org/greeninfrastructure.pdf

Birnbaum, Charles A. "Protecting Cultural Landscapes: Planning, Treatment and Management of Historic Landscapes" September 1994. Accessed May 21, 2012 http://www.nps.gov/hps/tps/briefs/brief36.htm

Bowker, J.M., Bergstrom, J.C. and Gill, J.K., *The Virginia Creeper Trail, An Assessment of User Demographics, Preferences and Economics*, USDA Forest Service and the University of Georgia Department of Agriculture and Applied Economics, 2004.

Cassin, Jan. "Hurricane Sandy Highlights Need to Protect Green Infrastructure" Ecosystem Marketplace. Nov. 2, 2012. Accessed December 13, 2012. www.ecosystemmarketplace.com/pages/dynamic/article.page.php?page_id=9401&section=news_articles&eod=1

Constanza, Jen, Earhardt, Todd, Terando, Adam, McKerrow, Alex. "Modeling Vegetation Dynamics and Habitat Availability in the Southeastern U.S. Using Gap Data." Gap Analysis Bulletin, North Carolina State University. Vol. 18, 2010.

Copeland, Holly E, Pocewicz Amy, Naugle David E, Griffiths Tim, Keinath Doug, Evans, Jeffrey, Platt, James, "Measuring the Effectiveness of Conservation: A Novel Framework to Quantify the Benefits of Sage-Grouse Conservation Policy and Easements in Wyoming." *PLoS ONE* (2013)8(6): e67261. doi:10.1371/journal.pone.0067261.

Correll, Mark R., Lillydahl, J., Jane H. and Singell, Larry D. "The Effect of Greenbelts on Residential Property Values: Some Findings on the Political Economy of Open Space." *Land Economics* 54(2), (1978): 207-217.

Crompton, J., Love, L., and Moore, T. (1997). "An Empirical Study of the Role of Recreation, Parks, and Open Space in Companies' (Re) Location Decisions." *Journal of Park and Recreation Administration* 15(1), (1997): 37-58.

Dale, Virginia H. "Ecological Principles and Guidelines for Managing the Use of Land." *Ecological Applications* 10, (3): 639–670.

Dale, V.H. and Haeuber, R.A. eds., *Applying Ecological Principles to Land Management*. New York: Springer-Verlag, 2001.

Dale, V.H. and English, M.R. eds., *Tools to Aid Environmental Decision Making*. New York: Springer-Verlag, 1999.

Dramstad, Wenche E., et al. *Landscape Ecology Principles in Landscape Architecture and Land Use Planning*. Washington, D.C.: Island Press, 1996.

Duerksen, Christopher and Snyder, Cara. *Nature Friendly Communities, Habitat Protection, and Land Use Planning*. Washington, D.C.: Island Press, 2005.

Duh, Steve. City of Vancouver Urban Forestry Management Plan. City of Vancouver. December 2007.

Fiorino, Daniel J. "Citizen Participation and Environmental Risk: A Survey of Institutional Mechanisms." *Science, Technology and Human Values* 15(2) (Spring 1990): 226-243.

Fischer, R.A. and Fischenich, J.C. *Design Recommendations for Riparian Corridors and Vegetated Buffer Strips*, (No. ERDC-T-N-EMRRP-SR-24). Army Engineer Waterways Experiment Station Vicksburg Ms Engineer Research And Development Center, April 2000.

Florida, Richard. "The Rise of the Creative Class." *Washington Monthly*. Last modified May 2002. Accessed May 2009. http://www.washingtonmonthly.com/features/2001/0205.florida.html

Forman, R. T. T. Land Mosaics. *The Ecology of Landscapes and Regions*. Cambridge: Cambridge University Press, 1995.

Frank, Lawrence, Engelke, Peter. and Schmid, Thomas. *Health and Community Design: The Impact of The Built Environment on Physical Activity*. Washington, D.C.: Island Press, 2003.

Frumkin H, Frank L, Jackson R. *Urban Sprawl and Public Health: Designing, Planning, and Building for Healthy Communities*. Washington, D.C.: Island Press, 2004.

Fulton, Pendall, Nguyen, Harrison. "Who Sprawls Most: How Growth Patterns Differ Across the U.S.," Brookings Institute(-July 2001) Accessed May 2006. http://content.knowledgeplex.org/kp2/img/cache/kp/2631.pdf

Gustafson, E. J., and G. R. Parker. "Relationships between landcover proportion and indices of landscape spatial pattern." (1992) *Landscape Ecology* 7:101-110.

Hellmund, Paul Cawood, Smith, Daniel Somers. *Designing Greenways: Sustainable Landscapes for Nature and People*. Washington, D.C.: Island Press, 2006.

Hinds, Joe; Sparks, Paul. "The Affective Quality of Human-Natural Environment Relationships." *Evolutionary Psychology* 9(3) (2011): 451-469.

Holling, Crawford Stannley. "Resilience and Stability of Ecological Systems" *Annual Review of Ecology and Systematics*, 4 (November 1973): 1-23.

Hopper Joseph R. and Mc Carl Nielson, Joyce, "Recycling as Altruistic Behavior: Normative and Behavioral Strategies to Expand Participation in a Community Recycling Program." *Environment and Behavior* 23(2) (March 1991): 195-220.

Howell, Andrew J.; Dopko, Raelyne L.; Passmore, Holli-Anne; et al. "Nature connectedness: Associations with well-being and mindfulness." *Personality And Individual Differences* 51(2) (July 2011): 166-171.

Huang, J., H. Akbari, and H. Taha. *"The Wind-Shielding and Shading Effects of Trees on Residential Heating and Cooling Requirements."* Paper presented at the Winter Meeting of the American Society of Heating, Refrigerating and Air-Conditioning Engineers. Atlanta, Georgia, 1990.

Johnson, Bart and Hill, Kristina, eds. *Ecology and Design*. Washington, D.C.: Island Press, 2001.

Kaplan, R. & S. Kaplan. *The Experience of Nature: A Psychological Perspective*. Cambridge: Cambridge University Press, 1989.

Kawachi I, Berkman LF. *Neighborhoods and Health*. Oxford(UK): Oxford University Press, 2003.

Kraus, We, Torgan CE, Duscha BD, Norris J, Brown SA, Cobb FR., Bales CW, Annex BH, Samsa GP, Houmard JA, Slentz CA. "Studies of a Targeted Risk Reduction Intervention Through Defined Exercise," *American Journal of Cardiology" Medicine and Science In Sports and Exercise* , 33(10) (December 15, 2007): 1774-1784.

Kurn, D., S. Bretz, B. Huang, and H. Akbari. The Potential for Reducing Urban Air Temperatures and Energy Consumption through Vegetative Cooling (PDF) (31 pp, 1.76MB). ACEEE Summer Study on Energy Efficiency in Buildings, American Council for an Energy Efficient Economy. Pacific Grove, California. 1994.

Little, Charles E. *Greenways for America*, Baltimore: Johns Hopkins University Press, 1995.

Louve, Richard. *Last Child in the Woods*. Chapel Hill: Algonquin Books, 2005.

Lynn, William S. The Ethics of Social Marketing for Conservation: A Learning Module. RARE Training Manual. London: RARE. 2001. Accessed January 10, 2012. May 2011. http://www.rmportal.net/library/content/tools/biodiversity-conservation-tools/putting-conservation-in-context-cd/communication-and-education-approaches-resources/The-Ethics-of-Social-Marketing-for-Conservation-A-Learning-Module/view

Lyman, Martha West. "Trust for Public Land, Quebec Labrador Foundation and the Northern Forest Community Forests: A Community Investment Strategy." San Francisco: Trust for Public Land, 2007.

Macie, Edward A.; Hermansen, L. Annie "Human Influences on Forest Ecosystems; the Southern Wildland-Urban Interface Assessment: summary report." General Technical Report SRS-64. Asheville, NC: U.S. Department of Agriculture, Southern Research Station. 13 pages. 2003.

McPherson, E.G., J. R. Simpson, P. J. Peper, S. E. Maco, and Q. Xiao. 2005. "Municipal forest benefits and costs in five US cities." *Journal of Forestry* 103(8), (2005): 411–416.

McHarg, Ian. *Design with Nature*. Garden City: American Museum of Natural History, Natural History Press, 1969.

Miller, Daphne, "Take a Hike and Call Me in the Morning." Washington Post Health Section. Tues, Nov 17, 2009. Accessed November 1969. http://www.washingtonpost.com/wp-dyn/content/article/2009/11/16/AR2009111602899.html.

Morris M, Duncan R, Hannaford K, Kochtitzky C, Rogers V, Roof K, Solomon J. Integrating planning and public health. Chicago: APA Planning Advisory Service, 2006.

Nolon, John. *Open Ground: Effective Local Strategies for Protecting Natural Resources*. Washington, D.C.: Environmental Law Institute, 2003.

Nowak, David J.; Greenfield, Eric J. "Tree and Impervious Cover Change in U.S. Cities." Urban Forestry and Urban Greening. (2012). USDA Forest Service/UNL Faculty Publications. Paper 240.

Nowak, David J; Hoehn, Robert E. III; Crane, David E.; Stevens, Jack C.; Walton, Jeffrey T., "Assessing Urban Forest Effects and Values", Washington D.C. USDA Forest Service, Northern Research Station, Newton Square, PA (24 pages). 2006

Peper, Paula J., McPherson, E. Gregory, Simpson, James R, Gardner, Shelly L., Vargas, Kelaine E., Xiao, Quinfu. New York City, New York Municipal Forest Resource Analysis. Center for Urban Forest Research. (March 2007).

Reiter, Susan. M. and Samuel, William. "Littering as a Function of Prior Litter and The Presence or Absence of Prohibitive Signs." *Journal of Applied Social Psychology*, 10 (February, 1980): 45–55.

Riley, Ann L. *Restoring Streams in Cities*. Washington D.C.: Island Press, 2001.

Roman, Lara A. "How Many Trees Are Enough? Tree Death and the Urban Canopy." Scenario Journal 04. Building the Urban Forest. (Spring 2014) Accessed January 2015. http://scenariojournal.com/article/how-many-trees-are-enough/

Stafford, Margaret. "Uprooted Town Moves To Higher Ground After Midwest Deluge Of '93. Disaster: Government Offered Pattonsburg, Mo., And Other Communities Millions To Move Out Of Harm's Way Rather Than Remain In Flood Plain." Associated Press. July 18, 1998. Accessed October 201. http://articles.latimes.com/1998/jul/12/news/mn-2946

Tassel, Sandra J. *The Conservation Program Handbook. A Guide for Local Government Land Acquisition*, San Francisco: Trust for Public Land, 2009.

Theobald, David M. Crooks, Kevin R. Norman, John B. "Assessing Effects of Land Use on Landscape Connectivity." *Ecological Applications*. 21(7), (2011): 2445-2458.

Ulrich, Roger S. "View Through A Window May Influence Recovery." *Science*. 224 (April 27, 1984):224-5.

Weakley, Allison, November 2012. Personal Communication.

Whitcomb, R. F., C. S. Robbins, J. F. Lynch, B. L. Whitcomb, M. K. Klimkiewicz, and D Bystrak. "Effects of forest fragmentation on avifauna of the eastern deciduous forest." Pages 125-205 in R. L. Burgess and D. M. Sharpe, eds. Forest Island Dynamics in Man-Dominated Landscapes (1981). Springer-Verlag, New York.

Weinstein, Netta, Przybylski, Andrew K, and Ryan, Richard M. "Can Nature Make Us More Caring? Effects of Immersion in Nature on Intrinsic Aspirations and Generosity." *Personal Social Psychology Bulletin 35* (October 2009): 1315-1329 (first published on August 5, 2009).

Winter, Patricia L., Sagarin, B. J., Rhoads, K., Barrett, D. W., and Cialdini, R. B. "Choosing to Encourage or Discourage: Perceived Effectiveness of Prescriptive Versus Proscriptive Messages." *Environmental Management*. 26(6) (December 2000): 589-594.

Winter, Patricia L., Cialdini, R. B., Sagarin, B. J. "An Analysis of Normative Messages in Signs at Recreation Areas." *Journal of Interpretation Research*. 3(1) (Winter 1998): 39-47.

Wolf, Kathleen L. "City Trees, Nature and Physical Activity," *Arborist News*, 17(1) (February 2008).

WEB SITES REFERENCED

EPA Healthy Watersheds Initiative: http://www.epa.gov/owow/nps/healthywatersheds/examples.html

Green Infrastructure Projects: www.greeninfrastructure.net

Green Infrastructure Center Projects: http://www.gicinc.org/projects.htm

Green Maps: http://www.greenmaps.org

Historic Vernacular Landscapes http://preservapedia.org/Historic_vernacular_landscape

Human Dimensions of Urban Forestry and Urban Greening. List of articles and presentations for download http://www.naturewithin.info/products.html

Landscope America: http://www.landscope.org/introduction/

Video: Green Infrastructure, Protecting Our Commonwealth. Available on YouTube at:
http://www.youtube.com/watch?v=fb7HLYPwJ4I&uid=Vr9xSKUIWQoQ0LjEFyYm-w&lr=1